IS GLUTEN MAKING ME ILL?

IS GLUTEN MAKING ME ILL?

REDUCE OR REVERSE THE SYMPTOMS OF
GLUTEN SENSITIVITY IN JUST 14 DAYS

DR. SHARI LIEBERMAN
WITH LINDA SEGALL

RODALE

This edition first published in 2007 by
Rodale International Ltd
7–10 Chandos Street
London
W1G 9AD

The moral right of Dr. Shari Lieberman to be identified as the author of this work has been
asserted in accordance with the Copyright, Design and Patents Act of 1988.

Printed and bound in the UK by CPI Bath using acid-free paper from sustainable sources.

1 3 5 7 9 8 6 4 2

A CIP record for this book is available from the British Library

ISBN-13: 978-1-4050-9987-5

This paperback edition distributed to the book trade by Pan Macmillan Ltd

Notice

This book is intended as a reference volume only, not as a medical manual. The information given
here is designed to help you make informed decisions about your health. It is not intended as a
substitute for any treatment that you may have been prescribed by your doctor. If you suspect that
you have a medical problem, we urge you to seek competent medical help. Mention of specific
companies, organizations or authorities in this book does not imply endorsement by the publisher,
nor does mention of specific companies, organizations or authorities in the book imply that they
endorse the book.

Addresses, websites and telephone numbers given in this book were accurate at the time the book
went to press.

LIVE YOUR WHOLE LIFE™

We inspire and enable people to improve their lives and the world around them

To my husband, Augusto,

whose love and support

make monumental tasks

so much easier.

CONTENTS

When Dr. Shari Lieberman asked me to write the foreword to her book on gluten sensitivity, I paused to think for a moment: I'm a specialist in matters of the heart, not gastrointestinal disease.

But in addition to being a cardiologist, I am a certified nutrition specialist, and so I am deeply entrenched in the dietary and nutritional issues of my patients. Combining a healthy diet with essential targeted nutrition is perhaps the most important way to prevent disease. Certainly in my specialty (preventive and metabolic cardiology), the Mediterranean diet has proven to be the healthiest dietary approach for preventing sudden cardiac death, as well as for reducing the incidence of subsequent cardiac events. The Mediterranean diet provides an abundance of precious omega-3 essential fatty acids that have a profound impact in reducing inflammation.

Silent inflammation as we know it today is the main factor in the development of cardiovascular disease, gastrointestinal problems, diabetes, cancer, Parkinson's disease and other neurodegenerative diseases. Although the many causes of silent inflammation include cigarette smoking, heavy metals, microbes, trans fatty acids and excessive radiation, dietary factors that cause surging insulin levels appear to top the list.

And then, of course, there are the insidious food allergies and intolerances and "leaky gut" type syndromes that cause immune-system dysfunctions that can slowly undermine our health.

I can attest to the fact that problems with indigestion, food allergies, malabsorption and excessive wind and bloating do, indeed, affect the heart. So, it is not uncommon for someone like me to be intrigued by Dr. Lieberman's book. I see multiple cardiovascular issues, such as heart irregularities, atypical chest pain and high blood pressure, in people with digestive problems. And, of course, there is the complex issue of gluten sensitivity, which can develop into coeliac disease (CD).

Dr. Lieberman's book is about a condition that is reaching epidemic proportions. Although this "malabsorption syndrome" was first identified way back in 1888, it is now believed that it may be the most common *genetic* disorder that sends people like you, looking for answers and relief, to specialists like me.

While many readers may be wondering what I'm leading up to, those of you diagnosed with this health-threatening disorder – or who know someone who is – have probably figured out that I am referring to coeliac disease. Don't worry if you haven't heard of this problem, because that's how uninformed the general public and some medical professionals still are about it.

This disorder is *not* a food allergy; it is an intolerance. The condition is also known by other multiple names – such as gluten-sensitive enteropathy, coeliac sprue, nontropical sprue, and Gee-Herter's disease/syndrome.

Regardless of what label it carries, the problem is consistent: an inability to tolerate the gluten found in wheat, barley and rye, with or without damage to the villi of the jejunum (upper part of the small intestine). The villi are microscopic, hairlike projections in the small intestine that provide the surface area needed to absorb the nutrients from the foods and supplements you ingest.

The link between this disease and diet wasn't made until 1944, when a Dutch paediatrician observed that children in his clinic started getting better after the Nazi invasion. Symptoms such as bloating, stomach cramping, diarrhoea and generalized fatigue gradually abated as bread disappeared from their diets, even though the children were starving for food.

Despite rising awareness of CD, many doctors think it is a low-incidence problem. And most doctors think *only* in terms of coeliac disease – the "ultimate" form of gluten sensitivity.

CD can be, and is, diagnosed at any age, from infancy to the last decade of life, but while the typically affected European is diagnosed by more CD–conscious doctors within a year, on average it may take up to 10 years of symptoms for that to happen in the United States.

I remember one of my patients, a Catholic nun who was diagnosed as having CD in her late 80s, after years of becoming ill after ingesting the communion wafer. The small amount of gluten in the wafer caused her to develop wind, bloating and diarrhoea. Unfortunately, she suffered for an enormous length of time before someone finally diagnosed her problem.

One year, 10 years, or *any* chunk of your life is a long time to suffer when no one knows what is wrong with you. Dr. Lieberman's book raises public awareness about this terrible condition that afflicts many people – some genetically predisposed, some not. One person in the latter category (not genetically predisposed) is my own son, who developed acquired coeliac disease after being exposed to toxic moulds.

As you can imagine, when my own grown child complained of GI symptoms of bloating, diarrhoea and wind, along with significant weight loss, I became concerned. I took him to more than a dozen top doctors and specialists across the country, but the puzzle pieces didn't fall into place.

Although laboratory tests showed multiple laboratory abnormalities, a diagnosis was still uncertain. Finally, he found a doctor-expert in environmental biotoxins, who diagnosed him with acquired gliadin allergy.

CD responds well when gluten – the trigger food-product ingredient – is removed from the diet. Now, I'm sure that many people are still undiagnosed and are still suffering, totally unaware about this bizarre form of acquired CD. But people with CD who continue to eat gluten risk tremendous health consequences, including a host of medical and autoimmune disorders and a higher risk of bowel cancer.

Furthermore, the longer they go undiagnosed, the more damage occurs to their intestines and the rest of their body. Clearly, when my son takes in *any* gluten, his health takes a step backward. Even though he does not have genetically predetermined CD, the acquired type of CD that he does have still requires the elimination of gluten from his diet.

Whenever making the diagnosis is obscure or difficult for me – whether I'm treating heart disease, psoriasis, gastrointestinal symptoms, or whatever – I've found that having the individual restrict or eliminate gluten from the diet has resulted in spontaneous improvement. The prescription to eliminate gluten even in the case of cardiomyopathy is well founded on science. Dr. Lieberman, in fact, cites published studies that show the beneficial effects of a gluten-free diet on patients who suffer from cardiomyopathy, as well as a host of neurological, dermatological and gastrointestinal problems.

Now, you may think that it's cruel to restrict flour and wheat from someone's diet for several months or even for a lifetime. But when you see the remarkable improvement in health a gluten-sensitive person gains when the offending substance is out of his or her system, all the dietary sacrifices are more than worth it!

If you were the person experiencing this for yourself and getting your life back, I'm sure you'd continue a gluten-free diet, just as my cardiac patients who have experienced a heart attack or gone through bypass surgery are motivated to stick to the Mediterranean diet that I insist they try.

Hippocrates was absolutely right when he said that "food is medicine, and medicine is food". We must understand that being aware of food choices is vital to maintaining health, aliveness and quality of life.

Permit me to tell you about Virginia, because her story is so typical of what I call a coeliac sufferer – someone struggling with symptoms of this disease until the diagnosis is made and the triggers eliminated.

Virginia told me that she felt as though she had been in a "brain fog" her entire life. Even now, she reflects on how, as a youngster, she felt like a "bad girl", recalling tantrums when she couldn't manage her irritability. As a teenager, she menstruated only three or four times a year, and it's never been unusual for her to go 6 months without a menstrual period.

As an adult, she blamed herself for feeling "out of it". Virginia engaged in years of personal psychotherapy, searching for insight into her mood and behaviour, and doctors placed her on antidepressants. Finally, a trusted psychologist, sensing that a physical source for her symptoms must have been overlooked, recommended that she undergo more medical evaluation.

A neurology checkup failed to confirm any reason for her exhaustion. It was probably easy enough for doctors to point to her long-standing anaemia and single-parent status for her symptoms, but why couldn't they resolve the anaemia – or the depression? Virginia continued to actively search for answers for *2 decades,* consulting doctor after doctor, including a gastroenterologist for her peptic ulcer and other gastrointestinal symptoms.

Then, one day, a lightbulb came on for her doctor during a routine office visit. He asked Virginia about her 23-year-old son, Aaron, who was also under his care for chronic diarrhoea. She told him of an incident that had occurred the night before. Aaron was forced to leave work early with an acute respiratory reaction and swollen and watering eyes. Aaron is a chef. He'd forgotten to turn down a mixer before adding some flour, and the dust that blew up into his face had triggered his immune system into a violent response.

Virginia will always remember how that doctor riffled through her chart on his desk and then proclaimed, "Oh, my God! I know what's wrong with you!"

The doctor didn't wait for tests to be done to confirm coeliac disease. Virginia and her son immediately eliminated grains from their diets. It took 2½ years on a gluten-free diet for Virginia's symptoms (including her depression) to remit *completely*. Finally, she had her life back!

There has been an alarming increase in the incidence of coeliac disease in the past decade. Successfully diagnosing more cases than before may be the reason that statistics reflect a higher prevalence of CD. In Europe, the condition appears in 1 in every 200 to 300 inhabitants. The University of Maryland's Dr. Alessio Fasano (CD researcher, paediatrician and gastroenterologist) reports rates in the United States to be as high as 1 in 133. That's downright shocking! Especially when you consider that, in 1994, we expected about 1 in 10,000 people to be affected by it.

What's even more shocking is that coeliac disease is the end stage of gluten sensitivity. Many, many more people are gluten *sensitive* who do not (and would not) test positive for coeliac disease. That's because blood tests (commonly used in the first instance to diagnose CD) do not always detect gluten sensitivity – and because gluten sensitivity masks itself behind symptoms of many other diseases and conditions. Obviously, we have a *long* way to go – and that's why Dr. Lieberman's book is so important. It uncovers all of these truths.

How do you know if you're at higher risk for inheriting this condition, which may be blocking your absorption of nutrients – and damaging your health? Well, because one cause is genetic, those whose blood relatives have coeliac disease are clearly at risk. Obviously, many of us could have a genetic predisposition without actually knowing anyone in our family whose CD was ever confirmed. It's also been observed that women are more vulnerable than men.

In one 2001 US study of 1,138 responding adults, most weren't diagnosed with CD until late in life, despite an average of 11 years of symptoms. Women predominated over men at a rate of nearly three to one. About 75 per cent surveyed had a biopsy to confirm their diagnosis, and 77 per cent reported an improved quality of life after their diagnosis was confirmed and they eliminated gluten from their diets.

There may be cultural tendencies, too. Northern Europeans have the highest incidence of CD. African Americans and Asians are least likely to have it. We do know that CD is common in Europeans – particularly the Irish. I have a now-adult friend who was diagnosed as a "failure to thrive" baby until her mother happened to visit family in Ireland. An Irish doctor quickly recognized the then 2-year-old's CD and put the toddler on a gluten-free diet. That doctor's diagnosis turned her life around.

My best advice to you is to read this book and learn how the multi-faceted personality of gluten sensitivity affects multiple organ systems, such as the skin, the neurological system, the muscles, and, of course, the gastrointestinal tract.

Should you discover that you have gluten sensitivity or CD, one thing is for certain: your body is not absorbing key nutrients. You will need to go on a strict gluten-free diet. And your doctor or nutritionist may decide that you should supplement your diet with an individualized, targeted vitamin and nutrient strategy to restore a state of health and balance.

The key to optimum health is the earliest possible identification of a health issue so that intervention can begin as soon as possible. CD is much more common than we think it is. And gluten sensitivity is even more prevalent than coeliac disease.

The good news is that the condition can be diagnosed and treated effectively. Dr. Shari Lieberman's book is a great place to learn about this poorly understood condition that could negatively impact millions of people's lives. She defines the problem clearly and provides you with simple solutions.

– Dr. Stephen T. Sinatra, FACC
Specialist in Preventive and Metabolic Cardiology,
Author of The Sinatra Solution: New Hope for Preventing and
Treating Heart Disease

INTRODUCTION

I am a nutrition scientist. I help people eat right to be healthy. As a private practitioner, I am frequently the professional of last resort. People come to me, often through medical referral, after they have unsuccessfully tried other, often easier, remedies for their health problems.

It was through these cases of last resort that I became intrigued with gluten sensitivity, also known as gluten intolerance. This intrigue eventually led to the writing of this book.

Gluten is a protein found in wheat, barley and rye. People who are sensitive to gluten have an autoimmune reaction to it: instead of the body digesting the protein as it should, it recognizes gluten as an enemy and tries to fight it off. If it is a minor intolerance, no symptoms are produced.

But autoimmune reactions are often cumulative: they get worse with additional introductions of the offending substance. Ultimately, in the case of gluten, the autoimmune reaction can lead to coeliac disease.

Researchers and doctors have associated gluten with medical problems for more than 50 years. But the problem they most often identified with gluten was coeliac disease. They did not grasp (and many still do not, unfortunately) that the culprit behind coeliac disease could be causing a myriad of other problems long before it manifests itself as a disease of the gut.

As a nutritionist, I recognize that people eat foods that nature never meant for them to eat. In today's society, this is especially true. Much of the food we have available to consume is changed from the way that nature made it. Biochemists have changed the seeds from which plants are grown. And food manufacturers have inundated our food supply with gluten, most notably wheat.

The majority of people can tolerate processed foods. But some cannot. They suffer the consequences of these easy-to-use foods.

And it is these "some" people who often come to nutritionists for help. As we work with them, we examine their diets for suspect foods, including milk, eggs, fish, crustacean shellfish, tree nuts, peanuts, wheat, soyabeans and nightshades (peppers, tomatoes, aubergines). Then we work with them to modify their diets, eliminate troublesome foods and their derivatives and introduce wholesome nutrition, including appropriate supplementation, to make up for possible deficiencies caused by their physical conditions.

It was through this type of course of action that I discovered the powerful effect gluten can have – and the even more dramatic effect that taking gluten out of a diet can have – on a person's health.

The best way to illustrate this power is to share some of my earliest cases with you, because more than 20 years ago, these cases alerted me to the need to enlighten people about gluten sensitivity. Here are some of them:

Saved from the knife. A 14-year-old Canadian girl was brought to me for help. She was suffering from Crohn's disease. (See Chapter 6, Digestive Disorders.)

Pharmaceutical intervention was limited in the US in early 1980s, and what was available had been ineffective for this girl. The doctors wanted to remove part of her colon; her parents wanted to avoid this last-ditch effort. (Surgery would have removed necrotic tissue, but it would not have halted the disease.)

Unlike most of my colleagues at that time, who only removed wheat and yeast from diets, I recommended eliminating *all* sources of gluten. I put the girl on a gluten-free diet. And within 30 days, *all* of her symptoms resolved.

She is still gluten-free today and has a healthy 3-year-old baby.

Controlling blood sugar. A young woman in her early twenties suffered from type 1 diabetes. (See Chapter 5, Other Autoimmune Diseases.) Although she took insulin and watched her diet carefully to avoid sugars, no matter what she did, her blood sugar levels soared, and she experienced diabetes-related problems, including retinopathy, a complication involving inflammation of the retina.

I put her on a high-fibre diet that included beans, lentils and oatmeal. We discovered that whenever she ate oatmeal (*without* added sugar), her blood sugar would skyrocket.

I switched her to a gluten-free diet that also eliminated oats. (Although oats in themselves do not contain gluten, they are often contaminated with gluten, because they are generally processed in the same factories that process wheat and often grow in the same fields where wheat has been grown.)

Within 2 weeks, my patient found that she could go days without taking insulin to regulate her blood sugar. And after several months, even her retinopathy substantially improved.

Modified ineffective Feingold diet. A distraught mother brought her 10-year-old daughter to see me. The girl exhibited behavioural problems typical of a child with an attention deficit disorder (ADD/ADHD). (See Chapter 4, Neurological Disorders.) She could not concentrate or sit still, and she was impulsive. Her schoolwork was greatly affected by her inability to concentrate.

The mother had tried everything except Ritalin, a medication that works as a stimulant on the central nervous system and is often prescribed to calm children with ADD/ADHD. The mother did not want to expose her child to the risks involved with pharmaceuticals.

Among her sincere attempts at solving the girl's behaviour problems was the Feingold diet, which eliminates foods with artificial colouring and flavouring, synthetic sweeteners and the artificial preservatives BHA, BHT and TBHQ.

The diet is effective with many children who have ADD/ADHD, but it was not with this girl. Although she did not have any physical symptoms to suggest a sensitivity to gluten, I put her on a gluten-free diet. Six weeks later, the mother called me. Not only had her daughter sailed through a maths test, her behaviour and learning were so greatly improved that she was being moved from a special education class to a normal class! The change in the girl was dramatic.

Overcome developmental delay. I was the "last stop" for a 4-year-old boy who was developmentally delayed and was diagnosed with a failure to thrive. He could not talk, but he could scream, which he did incessantly. Screaming was how he communicated with the world.

I put the boy on a gluten-free diet, accompanied by a dairy-free diet. Within 2 weeks, the parents called to report his progress. They cried tears of happiness as they told me that not only had his behaviour improved, but he had also spoken his first words! And he was already gaining weight.

One "side effect" the parents noticed: the boy was jealous of anyone who approached his "special" food. He knew it was making him normal, and he didn't want it to go away. He no longer felt like he was crawling out of his skin.

That case happened 25 years ago. The "boy" remains gluten-free to this day and is a normal young man.

Erased mask. A 30-year-old patient suffering from early-stage lupus (see Chapter 5, Other Autoimmune Diseases) asked for help. One of her primary symptoms was a "wolf mask" (discolouration on the face).

After 1 month of being on a gluten-free diet, her skin cleared up and she was in full clinical remission.

Halted MS. A woman with late-stage multiple sclerosis (MS) came to me for guidance. Although she had neurological damage and her left leg was impaired, she continued to exercise daily, determined to fight the disease that kept progressing, despite all her efforts.

When she went on a gluten-free diet, the neurological progression stopped. Her damaged left leg regained some of its feeling and her right leg returned to normal function. Even more important, her vision was restored! The diet stopped the MS progression.

Two-for-one treatment. A young lady who was diagnosed with ulcerative colitis and who was tired of feeling bad wanted help with her diet. She thought that if she could only eliminate the foods that made her digestive system disruptive, she could live a normal life.

When she came in for consultation, her male cousin, who had Crohn's disease and had already had surgery to remove necrotic tissue in his colon, accompanied her. Both of these young people were in their twenties.

I consulted with the young lady, who was my patient. The cousin – who came in only for moral support – listened as I advised her to start a gluten-free and dairy-free diet immediately.

Four weeks later, she returned, again accompanied by her cousin. Her bloody diarrhoea had completely resolved; she felt "normal" and appreciative.

Then came the surprise: her cousin told me, "I listened to what you said, and I also went gluten-free. It's the first time in my life that I've had normal bowel movements. I wish I had met you 10 years ago!"

Head-to-toe makeover. Perhaps one of the most visibly dramatic improvements I've seen was a case of a young man who had been diagnosed with Darier's disease.

Darier's is a rare psoriasis-like genetic skin condition that causes a scaly rash. The severity of the condition varies widely but this young man had the rash from head to toe. The condition was so extreme that he would not wear T-shirts or shorts. He kept as much skin covered as possible to avoid embarrassing stares.

I put him on a gluten-free and dairy-free diet. In less than 6 months, his skin cleared up completely. He even started going to the beach!

The response was so dramatic, and he was so grateful, that he kept in touch with me for 5 years to thank me. His skin lesions never came back.

I must again remind you that these were *early* cases, more than 20 years ago. At that time, there was no research that linked an intolerance to gluten to the conditions these individuals exhibited.

Today, that is changing. Much of the research is *still* focused on coeliac disease. Yet, more researchers are recognizing that gluten is a problem long before it causes deterioration of the digestive system.

The unfortunate thing about research into gluten intolerance is that it has not been collected into one place. And because gluten intolerance manifests itself in so many different ways – including skin disorders, neurological disorders, digestive disorders and disorders that have no apparent cause – the research gets published in too many places for the GPs who first see patients to know about it.

As a consequence, these doctors attempt to treat symptoms by applying pharmaceutical solutions to the problem. The wrong solution applied to a problem doesn't resolve anything! And their patients are left to cope.

This book is *not* about coping. I wrote this book to create an awareness that the problems you or your loved ones are experiencing may be due to something you ate – and can be resolved by eliminating that "something". It's as simple as that.

This introduction would not be complete without sharing a personal story about "creating an awareness".

As my co-author was researching the chapter on digestive disorders, she decided to find out what research had been done associating gluten sensitivity with colitis, in particular, lymphocytic colitis. Her husband, JC, had been diagnosed with that particular "brand" of colitis and had been taking mesalamine for it for more than 2 years.

Unfortunately, the drug provided minimal (if any) relief. Some days, he had to take the maximum dosage; other days, he seemed to be able to reduce the number of pills he swallowed. But never did the drug completely alleviate his diarrhoea. His gastroenterologist actually told him that the problem could be lifelong and that he would have to cope with it.

My co-author found a study conducted in 2001[1] indicating that 15 per cent of patients with lymphocytic colitis had coeliac disease. The authors wrote, "There is a high frequency of coeliac disease in patients with lymphocytic colitis. Given the importance of the early detection of coeliac disease, it should be excluded in all patients with lymphocytic colitis, particularly if diarrhoea does not respond to conventional treatment."

JC showed the study to his doctor, who ordered a coeliac panel blood test. It came back negative. That meant he did not have coeliac disease. But the blood test did *not* rule out gluten sensitivity.

At my urging, he then took a stool-sample test, available only at one laboratory and (unfortunately) not well known among medical doctors, including his gastroenterologist. (See Chapter 10, Am I Gluten Sensitive?)

The test came back positive. He went on a gluten-free diet. Within a few days, he reduced the amount of mesalamine he had been taking. And within 2 weeks, he was symptom-free and medication-free!

But there's more to this story. Because her husband was on a gluten-free diet, my co-author decided that she, too, would abstain from all gluten. She had vaguely wondered if she could be gluten sensitive, although her only "symptoms" were minor colon disturbances and frequent wind that she had not given much thought to.

Two weeks after starting the diet, she realized that she hadn't felt so good in years! Her symptoms were gone – another gluten-free victory.

The discoveries my co-author made are ones that you can make, too. That is my goal in writing this book – to make you aware that good health may be restored to you just by eliminating a nonessential food from your diet.

I've written this book in four parts:

Part 1 deals with "something you ate" – gluten. You'll learn about its proliferation and the difference between an allergy and an intolerance.

Part 2 explores how gluten sensitivity is often mistaken for other disorders. For doubters (including medical doctors!), we've pulled together scientific proof that gluten is the cause of a myriad of conditions that perplex and plague people. Research aside, I know you will be amazed at the anecdotal evidence and testimonies of medical doctors who have had gluten-sensitive patients – and have successfully treated them by putting them on a gluten-free diet.

Also in the second part, in a chapter devoted to testing, you will read about how you can discover if you are gluten sensitive. (You'll also find out why blood tests don't tell the story about gluten sensitivity.)

If you discover that your condition may be caused by something you ate, what do you do? That's what Part 3 of this book is about. Its goal is to put you on the road to healthy, gluten-free eating.

You'll also discover what to do if eliminating gluten *still* doesn't make you feel better. (Yes, you have more options.)

Finally, Part 4 deals with cooking. When I recommend a gluten-free diet to my patients, their reaction invariably is, "What am I going to eat? Am I going to have to give up *everything*?" This part will show you that you don't have to give up taste or good food to go gluten-free. You'll find recipes for people who don't have much time or interest in cooking, as well as recipes for people who enjoy cooking. And you'll also find a 14-day gluten-free diet.

Are you sick and tired of being sick and tired? Then what do you have to lose? You don't need wheat, barley or rye to be healthy. You *can* live without them. And as I and my co-author and her husband have quickly learned, "After a few days, you don't really miss them".

So, pull out your reading glasses, prop up your feet, and find out if gluten is the hidden cause of your health problems.

To your good health!

PART 1

IS IT SOMETHING I ATE?

It has been said, "Man cannot live by bread alone." But some men (and women, of course) cannot live by *eating* bread. To them, bread is *not* the staff of life. It is a slow-working poison.

As a way of introducing you to the dangers of grain and setting the stage to explore gluten sensitivity, I invite you to take a short quiz, which I hope will jump-start your curiosity:

Q.   *What is gluten? (a) glue (b) something used in making bread (c) a protein found in some grains*

A.   In a sense, all three answers are correct. Most people have heard of gluten in the context of baking bread. Gluten is the stuff that makes dough sticky. In that regard, it *is* a glue – and, in fact, it is sometimes used as a binding agent in the glue found on envelopes and stamps. But in terms of physiological composition, *gluten is a protein,* which is found in wheat, barley and rye.

Q.   *Is wheat safe to eat? (a) yes (b) no*

A.   This is a "yes, but" answer. Whole wheat, eaten in moderation and used in heat-treated cooking or baking, is safe to eat, *but only if you are not gluten sensitive.* Wheat as a raw grain or even in its processed (flour) form is not safe to eat. That is because the grain contains enzyme blockers and lectin, chemicals that are toxic to animals, including human beings. Heat, however, destroys these toxins to a safe level for consumption.

Q.   *Is the wheat that is grown today the same as wheat that was cultivated 100 years ago? (a) yes (b) no*

A.   No! Bioengineers continually work to produce wheat that has more gluten and "better" gluten, in other words, gluten that is stickier. Wheat has been genetically altered so that the wheat that is planted and harvested today is considerably different from the wheat that even our grandparents harvested, milled and used for baking.

Q.   *Which of these grains has gluten?(a) wheat (b) spelt (c) durum (d) semolina (e) rye (f) barley (g) oats*

A.   Spelt, durum and semolina are all types of wheat, and wheat contains gluten. Rye and barley are also gluten-containing grains. Oats are also a grain, but they do not have gluten. *However* – oats often become cross-contaminated when they are planted in fields that have grown wheat or when they are processed in factories that refine wheat. So although oats themselves do not contain gluten, they may not be safe for gluten-sensitive individuals to consume, unless certified to be gluten-free.

Q. *If you are gluten sensitive, should you (a) become desensitized to gluten just as you might with bee venom (b) take a special "gluten pill" before eating bread (c) eliminate all gluten from your diet forever?*

A. Since gluten sensitivity is not an allergy – it is an intolerance – it is not possible to outgrow it or to become desensitized to it. Most gluten-sensitive people probably wish they could take a pill so that they could eat bread or cake, but no pharmaceutical remedy is available. *The only solution to gluten sensitivity is to eliminate all gluten from your diet.*

In Part 1 of this book, you'll discover:

CHAPTER I: GRAIN DANGER. This chapter points out the menace of grains to nutrition today.

CHAPTER 2: ALLERGY OR INTOLERANCE? In this chapter, you'll see why gluten sensitivity is not considered an allergy and will understand why lifelong abstinence from gluten is physiologically important for gluten-sensitive individuals.

CHAPTER 1

GRAIN DANGER

We Westerners love food. We love food so much that we make sure we are never far from it.

In every town centre, you'll find at least one fast-food restaurant. In most supermarkets, there is a deli counter. Every 15 minutes on television, adverts for McDonald's, Burger King, Pizza Hut and Kentucky Fried Chicken bombard viewers. Adverts shown during Saturday morning cartoons tempt children with sweet treats and breakfast cereals.

And if viewers fail to satiate their visual appetites with the adverts, they can turn on TV's Food Channel to drool over all types of concoctions, from pastas to French pastries.

Years ago, our grandparents ate a basic diet of meat, poultry, fish, potatoes and other root vegetables and a variety of garden-fresh vegetables. Their meat was free from hormone enhancements. The fish came directly from the sea or from crystal-clear lakes and rivers, which did not experience fertilizer runoff. And their vegetables were exposed to few (if any) pesticides and herbicides.

They ate bread, cakes and pies, of course. But they baked these goods in their own kitchens, using wheat that had not been genetically altered.

What a difference a few decades have made! Today, we eat out almost as often as we cook at home. And we eat fast food more than we eat well-balanced meals.

Food-manufacturing companies have made sure that we can open a box or a tin, or pop a frozen meal into the microwave oven and enjoy it within minutes and without any cooking skill, whatever type of delicacy takes our fancy.

Food nourishes. It comforts. And when it tastes good, it makes us feel good.

But the same food that you enjoy putting into your mouth may be making you sick!

The culprit? *Gluten.*

If you have heard the word *gluten,* it was most likely in context with baking, as in "kneading dough to develop the gluten". Gluten – a protein – is the stuff that makes dough sticky.

Unfortunately, this chewy, gluey protein that makes bread and bagels taste so good is poison to a large segment of the population who cannot tolerate it. *These people are gluten sensitive.* They suffer from a systemic autoimmune disorder. When they eat *anything* with gluten in it – and that is virtually all processed and prepared foods – their immune system reacts.

For more than 50 years, doctors have pointed to gluten as the cause of coeliac disease (CD) – an autoimmune disorder centred in the gastrointestinal system.

Worldwide, coeliac disease has been studied extensively, almost since it was discovered and named. As testing became more sophisticated and as the definition of coeliac disease was expanded to include more than individuals who had overt symptoms, researchers have shown that coeliac disease afflicts approximately 1 per cent of the world's population, or anywhere from 1 in 100 to 1 in 200 worldwide,[1] with much higher rates in some countries.[2]

In the general populations of Western Europe, the prevalence ranges from 0.5 to 1.26 per cent (1 in 200 to 1 in 79).[3]

For example: a report published in 2001 said that the prevalence of CD (identified through screening methods) in the United Kingdom was 1 in 112 people; in Finland, it was 1 in 130; in Italy, 1 in 184; and in the Sahara, an astonishing 1 in 70.[4]

In the US, medical researchers and practitioners had believed this disease was confined to a relatively small number of people, primarily children. Within the past few years, those beliefs have been put down.

Researchers have discovered that coeliac disease afflicts just under 1 per cent of the population in the United States. A large-scale study of 13,145 individuals[5] showed that 1 out of 133 people in the general population has CD.

The odds are even worse that you will have this disease if you have a first-degree relative with CD (1 out of 22), if you have a second-degree relative with it (1 out of 39), or if you have digestive-disorder symptoms (1 out of 56). If you are one of these unfortunate individuals and continue to eat gluten, you can waste away from malnutrition and may even suffer premature death.

But the gluten problem touches *far more* people than those who have coeliac disease. Some researchers now speculate that in the US *as many as 29 per cent*[6] of the population – almost 3 out of 10 people – are gluten sensitive! And approximately 81 per cent[7] of Americans have a genetic disposition toward gluten sensitivity.

If you are gluten sensitive, you can have a low level of intolerance and function for years – perhaps your entire life – without any identifiable symptoms or with symptoms so mild that you pay no attention to them. Feeling less than 100 per cent is so normal that you don't know you can feel better.

But many people (most of the 2.9 out of 10 who are gluten sensitive) suffer from a variety of physical problems that you and your doctors have *not* linked to the "killer cause", gluten – problems such as diabetes, multiple sclerosis, lupus, arthritis, osteoporosis, chronic fatigue syndrome and some forms of dermatitis and psoriasis, to name a few. (Part 2 of this book details the variety of problems that gluten can cause.)

Gluten sensitivity is a *huge* problem contributing to the chronic diseases that plague Western society today. We are only now discovering its extent.

But, like any other problem, if we understand its origin and its cause, we can fix it. All problems, after all, have a solution. Gluten sensitivity is no different.

AN EVOLUTIONARY PROBLEM

The problem with gluten can be traced back to the agricultural revolution and the cultivation of grains more than 10,000 years ago. Until that time, Paleolithic man subsisted off the land: he was a hunter-gatherer – getting his needed protein, fat and carbohydrate requirements by hunting game and fish and gathering fruits, nuts and vegetables. Nature provided him with all of his needed nutrients; all he had to do was find them.

Although the life span of early *Homo sapiens* was short (his life expectancy was only about 20 years), his health was relatively good, especially when food was plentiful. When food was scarce, early man did suffer from nutritional deficiencies, which contributed to early demise, but death was caused largely by infection, parasitic infestation and by accident.

Enter the age of agriculture. When Neolithic man, a successor to Paleolithic man, discovered how to cultivate and mill grain and how to use fire to cook his food – which destroyed toxins in otherwise inedible foodstuffs – his life changed. No longer dependent on the abundance of nature, he could now control much of his food source. This resulted in allowing more people to exist on a smaller amount of land – a *good* consequence of agricultural technology.

A *bad* consequence was that with the planting, harvesting and milling of grain – particularly wheat, but also barley and rye – man introduced a new plant protein into his digestive system. *That protein was gluten.*

Many nutritional scientists trace the cause of today's chronic health problems to the advent of the agricultural revolution. Two researchers, Dr. James H. O'Keefe Jr., and Loren Cordain, PhD, observed, "Humans evolved during the Paleolithic period, from approximately 2.6 million years ago to 10,000 years ago. Although the human genome has remained largely unchanged…our diet and lifestyle have become progressively more divergent from those of our ancient ancestors. These maladaptive changes began approximately 10,000 years ago with the advent of the agricultural revolution and have been accelerating in recent decades. Socially, we are a people of the 21st century, but genetically, we remain citizens of the Paleolithic era."[8]

Our genetic similarity to Paleolithic man – and our inability to tolerate gluten – began to create a serious problem when we left our agricultural society behind and entered into another significant stage of human development: the Industrial Revolution.

Technology stimulated a change in grain consumption with two significant inventions:

The mechanical reaper. The invention of the mechanical reaper in 1831, meant that wheat could be harvested more efficiently than by hand – eight acres a day by the reaper, only two by hand. That resulted in the greater abundance of grain to feed the growing populations of the Western world.

The roller mill. Until the Industrial Revolution, milling had been done through stone grinding in a process not dissimilar to that used by Neolithic man (although on a larger scale): the heads of grain were crushed between two big stones to make flour. The flour that resulted was wholegrain flour that included all parts of the wheat kernel.

In 1873, the milling process changed. At that year's World's Fair, the world was introduced to the roller miller,[9] which used steel rollers to mill grain and refined flour better and more cheaply. With the widespread adoption of this technology, the majority of the Western population suddenly could afford to buy refined flour. And they quickly acquired a taste for white bread.

Because of the availability of refined flour, as well as the invention of new types of mechanizations, people no longer had to live off the land; the "land" came to them through processed meats, vegetables and grains. Their hunting and gathering consisted of finding a shop or supermarket and putting tins into a shopping bag.

In the United States in particular, as the 20th century began and the emigration of Americans from the land to the cities intensified, the demand for more-processed foods continued to increase, initially for tinned goods, later – once households had electric refrigeration – for frozen goods. In the 1950s, TV dinners became popular, along with frozen bakery treats.

Today, of course, every type of food you desire is available in a convenient form, ready to be popped into a microwave or an oven.

This demand for convenience caused grain consumption to escalate.

If you think that you don't eat that much grain (and gluten), think again: much of the gluten that you consume is hidden. You don't know you are eating it! For example:

• Food manufacturers *add* "vital gluten" (gluten that is specifically processed from high-gluten-containing wheat) to wheat flour to give it more binding power.

• Gluten is used in the manufacturing of virtually all boxed, packaged and tinned processed foods to create textures that are more palatable to our taste buds, or is used as binders, thickeners and coatings. It is even used as glue on envelopes and stamps!

• Even if you were consuming the same amount of grains today as you did last year or 10 years ago, you would be ingesting more gluten. That is because bioengineers continually work to "improve" gluten and make it a larger and more potent part of edible grain. It is estimated that today's wheat contains nearly 90 per cent more gluten than wheat did from a century ago!

To get an idea of how much hidden gluten you consume, take a walk down the aisles in your supermarket. Stop to read the labels. You'll find wheat, barley or rye in products such as:

- Barbecue sauce
- Biscuits and cakes
- Breaded fish, chicken and seafood
- Bread – even "potato bread" or "rice bread"
- Cereal
- Couscous
- Crackers
- Flavoured potato crisps
- Frozen dinners
- Pasta
- Pies
- Rice mixes
- Sauces and gravies
- Some ice creams
- Some salad dressings
- Soy sauce
- Teriyaki sauce
- Tinned and dried soups
- And many, many more items

INCREASED JEOPARDY

Have you heard the expression, "Just because you *can,* doesn't mean you *should*"? The expression may well apply to the consumption of grain, especially wheat, barley and rye.

The danger that grains presents to us is probably best evidenced by looking at the effect that a modern diet has had on modern-day hunter-gatherers, whose diet is significantly different from that of Westerners.

All people require foods that provide energy. According to The Economic Research Service in the US,[10] the energy sources of Americans in 2000 came from:

- Fats and oils (22 per cent)
- Grains (24 per cent – that's a quarter of the overall diet!)
- Meat, poultry and fish (14 per cent)
- Processed foods (21 per cent)
- Sugars and sweeteners (19 per cent)

This is fairly representative of the modern Western diet as a whole and is considerably different from hunter-gatherers (yes, some tribes still exist today), who consume:[11]

- Fruits, vegetables, nuts and honey (65 per cent)
- Lean game, wild fowl, eggs, fish and shellfish (35 per cent)

Noticeably absent from the hunter-gatherer diet are three types of foods:

- Dairy (Typically, they use only fermented dairy products or dairy straight from their own livestock – more often goats than cows.)
- Processed foods (They eat off the land.)
- Refined grains (If they eat grains, they eat them as wholegrains and in moderation.)

A number of nutritional anthropologists have studied the danger of grains (and remember – grains are the source of gluten!) on society.

A Dentist's Observations

In the 1930s, Dr. Weston A. Price,[12] an American dentist with a passion for nutrition, roamed the globe to study primitive hunter-gatherer cultures. Dr. Price suspected that poor nutrition played a part in physical degeneration, manifested in tooth decay and deformed dental arches. To test his hypothesis, he decided to travel the world and observe isolated primitive peoples – those who were largely (although not exclusively) hunter-gatherers.

His travels took him to sequestered villages in Switzerland and Gaelic communities in the Outer Hebrides; Eskimos and Native Americans; Melanesian and Polynesian South Sea islanders; African tribes; Australian Aborigines; New Zealand Maori; and Indians of South America.

Dr. Price observed that people who ate native diets had beautiful, straight teeth with no decay and strong bodies; and a high resistance to disease. One of the key characteristics Dr. Price noted about traditional diets: *These diets did not include refined or denatured foods, such as refined sugar, white flour and tinned foods.*

He contrasted these healthy native people with those who no longer lived in complete isolation but had been introduced to modern diets that included sugar, white flour, pasteurized milk and convenience foods filled with preservatives and additives.

Dr. Price observed that "modern-day" natives experienced more tooth decay and exhibited deformed and narrow dental arches, tooth crowding and pinched features. He also noted an increase in birth defects and a susceptibility to illness. Diseases that had previously left these societies untouched now took their toll.[13]

Dr. Price recorded the physical changes in the new generations and compared them with the faces of healthy ancestors. He published his photographs in his book, *Nutrition and Physical Degeneration.*

Diet and Diabetes

A paper published in 2001 in the *Asia Pacific Journal of Clinical Nutrition* reported on the dietary trends of indigenous Fijians. The author stated that the diet of the Fijians changed drastically over 50 years and adversely affected the population:[14] "The total energy derived from cereals and sugar increased dramatically with a reduction in consumption of traditional foods. The prevalence of diabetes among the urban indigenous population in 1965 was very low compared to the 1980 figure, while the National Nutrition Survey of the same ethnic group showed a *433 per cent increase* in urban diabetes from 1965 to 1993."

Gluten sensitivity can affect the functioning of the pancreas – the organ that regulates sugar metabolism. When this happens, the symptoms resemble diabetes.

Grain Damage

In their 2004 paper, medical and nutritionist researchers O'Keefe and Cordain state that historical evidence indicates that hunter-gatherers were generally fit and free from chronic diseases.[15] That condition, however, changed when these primitive peoples transitioned to an agrarian society. Among the effects grain had on them were:

- Diminished stature
- Greater incidence of osteoporosis, rickets and other mineral- and vitamin-deficiency diseases
- Higher childhood mortality
- More obesity, diabetes and other diseases of civilizations
- Shorter life spans

Native American Travesty

North America had its share of hunter-gatherers – the Native American tribes. When the federal government took the land away from these tribes and placed them on reservations – most of which did not have the resources for hunting nor for agriculture – their diet changed radically.

Regardless of their origination, traditional Native American diets consisted of wild game, berries, roots, teas and indigenous vegetables. When Native Americans cultivated grain, it was corn – *a non-gluten-containing grain*. Wheat was not a traditional part of their food intake.

When the government placed Native Americans on reservations, bureaucrats provided "food" for them – processed food, tinned fruits and vegetables, refined flour and refined sugars.

The diet of Native Americans today remains high in fat and refined starches and sugars.[16] Popular among them is white bread, white flour and white rice. The change in diet among Native Americans has resulted in some of the highest rates of diabetes and chronic diseases of any groups in the United States.[17]

In fact, the American Diabetes Association reports that 14.5 per cent of Native Americans and Alaska natives who receive care from the Indian Health Services have diabetes.[18] The Pima tribe in Arizona has the highest rate of diabetes in the world. About 50 per cent of adults between the ages of 30 and 64 suffer from this chronic disease.[19]

BACK TO GLUTEN

All around the world – from Fiji to North America – a change in traditional diet to the diet "enjoyed" by us today has resulted in chronic health problems that plague "advanced" Western cultures. It would be ludicrous to assert that *all* of these chronic problems are due to gluten. But it would also be naïve to think that grain (in particular, wheat, which is the number one staple in the Western world) is an "innocent bystander".

Just because we *can* eat more grain – and gluten – doesn't mean we *should*. Too much of a good thing is bad. Perhaps that is what has happened with our love affair with grain (and gluten). Perhaps we just got carried away with it.

So, now we have a situation: the incidence of chronic illness is rising. And the number of people with gluten sensitivity is rising. A coincidence? I don't think so.

So, your question remains, "Is gluten making me ill?"

It just might be.

UNDERSTANDING GLUTEN SENSITIVITY

Gluten causes problems. That's an understatement. Comprehending *why* gluten causes so many health problems for those who are sensitive to it and how you can ascertain if you are gluten sensitive requires having a basic understanding of what happens in your digestive system.

Digestion, of course, begins when you put food into your mouth. Chewed food passes from the mouth down the oesophagus (a tube that connects the throat to the stomach) to the stomach, where it is churned and mixed with some gastric juices to create a very sloppy type of soup.

This soup then passes into the small intestine, where more juices from the pancreas and the gallbladder help break down the food's various components (proteins, carbohydrates and fats) into their respective amino acids, monosaccharides and fatty acids. Once the food is broken down into these soluble components, it is absorbed by fingerlike projections called villi in the small intestine. These thousands of villi are composed of capillaries and lymphatic tissue, which pass the nutrients to the bloodstream.

The parts of the food that cannot be broken down into amino acids, monosaccharides and fatty acids pass on to the large intestine and are eliminated in a matter of hours.

That's what happens when we eat nutritious food. But unfortunately, not everything we take in as food is healthy for us. We sometimes ingest antigens – foreign substances, such as toxins or bacteria, or (for some people) *actual foodstuffs such as gluten*. In childhood, especially, we are exposed to a plethora of food antigens.

When we take in food antigens, the body goes to work to fight them off. The regulatory T-cells (white cells in the blood) in our immune system easily recognize these antigens and destroy them so that they will not cause us any harm.

Sometimes, however, the balance in our immune system is disrupted by infections, medications, stress and other factors. This disruption causes our T-cells to stop regulating properly.

When this occurs, the antigens from a food we have eaten all our lives can suddenly produce a significant amount of inflammation, which can cause some atrophy (deterioration) of our intestinal villi, thus allowing the food antigens to enter our bloodstream.

The antigens that enter the bloodstream then cause the body to produce antibodies, which attempt to fight the antigens.

Let's bring this home to the problem of gluten sensitivity.

If you are gluten sensitive, your digestive system does not have the ability to break gluten down into soluble proteins (amino acids). Consequently, whenever you eat wheat, barley or rye in *any* form and *any* amount (not necessarily as a big slice of bread or cake!), your body reacts to the gluten because it interprets the gluten to be an antigen. The gluten fails to be broken down and passes into the bloodstream.

When the gluten gets into your bloodstream in this "raw" form, your body forms antibodies to combat it. These antibodies, which reside in the intestine as long as the villi are functioning properly, may be:

- Anti-endomysial antibodies

- Anti-gliadin IgA antibodies

- Anti-tissue transglutaminase antibodies

As your body valiantly but unsuccessfully tries to break down the gluten into its component amino acids, and the antibodies fight the invader gluten, the lining of the intestine becomes inflamed. If the inflammation in your intestine progresses to the point of the villi becoming flattened, the antibodies that formed to fight the gluten also pass into the bloodstream.

Gluten sensitivity is not necessarily something you are born with. You may acquire it at any point during your life. Unfortunately, even though the prevalence of coeliac disease (the worst case of gluten sensitivity) is higher than anyone ever envisioned, most doctors do not screen their patients for CD. A significant number of doctors still erroneously believe that CD is rare and a disease of childhood, despite the scientific evidence to the contrary.

You may be asking yourself, "How can I tell if I am gluten sensitive?" You have two options:

- You can eliminate gluten from your diet. Grains are not essential foods! You can give them up without any bad effects on your overall health. If you feel better and any suspect symptoms go away, you are probably gluten sensitive.

- You can be tested for gluten sensitivity – but you must ask for the *right* test. The right test can tell you definitively if you are gluten sensitive. (How to test for coeliac disease and gluten sensitivity is covered in detail in Chapter 10, Am I Gluten Sensitive?)

Before we get to that important topic, however, we need to look at who really needs to find out if they're gluten sensitive and why. You'll be amazed.

CHAPTER 2

ALLERGY OR INTOLERANCE?

Nutritionists are dietary sleuths. We examine health problems in the context of food, and we make recommendations for dietary changes and supplementation to achieve optimal nutrition and health.

Throughout the years, a number of my patients have been individuals whose health problems and symptoms have failed to respond to traditional medical intervention. When I suggest to these patients that they may be gluten sensitive, they typically react, "Does this mean I have an allergy?"

The answer is "No!"

Gluten sensitivity is *not* an allergy. It is a food intolerance. Allergies and intolerances are both reactions by your immune system, but those reactions are completely different. It's important for you to understand the difference between an allergy and an intolerance, because understanding is critical to accepting and subsequently dealing with it.

WHAT IS AN ALLERGY?

A food allergy is an exaggerated response by your body's immune system to a food that you have consumed. According to the medical charity Allergy UK, approximately 2 per cent of the UK population suffer from food allergies.

Although *any* individual may be allergic to *any* food – even the "safest" of foods – 90 per cent of food allergies result from eating foods belonging to eight categories: milk, eggs, fish, crustacean shellfish, tree nuts, peanuts, wheat and soyabeans.

Normally, when your body senses a foreign invader, such as a dangerous bacteria, a virus or even an offending food, it calls upon its immune system – specialized white blood cells, chemicals and proteins and enzymes – to defend against the invader. Specialized white blood cells produce antibodies, which attach to a specific antigen (invader), to make it easier for other specialized white blood cells to destroy it.

But sometimes, the "normal" thing doesn't happen, especially if you come from a family with a propensity toward allergies. Instead, you experience an immediate-onset allergy.

When you are exposed to a food to which you are allergic, several things happen:

- Your body produces a food-specific antibody called immunoglobulin E (IgE), which is a type of protein.

- One side of the IgE antibody recognizes the allergic food and tightly binds to it in an effort to destroy it.

- The other side of the IgE antibody attaches to a mast cell, which is an immune cell loaded with histamine and found in all body tissues. (Most mast cells are found in your nose, throat, lungs, skin and gastrointestinal tract.)

- The next time you eat the allergic food, the IgE antibodies immediately attach themselves to the food, and this causes histamine and other allergy-related chemicals to be released from the mast cell.

The allergic reaction occurs within minutes or up to an hour or so after eating the offending food. Depending upon the severity and the particular food, you may experience tingling or itching in your mouth; stomach cramping, diarrhoea or vomiting; or a skin rash or hives.

And in severe cases, as the histamines travel through your bloodstream, your blood pressure may drop. When they reach the lungs, they can cause an asthmatic attack.

It is the histamine released from mast cells that causes the adverse reaction (hives, diarrhoea, gastric symptoms, etc.). To stop the reaction, it is necessary to counteract the histamine. A dose of over-the-counter antihistamine medication is usually sufficient to return the body to normal. In severe cases, more drastic measures must be taken.

For example, people who are allergic to peanuts are at high risk of anaphylaxis, a severe type of life-threatening allergic reaction. They must carry a syringe of adrenalin with them at all times, in case they are unknowingly exposed to some form of peanuts. If they don't inject themselves with the adrenalin immediately, their reaction is so severe that their breathing can become completely obstructed and they can die.

Other people may find that when they eat seafood, their tongue or throat swells, or they get a rash or one or more of the other symptoms rather quickly after eating the offending food. Quick reaction with an antihistamine is necessary to avoid a trip to hospital or phoning an ambulance.

Children often outgrow minor allergies, but adults who have food allergies own them for life. The **only way** to avoid an allergic reaction is to avoid the offending food.

FOOD INTOLERANCE

Although many people think they have a food allergy, they actually have food immune reactivity (FIR), or food intolerance, which is a delayed reaction from eating some foods or ingredients. Common types of FIR occur from eating gluten in wheat, barley and rye; dairy products; nightshades (tomato, potato, aubergine, tobacco and peppers); and soya products.

FIR is much more complicated than an allergic reaction:

- Symptoms are sometimes similar to those resulting from an allergic reaction, but the cause is not easily identified. Reactions to ingesting an offending food are delayed – by hours or even days, and symptoms generally become apparent over time.

- FIR does *not* involve IgE reactions; no histamines are released. Consequently, antihistamines have no effect. There are no pills or medications you can take to alleviate the symptoms.

- An allergic reaction can evoke a violent effect (as in the case of anaphylaxis), but it incurs no long-term damage to organs. FIR, on the other hand, is insidious, and its long-term effects on organs throughout the body can be devastating, even leading to premature death.

Let's look at these differences between immediate-onset reaction and gluten-derived FIR more closely.

Symptoms

The most common symptoms of an allergic reaction, as we have already described, are an immediate reaction to food, which shows up as tingling or itching in your mouth, swelling, or difficulty in breathing; stomach cramping, diarrhoea or vomiting; or a skin rash or hives.

If you are gluten sensitive (cannot tolerate the protein gluten in wheat, barley or rye), you may also experience any of those symptoms – as well as a number of others that masquerade as symptoms of other physical conditions. (Part 2 elaborates on the symptoms of gluten sensitivity.)

Because of the immediacy of an allergic reaction, it is relatively easy to see cause and effect between an offending food and the reaction to it. But in FIR, especially with gluten sensitivity, the reaction will not be seen for some time. It may take many exposures over a long period of time before any symptoms appear. That makes FIR difficult to diagnose but even more important to identify, because of long-term consequences.

Different Antibody Production

In an allergic reaction, the body forms IgE antibodies, which cause histamine to be released. That histamine then causes the specific allergic reaction, such as hives or swelling. Taking an antihistamine makes the symptoms go away.

In FIR, specifically gluten-sensitivity FIR, the body may also produce antibodies – but the antibodies are of a different type: anti-gliadin IgA antibody (AGA), anti-tissue transglutaminase antibody (tTGA) and anti-endomysial antibody (EMA).

These antibodies do *not* trigger histamines. Rather, they cause a chronic inflammation and eventually can lead to the complete flattening of intestinal villi – the fingerlike projections in the intestine that absorb nutrients. When that happens, gluten sensitivity becomes all-out coeliac disease.

Long-Term Effects

Aside from anaphylaxis, which is violent and must be counteracted quickly to avoid death, the effects of an allergic reaction are not long-term. Once you recover from the allergic reaction, your body resumes normal functioning. As long as you stay away from the offending food, you will not suffer any other effects.

Not so with food immune reactivity. The long-term effects can play havoc on your health, especially in the case of gluten sensitivity. Here are some examples:

Permanent organ damage. As we have already stated, undiagnosed gluten sensitivity can result in coeliac disease. But it can also cause other organ damage, such as damage to the pancreas or to the neurological system. Left unchecked, some of the effects of gluten intolerance can be irreparable.

Severe tissue damage. When gluten causes FIR, an extreme inflammatory response results. Ingestion of gluten sparks T-cell mediated inflammation and an abnormal increase in the production of nitric oxide, which can result in severe tissue damage if not controlled.

Hyperactivated immune system. If you have gluten-caused FIR, any gluten you eat triggers reactions within the body. For example: gluten stimulates an overproduction of pro-inflammatory cytokines (such as interferon, which regulates immune responses). The result is inflammation.

Gluten may also cause the production of antibodies that affect the balance of inhibitory and excitatory neurotransmitters in the central nervous system, resulting in symptoms of ataxia and neuropathy. (See Chapter 4, Neurological Disorders, for more information on these conditions.)

ONE SOLUTION FOR BOTH PROBLEMS

Although it is true that you can take an antihistamine to counteract the effects of a food allergy, you can't "cure" the allergy. The only cure is to abstain from eating the offending food.

The same holds true for FIR. In gluten sensitivity, no medications alleviate symptoms. The only treatment is to eliminate *all* gluten (wheat, barley and rye) from your diet – for life.

The intolerance your body has for gluten remains with you forever. This intolerance is insidious. Don't be fooled into thinking you are cured if you go off gluten for a time and your symptoms go away. The intolerance is just waiting for you to relapse into a gluten-containing diet again! And if that happens, the symptoms and inflammation – resulting in potential bodily damage – will return.

PART 2

GLUTEN SENSITIVITY'S MASQUERADE

Gluten sensitivity is a chameleon-like disease. Instead of confining itself to one area of the body – such as the gut, where it was first described by the ancient Greek doctor Arataeos in AD 100[1] – and exhibiting one set of defining characteristics that can be easily diagnosed, it can develop in many different, unsuspected ways.

The condition's ability to hide behind a variety of symptoms makes it difficult – but not impossible – to diagnose correctly. Obviously, without the correct diagnosis, it is impossible for a doctor to prescribe the right remedy, which in the case of gluten sensitivity is *one* thing: *a gluten-free diet.* And prescribing the *wrong* remedy (harsh pharmaceuticals) can often cause even more complicating problems than the original disease!

Misdiagnosis, because of gluten sensitivity's ability to masquerade as – and, in some cases, piggyback onto – the symptoms of other diseases and disorders, can have devastating effects. Not only are people who are misdiagnosed relegated to "living with" a disease (when they may be able to be free of it), but living with this condition can lead to severe consequences – such as the irreversible crippling of rheumatoid arthritis, bone loss and breakage, infection or even death.

In this part of the book, we're going to take a look at a number of different diseases and conditions to uncover gluten sensitivity's masquerade:

CHAPTER 3: GLUTEN AND SKIN DISEASES. These include dermatitis herpetiformis, psoriasis, eczema, acne and hives.

CHAPTER 4: NEUROLOGICAL DISORDERS. These include ataxia (loss of muscle coordination), severe headaches and behavioural problems such as attention deficit hyperactivity disorder (ADHD).

CHAPTER 5: OTHER AUTOIMMUNE DISEASES. These include lupus, multiple sclerosis, diabetes, scleroderma, thyroid disease, osteoporosis, rheumatoid arthritis and ankylosing spondylitis.

CHAPTER 6: DIGESTIVE DISORDERS. These include the all-encompassing irritable bowel syndrome (IBS), Crohn's disease, ulcerative colitis, proctitis, gastro-oesophageal reflux, ulcers and giardiasis, in addition to classic coeliac disease.

CHAPTER 7: UNDIAGNOSED DISEASES AND CONDITIONS. These include such catch-all conditions as chronic fatigue syndrome, fibromyalgia, weight loss that cannot be accounted for, anaemia, chronic infection and asthma.

CHAPTER 8: A WORD ABOUT FIDO. As you'll learn, gluten sensitivity affects pets as well as people.

CHAPTER 9: FROM THE FILES OF HEALTH PROFESSIONALS. Doctors share their success stories treating gluten-sensitive patients who come to them with a variety of symptoms.

CHAPTER 10: AM I GLUTEN SENSITIVE? We look at the reasons why blood tests cannot tell the story about gluten sensitivity, and we identify new tests that are highly sensitive for pinpointing this condition.

CHAPTER 3

GLUTEN AND SKIN DISEASES

What is worse than an itch? Well, a lot of things. But to someone who has a rash that won't go away, an itch is unbearable, especially if it spreads and refuses to respond to "normal" lotions, ointments, or even steroids.

In this chapter, we'll examine gluten sensitivity and how it expresses itself in skin disorders, often masquerading as other more common autoimmune dermal problems.

DERMATITIS HERPETIFORMIS

One of the itches that won't go away (without proper treatment) is the now-recognized and well-accepted form of gluten sensitivity, dermatitis herpetiformis (DH). DH was first described as a distinct *clinical* entity in 1884 by an American dermatologist, Louis Duhring.[1] But it wasn't until 1967 that it was actually linked to gluten sensitivity.

Typically, DH is characterized by small groups of itchy blisters, often on red plaques, located on the back of the elbows and forearms, on the buttocks and in the front of the knees. But, the rash can occur in other places on the body, including the face, scalp and trunk. Anyone can get this skin disorder, but its initial outbreak seems to occur more often in younger people.

DH occurs as an immune-system reaction to gluten. Instead of digesting this protein, the body fights it with an antibody (called IgA) that is produced in the lining of the intestines. When IgA combines with ingested gluten, the combined antibody/gluten substance circulates in the bloodstream and eventually clogs up the small blood vessels in the skin. The clog attracts white blood cells brought in by the body to fight the invasion. The white blood cells, in turn, release powerful chemicals that create the rash.[2]

The interesting thing about DH is that although it is caused by gluten sensitivity, affected individuals may not have *classic* signs of gluten intolerance such as distress to the gastrointestinal system. In other words, their gut may *not* be affected. That's why doctors for years did not think to associate the mysterious skin rash, which failed to respond to "normal" protocols, with gluten sensitivity.

If you have DH, you know how bad it is. One sufferer described that it was "…like rolling in stinging nettles naked with a severe sunburn, then wrapping yourself in a wool blanket filled with ants and fleas…"[3]

Imagine suffering from this type of rash and having it misdiagnosed for years! That's what has happened to countless DH sufferers. Here are a few cases of misdiagnoses:[4]

A 5-year+ problem. During the year he was an exchange student in Germany, Eric ate a lot of bread and pastry. Shortly after he returned to the United States, he developed a small purple blister on his right buttock. Within a year, the rash grew to include his other buttock and each of his knees and elbows.

The diagnosis his doctor made: a strange case of poison ivy, which he treated with prednisolone, a corticosteroid that can have serious side effects, such as upset stomach, stomach irritation, vomiting, headache, dizziness, insomnia, restlessness, depression, anxiety, acne, increased hair growth, easy bruising, swollen face and ankles, vision problems and muscle weakness.[5]

After another year of unrelenting itching and pain and the spreading of the rash, which did not respond to the cream, Eric went to another doctor, who said he had a rare form of pustular psoriasis. The remedy – another type of topical corticosteroid cream.

He used the cream for 5 years, yet the rash continued to spread, and he developed a secondary staphylococcal (or bacterial) infection. Eric finally found a doctor who was able to diagnose the problem correctly – dermatitis herpetiformis. A gluten-free diet cleared up the condition.

Not a mite problem. According to the first doctor Bill consulted, the rash that began to plague him was shingles. Shingles (herpes zoster) is characterized by an outbreak of a rash or blisters on the skin caused by a virus – the same virus that causes chickenpox, the varicella-zoster virus. Anyone who has had chickenpox is at risk of getting shingles, which is described as being intense and unrelenting. The symptoms of shingles can be relieved, at least temporarily, by taking antiviral drugs, but the disease must run its course, usually 3 to 5 weeks.[6] The virus continues to be harboured in the body even after the condition has cleared up.

Bill didn't have shingles, so the treatment the doctor prescribed did him no good and the rash persisted. He then went to a dermatologist, who told him he had *scabies*!

Scabies is caused by a tiny mite that burrows under the skin and causes severe itching. The effective cure for scabies is a topical insecticide cream, which the doctor prescribed. Of course, the lotion didn't work.

Bill consulted several different doctors over the course of months. More than one gave him the same scabies diagnosis. Frustrated, he finally returned to his original dermatologist, who this time did a biopsy and discovered that Bill didn't have scabies after all. He had dermatitis herpetiformis. He went on a gluten-free diet, and his skin condition went away.

Cure worse than the problem. David began to develop tiny water blisters, which burst and left scabs. Because he had been working long hours in a stressful job, his family doctor initially diagnosed stress-related psoriasis. The condition did not clear up.

For *18 years,* David endured the problem, with only periodic, short-term relief. One doctor prescribed a corticosteroid cream. This, however, was a case of the cure possibly being worse than the problem.

As already mentioned, corticosteroid cream can have harsh side effects if used long term on large areas of the skin, especially on raw skin and in skin folds. The particular cream David used, Fucibet, can cause the adrenal glands to decrease the production of natural hormones and also cause the skin to thin.[7] After using the cream daily for 2 years, he began to experience side effects, including sore eyes and dry skin on his cheek bones.

David finally found a new doctor who correctly diagnosed the problem as DH caused by gluten sensitivity. A gluten-free diet cured his 18-year condition.

DH *can* be cured. For immediate relief, doctors may prescribe drugs

– Dapsone, sulphapyridine or sulphamethoxypyridazine. All of these drugs are actually antimicrobials that were developed in the 1930s and 1940s. It is not understood exactly *how* they work on DH, but they act as agents to address the skin condition. Although the drugs control the rash within days, DH returns quickly when the drugs are discontinued.

In other words, these drugs are used to produce immediate relief from the itching but do not cure the condition.[8]

The cure for DH, like any other gluten sensitivity, is a gluten-free diet. When the individuals mentioned in the previous cases went on a gluten-free diet, their DH disappeared.

PSORIASIS

In the case studies we just cited, DH was misdiagnosed as psoriasis, a noncontagious skin disease that afflicts approximately 2 per cent of the UK population. Misdiagnosis is understandable, because psoriasis and DH have two things in common.

Similar appearance. The conditions look the same – a recurrent skin condition that appears as raised red patches of skin and is often itchy.

Caused by an immune-system response. Both DH and psoriasis are caused by an immune-system response. A number of different things, such as stress, infections, reactions to some medications and heat, may trigger psoriasis. DH, on the other hand, is triggered by the immune system's response to gluten.

With these similarities, it is no wonder that doctors may assume that a person suffering from psoriasis-like symptoms actually has the more common condition.

However, that assumption is not valid. In one screening study, researchers found that 16 per cent of people with psoriasis also had antibodies (IgA and/or IgG) to gliadin (gluten).[9]

In another study, researchers had observed that because gluten antibodies (AGA) were often present in people who had psoriasis, they conducted a study of 130 patients with psoriasis. They found that people who had a higher level of AGA had more-severe cases of psoriasis.[10] Put another way – *some people who have psoriasis also have gluten sensitivity, and the gluten sensitivity aggravates the psoriasis.*

The treatment for psoriasis is considerably different than the treatment for DH. Psoriasis may be treated in a variety of ways, including using creams and ointments to reduce swelling and itching, exposing the affected skin to natural ultraviolet light and, in severe cases, taking drugs or getting injections for systemic treatment.

Despite the variety of treatments for psoriasis, none cures it.

However, people with psoriasis (without arthritis) who have gluten sensitivity recover from their psoriasis when they go on a gluten-free diet. In a 2003 study,[11] individuals showed a clinical improvement in their psoriasis when they went gluten-free for 3 months. When they went back to a regular diet, the psoriasis worsened. The study confirmed that a gluten-free diet can influence psoriasis in people who have gluten antibodies (IgA or IgG).

Unfortunately, a gluten-free diet will not help all people who have psoriasis – only those with gluten sensitivity. A study of 33 individuals who had anti-gliadin antibodies and six who did not proved that a gluten-free diet helped clear up psoriasis in the gluten-sensitive patients but did not have any effect on those who were not gluten sensitive.[12]

ECZEMA, ACNE AND ACNE ROSEA

What about eczema, acne and acne rosea – skin conditions that are similar in their symptoms to DH and are also caused by an autoimmune response? Doctors know that diet affects these conditions, and some doctors have observed that when some individuals with these conditions go on a gluten-free diet, their skin condition improves, similar to what occurred in the following two cases[13] of pemphigus (a type of eczema), a rare autoimmune blistering disease of the skin:

Gluten sensitivity late in life. An 82-year-old woman broke out in blister-like lesions. She had not been taking any drugs that might have accounted for the eczema, and she had been in good health. Laboratory tests showed she had gluten antibodies (IgA). Her doctor put her on a gluten-free diet, and 22 days later, the lesions had cleared.

Sensitivity in a teenager. An 18-year-old woman broke out in fluid-filled skin lesions on her chest, abdomen, neck and lower back. The lesions were even present on her arms and legs. She had no other abnormalities. Testing showed the presence of gluten antibodies, and she was placed on a gluten-free diet. Within a month, the lesions disappeared.

HIVES (URTICARIA)

Urticaria – commonly known as hives – affects approximately 20 per cent of people at some stage of their lives. This condition may also be a clue for undiagnosed gluten sensitivity.

Most hives are caused by an allergic reaction to eating certain foods, such as shellfish or strawberries. Usually within minutes or sometimes hours of eating the food, the person breaks out in itchy welts or pimples. Generally, these acute hives last only a short time and go away on their own. If relief from the itching is needed, an oral or ointment antihistamine is effective.

When hives become chronic, however, and the cause is difficult if not impossible to pinpoint, sensitivity to gluten should be considered, as these cases suggest:

From hay fever to hives.[14] A 24-year-old woman went to her doctor because she was experiencing hay fever. Pinprick tests showed that she was allergic to pollen. She was successfully treated with antihistamines. Three months later, she returned to the doctor, this time with generalized hives. The doctor took a detailed medical history, which did not reveal any allergies to food, food additives or medications. She was in otherwise good health, with no other symptoms of any other condition. The doctor treated her hives with an oral antihistamine.

After taking the drug for a month with no improvement, her hives worsened to the point that she was admitted to the hospital. A complete physical examination, including blood tests for anti-gliadin antibodies, was given. The diagnosis: coeliac disease.

The woman began a gluten-free diet. Her hives improved after a month and completely disappeared after 3 months.

Seven months of itching.[15] An 11-year-old boy came down with a case of chronic hives that persisted for 7 months. He had weals on his trunk, face and extremities that did not respond to conventional therapy.

The doctors took a skin biopsy and found that he had dermatitis herpetiformis. At the time of diagnosis, he had no other symptoms of gluten sensitivity.

If anecdotal case studies are not convincing enough, consider this: in a study published in 2005, researchers found that 4 out of 79 children (5 per cent) with chronic hives were gluten sensitive.[16] This represented a much higher incidence than in the control group (0.67 per cent). When the newly discovered gluten-sensitive patients were put on a gluten-free diet, their hives went away.

Not all skin disorders are caused by gluten sensitivity, but for those that cannot be traced to specific causes, gluten should be considered a culprit.

CHAPTER 4

NEUROLOGICAL DISORDERS

Neurological disorders include such diverse problems as lack of muscle coordination, unexplained severe headaches and psychiatric problems that are exemplified by bizarre behaviour.

Not all of these types of neurological disorders can be attributed to a sensitivity to gluten, of course. But gluten sensitivity can take on the same types of symptoms.

When symptoms persist and medical remedies are ineffective, it may be time to consider gluten intolerance.

ATAXIA (LOSS OF MUSCLE COORDINATION)

Idiopathic sporadic ataxia is a fancy name for irregular loss of muscle coordination (sporadic ataxia) that has no known cause (idiopathic).

People who have idiopathic sporadic ataxia may exhibit a number of symptoms, such as:

- Darting, unfocused vision

- Difficulty walking because of leg-muscle control

- Drooling

- Jerky arm and hand movements

- Slurred speech

- Sporadic leg movements

Ataxia is uncommon. In the US, for example, an estimated 150,000 people are afflicted with hereditary and sporadic ataxia.[1] Through testing, doctors can correctly identify and label some forms of this disorder.

But when they can't pinpoint a specific cause, such as genetics, stroke or alcoholism, doctors dub the syndrome "idiopathic sporadic ataxia".

One cause they often overlook but *should* consider is gluten sensitivity.

Idiopathic sporadic ataxia accounts for nearly 74 per cent of all patients who have ataxia.[2] That's a lot of people. But even more important – research published in 2002 showed that approximately *41 per cent* of people with idiopathic sporadic ataxia have gluten sensitivity, as defined by the presence of circulating anti–gliadin antibodies![3] *The correct diagnosis for these 41 per cent is gluten ataxia.*

Another common ailment similar to ataxia is peripheral neuropathy – damage to the peripheral nervous system, which sends messages from every part of the body to the brain.

More than 100 different types of peripheral neuropathy have been identified, each with its own characteristic set of symptoms, pattern of development and prognosis.[4] Most commonly, a person having peripheral neuropathy may have muscle weakness, cramps, muscle twitching and loss of coordination.

Just like ataxia, the condition can have many different causes, ranging from shingles to Lyme disease. But one that should not be discounted – or rather, *should be counted immediately* – is gluten sensitivity.

A review of all reports from 1964 to 2002[5] showed that ataxia and peripheral neuropathy were the most common neurological manifestations observed in people with *established* coeliac disease (CD). These were individuals in whom CD had been diagnosed with a biopsy of the small intestine. (*Remember: All people who have coeliac disease are sensitive to gluten – gluten intolerant – but only some people who are gluten sensitive have CD, which results from gluten sensitivity gone awry!*) Research was conducted to see the extent of gluten sensitivity in patients with *unknown* neurological causes.

The authors of the study stated, "The evidence was statistical: patients with neurological disease of unknown etiology [cause] were found to have a much higher prevalence of circulating anti–gliadin antibodies (57 per cent) in their blood than either healthy control subjects (12 per cent) or those with neurological disorders of known etiology (5 per cent)."[6]

Translation: More than 50 per cent of people with unknown causes of neurological disorders have a sensitivity to gluten.

The treatment for dermatitis herpetiformis, the severe skin disease that we discussed in the previous chapter, and CD is a gluten-free diet. When this type of diet is introduced, the skin condition caused by dermatitis herpetiformis clears up and the gut heals itself. Would this same diet relieve symptoms in individuals who have gluten ataxia and other similar neurological gluten-sensitive disorders? Research confirmed it would.

In one study, scientists identified 43 people who had gluten ataxia and anti-gliadin antibodies in their blood. Before putting them on a gluten-free diet, they assessed the extent of ataxia in each individual by using five different neurological assessments:[7]

Computerized finger-nose test. People in the study sat at arm's length from a touch-sensitive computer screen. They were asked to put their right index finger on the tip of their nose and were instructed to touch, as quickly and accurately as possible, the centre of a flashing cross that appeared on the monitor. When they touched the cross, the picture disappeared. They were told to repeat the task nine more times as the cross changed positions on the screen. The computer recorded the mean response time in milliseconds.

Grooved pegboard test. This test measured manipulative dexterity. People in the study had to insert pegs into holes, using only one hand and without additional help from the other hand, as fast as possible. The time it took for them to complete the task was recorded. The task was repeated with the other hand.

Tapping test. Study participants were asked to press a button on a counter with their index finger as rapidly as possible for 30 seconds. The task was repeated with the other hand. The total count for both hands was recorded. They then repeated the task using each foot.

Quantitative Romberg's test. These individuals were asked to stand with their feet together and their eyes closed. They were then told to stay that way as long as possible. The time to first foot movement or eye opening was recorded.

Subjective global clinical impression. Study participants were instructed to mark on a visual analog scale their impression of their symptoms of imbalance over the past month.

The testing established a baseline of the patients' symptoms. After the initial testing, the patients were introduced to a gluten-free diet. During the course of the study, which lasted 12 months (with 6-month and 12-month neurological assessments conducted), 26 individuals adhered to a strict gluten-free direct; 14 refused the diet. These 14 were considered the control group.

The result? Individuals on the gluten-free diet showed a significant improvement in performance in *all* the neurological tests, whereas those in the control group generally worsened. The research confirmed that a gluten-free diet is an effective treatment for gluten ataxia.

SEVERE HEADACHES

Gluten sensitivity can also cause severe headaches – a symptom that can pop up in other systemic diseases such as lupus (discussed later).

In 2004, a study was conducted to identify the association of coeliac disease with "soft" neurologic conditions such as headaches in young adults and children.[8] The researchers found that headaches were the most commonly found neurologic disorder in the 111 patients with CD (confirmed by biopsy) who participated in the study; 64.5 per cent (20 patients) with headaches had late-onset symptoms of CD or were asymptomatic (gluten sensitive), and 35.5 per cent (11 patients) had the classical early infantile form of coeliac disease.

The study further broke down the types of headaches these individuals experienced:

- Migraine, 45.1 per cent

- Non-specific, 35.5 per cent

- Tension-psychogenic, 19.4 per cent

In 16 patients (nine with migraines and six with non-specific headaches), a gluten-free diet relieved the symptoms.

Speculate, if you will, what the results could have been if all the patients who were gluten sensitive – not just those diagnosed with CD – had been placed on a gluten-free diet!

In an earlier study conducted in 2001,[9] 10 patients who suffered from severe headaches and who had MRI tests suggesting inflammation of the central nervous system were found to be gluten sensitive. When these patients were told to go on a gluten-free diet, *all but one found relief.* Seven of the 10 patients had a *complete* resolution of their headaches, and two experienced partial improvement. The one person who continued to suffer headaches? He refused to try the gluten-free diet.

The following case from that study illustrates the power of going gluten-free:

A 50-year-old man whose medical history did not disclose a disposition toward migraines experienced unexplained headaches for 4 years. When his headaches increased in severity and frequency, he agreed to undergo a blood test, which showed that he had anti-gliadin antibodies.

When he started on a gluten-free diet, his balance improved and his headaches resolved completely. But 2 years later, his symptoms returned. Upon being questioned, the man confessed: he had fallen off his gluten-free diet. A repeat of tests confirmed a return of anti-gliadin antibodies.

The tests convinced this man that gluten was the culprit behind his headaches. He went back on a gluten-free diet and has remained headache-free since then.

If this weren't enough evidence to suggest that gluten can be the culprit in headaches, consider this account:[10]

One individual said that he had suffered from migraine headaches for more than 10 years. The problem, for which the neurologists he had consulted could find no cure, intensified to the point that he had to take early retirement. By 2002, his three-headaches-a-week syndrome had escalated to an almost non-stop headache. In 1 month, he was headache-free for only 3 days. Migraine medications did nothing to alleviate the pain.

Then his family doctor suggested a gluten-free diet. The headaches gradually became less frequent, and after several months, he was 98 per cent headache-free.

Gluten-free wins again.

AUTISM

No parent wants to hear a paediatrician say, "I'm sorry. Your child is autistic." But sadly, that is the message given to increasing numbers of parents. According to The National Autistic Society one in 110 children has autism.[11]

A look at the statistics from the US shows that the situation is also getting worse: in 1996, data from a large surveillance system in Atlanta indicated that autism affected 3.4 per 1,000 children 3 to 10 years old.[12] That number increased to 6.7 per 1,000 children 3 to 10 years old according to a 1998 community study.[13]

Autism and related conditions are lifelong developmental disabilities. They are characterized by repetitive behaviours and social and communication problems. Individuals who have autism tend to have unusual ways of (or difficulty in) learning, paying attention or reacting to different sensations.

Although scientists speculate about the reasons for the increase in autism, the exact cause is not yet known. Doctors and parents have reached out for a number of different treatments, among them dietary control – more specifically, the elimination of gluten and casein (from dairy products) from the diet.

When parents discover that they have an autistic child, they often take desperate measures, including using drugs to control or counteract the autistic patterns. In the US the Autism Research Institute (ARI) collected information provided by more than 23,700 parents who completed a questionnaire. ARI wanted to find out which remedies were most effective in treating the autism.

One of the most effective treatments was following a special diet: removing gluten and casein from the child's diet, with 65 per cent of parents reporting that their child got better.[14]

Parents themselves report excellent results from a gluten-free, casein-free (GF/CF) diet.[15] (Casein is the major protein found in milk.)

Nine years of noncommunication. A 9-year-old boy was diagnosed as autistic when he was 3. He never learned to talk, had difficulty focusing and had trouble responding to communication. At the age of 7, he finally started saying words spontaneously. When he was 9, however, his parents put him on a GF/CF diet at the urging of some friends. Within *4 months,* the boy was potty-trained, started reading, began talking in long and sophisticated sentences and was able to interact with other children and adults.

Tantrums and more. A 10-year-old boy who had been diagnosed as autistic at age 4 had typical autistic behaviour: temper tantrums, biting himself, kicking, pushing and screaming. His mother put him on a GF/CF diet on her own. Within *3 weeks,* the boy started to talk clearly in long sentences. His temper tantrums diminished, and he became friendly and lovable.

A 2-year trial. A mother reported that her baby boy seemed entirely normal at birth, and for the first 5 months, his development was "by the book". Then, by 6 months old, he stopped developing and actually regressed in his behaviour. He did not move around on his own until he was almost 11 months old and did not walk until 18 months. At that age, he had only one word in his vocabulary: dog. The mother heard about the benefits of a GF/CF diet shortly after her son's second birthday. *Ten days* into the diet, the boy started talking, and his development has continued from that day on. Now, at age 4, he is enrolled in normal pre-school and "fits in fine". He is potty-trained, speaks conversationally, has a sense of humour and plays games.

How do these miracles happen? Researchers have found that autistic children excrete more opioid peptides – naturally occurring peptides that have pain-relieving and sedative effects – than nonautistic children and that some of these peptides are derived from gluten, gliadin and casein.[16]

The implication of this discovery is that the presence of these peptides may cause the signs and symptoms of autistic disorders[17] and that excessive peptides from undigested casein and gluten exert significant toxicity.[18]

A 2004 study[19] found that children with autism had significantly higher levels of gluten antibodies in more than 80 per cent of the cases. The researchers concluded: "The results of these studies further support dietary intervention, including a gluten-, gliadin- and casein-free diet, in children with autism".

BEHAVIOURAL PROBLEMS

Imagine not being able to sit still, always needing to be on the go – actually being compelled to move. That's what happens to children and adults with attention deficit disorder (ADD), also known as attention deficit hyperactivity disorder (ADHD).

The difference between ADD and ADHD is mainly that of labelling: according to the Attention Deficit Disorder Association, the "official" clinical diagnosis is ADHD. In turn, ADHD is sub-categorized into three types: combined type, predominantly inattentive type and the predominantly hyperactive-impulsive type.[20] Most people use ADD as the generic term to refer to all types of these conditions.

It is estimated that approximately 2 million children in the US – about 1 in every classroom of 25 to 30 children – have ADD.[21] The condition usually persists into adulthood, affecting between 4 per cent and 6 per cent of the US population.[22] In the UK the estimated prevalence of ADHD in schoolage children is between 2 and 5 per cent.[23]

Some research has been conducted that shows an association between coeliac disease and ADD. Mind you, the research has concentrated on diagnosed coeliac disease – not gluten sensitivity.

One study, for example, published in 2004,[24] showed that people with coeliac disease were more prone to develop neurologic disorders (51.4 per cent) compared with control subjects (19.9 per cent). The researchers included a number of different neurologic disorders in the study: hypotonia, developmental delay, learning disorders and ADHD, headaches and cerebellar ataxia.

Of special interest, however, is the comparison of people with learning disabilities and ADHD with controls: twice as many of the coeliac patients (20.7 per cent) had learning disabilities/ADHD than the control group (10.4 per cent).

Again: I cannot emphasize enough that these studies showed dramatic results with coeliac patients. The results would have been even more dramatic if gluten sensitivity had been included.

Another type of behaviour problem that afflicts both children and adults is obsessive-compulsive disorder (OCD). It is estimated that approximately 3 per cent of the UK population suffer from OCD.[25]

People with OCD can't stop performing rituals. If they do, they become anxious and may become plagued with persistent, unwelcome thoughts or images. They may be obsessed with germs and dirt, order or symmetry.

It is not known how many people with OCD may be gluten sensitive, but gluten does play a role in the obsessive behaviour of some individuals. A case study illustrates:[26]

From the time that Tom was a child, he exhibited behaviour problems. By age 13, his problems had become so pronounced that he met the criteria for OCD.

At age 14, he was tested for CD because both of his parents had been diagnosed with the disease. At that time, the tests showed an elevated level of anti-gliadin antibodies – suggesting gluten sensitivity – *but no action was taken at that time.*

At age 15, however, Tom's mother insisted on another CD test. The test showed that his gluten sensitivity had progressed to the point of coeliac disease.

Five months after starting a gluten-free diet, the boy's depressive tendencies remitted, his sleeping problems subsided and he was able to attend school normally. His school performance improved, and he learned to control his obsessive thoughts and fears.

The gluten-free diet worked to free this boy of OCD. Too bad he didn't start the diet when gluten sensitivity was discovered.

The power of gluten – and a gluten-free diet – can be seen in these reports:[27]

New toddler in town. A mother reports that her toddler is like a new child since he went on a gluten-free diet. "I had been told he was autistic. He did all the classic things autistic kids do – screaming, biting, spinning and not looking you in the eye. Since going gluten-free, his behaviour is nothing less than miraculous."

Accidents happen. A parent says that her daughter behaved so badly that they took her to a psychologist, who then wanted to refer her to a psychiatrist who could prescribe a pharmacological solution. The parents discovered that gluten might be the culprit and put her on a gluten-free diet. But gluten accidents have happened. The parents say: "She has had a couple of accidents – eating something with gluten – and her behaviours come right back. She gets moody, cries and clings."

A bad transformation. Another mother relates to accidents: "After being totally accident-free for 3-plus months, gluten totally transformed my sweet baby girl into a different child. I would not have been surprised to see her head spinning around. She threw things, hit the wall and pulled her hair. The reaction lasted about a week."

It's powerful stuff, gluten – bad stuff for people who are gluten sensitive.

CHAPTER 5

OTHER AUTOIMMUNE DISEASES

Gluten sensitivity looks like a lot of other autoimmune diseases, which by themselves create a variety of symptoms. This makes it difficult for doctors to correctly diagnose and treat the real disease.

LUPUS

To this point, we have been examining symptoms of neurological disorders exhibited by individuals who have gluten sensitivity. Once the sensitivity is discovered, a gluten-free diet resolves the problem. However, that discovery is not always easy, nor is it fast, because, as we have stated several times, gluten sensitivity is a chameleon-like disorder. It mimics the characteristics of other autoimmune diseases or may actually piggyback on those diseases. One such disease is systemic lupus erythematosus, more commonly known as lupus.

Lupus itself is a chameleon. As a systemic disorder, it manifests itself in different parts of the body and mimics symptoms of many other diseases, making it difficult to diagnose.

This disorder can affect a number of different parts of the body concurrently or at different times, including the joints, skin, kidneys, heart, lungs, blood vessels and brain. When people come down with lupus, they may suffer from extreme fatigue, painful or swollen joints (arthritis), unexplained fever, skin rashes and kidney problems[1] – and they may have any, some or all of these symptoms. Consequently, people with lupus may appear to be suffering from diseases ranging from arthritis to dermatitis or kidney disease.

One disorder that should be considered early when such symptoms appear is gluten sensitivity. A study conducted in 2001 showed that 23 per cent of people with lupus tested positive for anti-gliadin antibodies.[2] That means that almost one in five individuals with lupus is gluten sensitive. Those one in five may be misdiagnosed as having lupus, just as these patients were:[3]

From toddler to teen. A 17-year-old girl's symptoms first started when she was a toddler of 20 months – poor weight gain, eczema and a facial rash that her parents attributed to sun exposure.

She was treated with steroids, from which she developed side effects, including badly formed tooth enamel.

At 17, suffering from a psoriatic skin rash on the palms of her hands, she was sent to an adult lupus clinic, where doctors decided to consider gluten sensitivity. Testing confirmed anti-gliadin antibodies, and she was placed on a gluten-free diet.

Six months later, the symptoms she'd had for nearly 15 years went away. She got off drugs, her tests were normal and the skin rash disappeared – all because she excluded gluten from her diet.

Recurrent neurological symptoms. From the time she was 20, a 53-year-old woman had suffered from periodic headaches, blurred vision and general weakness. The symptoms would be severe, then would spontaneously clear up. When the symptoms began to persist, however, doctors ran her through a gamut of tests, including MRIs, CT scans, cerebrospinal fluid exams and blood tests. When she was 23, the doctors decided she had lupus.

Her symptoms would come and go for years at a time – typical of lupus. Finally, when symptoms returned in full force and she began to suffer from wobbliness (ataxia), doctors ran an immunological profile. It showed she had anti-gliadin antibodies.

She went on a gluten-free diet and *in 6 months,* she was able to discontinue her medications. Her headaches subsided, and she was symptom-free after nearly 30 years of suffering.

A variety of symptoms. At the age of 40, a woman began to have severe headaches, as well as a number of other complaints. Headache was the chief concern, however, so her doctors ran a CT scan to see if she had any brain abnormalities. She did not.

Nine years later, she complained of severe itching around the anal area (pruritus) and intermittent facial oedema (swelling). This was diagnosed as hives. Her main complaints, however, continued to be bad headaches and abdominal discomfort. The doctors diagnosed lupus.

Her complaints did not go away. Finally, at age 54, a gastroenterologist who performed a colonoscopy on her reviewed her history and suggested she might be gluten sensitive. Immunological tests confirmed the diagnosis. The woman began a gluten-free diet, and her headaches and gastrointestinal symptoms disappeared.

MULTIPLE SCLEROSIS

Another disease that is difficult to diagnose, because it has many symptoms and unknown causes, is multiple sclerosis (MS).

Multiple sclerosis is thought to be an autoimmune disease, the same as gluten sensitivity. This disorder, however, affects the central nervous system, which consists of the brain, spinal cord and optic nerves.

A key part of the nervous system is a fatty tissue called myelin. This tissue helps nerve fibres conduct electrical impulses, which control muscles. In MS, myelin is destroyed in many (multiple) places. It is replaced with scar tissue, known as sclerosis – hence, the name multiple sclerosis.

Individuals who come down with MS can display a number of different symptoms, including some shared with gluten sensitivity. Some of these symptoms include fatigue, problems with balance and coordination, spasticity and headache.[4]

MS typically follows one of four different clinical courses, each of which might be mild, moderate or severe:[5]

Relapsing-remitting characteristics. People with relapsing-remitting MS have clearly defined relapses (attacks), in which they suffer an acute worsening of neurological functions. These relapses are followed by partial or complete recovery periods that are free from the disease progression. Relapsing-remitting MS is by far the most common type of MS, affecting about 85 per cent of those who have the disease.

Primary-progressive characteristics. Individuals with the primary-progressive form of MS experience slow but continuous worsening of the disorder from the onset, with no distinct relapses. The rate of progression varies, however. About 10 per cent of those with MS fall into this category of characteristics.

Secondary-progressive characteristics. People with secondary-progressive MS have an initial period of relapsing-remitting disease, which is followed by steadily worsening conditions. About 50 per cent of people with relapsing-remitting MS develop this form of the disease within 10 years of the initial diagnosis.

Progressive-relapsing characteristics. People with the progressive-relapsing form of MS – a relatively rare form (about 5 per cent of those who have the disease) – have a steady worsening of symptoms from the onset. However, they also experience clear acute relapses with or without recovery. In contrast to relapsing-remitting MS, the periods between relapses are characterized by continuing disease progression.

Sensitivity to gluten is most likely not a cause of MS.[6] However, researchers have found cases of people who fall into the primary-progressive or atypical MS-like illnesses who also had gluten sensitivity. In five such cases, the doctors reported that the primary feature was ataxia (lack of muscle coordination), although other neurological symptoms were also present.

The conclusion of the authors: gluten sensitivity may be considered the cause of "atypical" primary-progressive MS, especially if ataxia is the prominent feature. In those cases, a gluten-free diet can result in a stabilization of neurology. In other words, the symptoms will not get worse.

Perhaps more important to keep in mind, however, is that *it can be impossible to distinguish between the symptoms of MS and those of gluten sensitivity.* For people who have MS symptoms, a gluten-free diet is worth trying.

OSTEOPENIA AND OSTEOPOROSIS

Did you break your arm when you were a child? If you did, you know that the novelty of wearing a cast soon wears off. You couldn't wait to get the cast off and get back to normal again. The bones of children (at least children who don't have coeliac disease [CD]) heal fairly rapidly. Those of adults may not, especially if the adult has osteopenia or osteoporosis.

The difference between osteopenia and osteoporosis is essentially one of degree: osteopenia is a mild thinning of bone density, a precursor to osteoporosis. Osteoporosis, by definition, means "porous bones". It is a disease characterized by low bone mass and structural deterioration. This can lead to bone fragility and an increased risk of fracture, especially of the hip, spine and wrist. Fractures are painful and may not heal fully, leading to disability.

According to The National Osteoporosis Society,[7] an estimated 3 million people in the UK have osteoporosis. Women over age 50 who are menopausal are particularly at risk.

Other risk factors include:

• Being thin or having a small frame

• Drinking too much alcohol

• Having a family history of the disease

• Not getting enough calcium

• Not getting enough physical activity

• Smoking

• Using certain medications, such as glucocorticoids

Significantly, some autoimmune diseases such as rheumatoid arthritis can cause osteoporosis. *So can gluten sensitivity.* In a study published in 2005,[8] researchers evaluated 266 individuals with osteoporosis (and 574 without the condition) to identify the prevalence of coeliac disease. They discovered that almost 5 per cent of people with osteoporosis had a positive blood test for CD – a number significantly higher than those without osteoporosis (just 1 per cent). Their findings were dramatic enough that the researchers recommended blood tests for gluten antibodies in *all* patients with osteoporosis.

As we consider this statistic, as amazingly high as it is, we need to keep in mind that blood testing for coeliac disease misses a significant number of individuals who are gluten sensitive. And these individuals may be on the way to losing bone density. (For more information on testing for gluten sensitivity, see Chapter 10, Am I Gluten Sensitive?)

Osteopenia and osteoporosis can often be reversed – but the condition must be treated with the proper remedy. That does not always happen, because of misdiagnosis, as the following case illustrates:[9]

Because osteoporosis ran in her family and because she was thin and small-boned, Willow, a post-menopausal woman, had her first bone scan in 1991. She was not surprised that she was diagnosed with osteoporosis. In an attempt to curb and reverse the disorder, her rheumatologist tried the medications available at that time – Fosamax and Actonel. They failed to help her.

Several years passed, and the disease progressed. In 2003, her osteoporosis specialist prescribed another medication (yet another bisphosphonate). Despite her diligence in taking this course of treatment, it also failed to stop the degeneration of her bones.

It was either by luck or by instinct that the woman demanded to be tested for coeliac disease. Her husband had been diagnosed with CD in 1982, so she had kept up-to-date on CD research. Although she had not experienced any symptoms of CD – she did not have diarrhoea, weight loss, anaemia or other symptoms – she asked her doctor to run a tissue transglutaminase blood test – a test for gluten sensitivity. The doctor and laboratory were unfamiliar with the blood test, but they learned how to do it.

To everyone's surprise (except possibly Willow's), the tests came back positive. She went on a gluten-free diet, gained over 6 kg (1 st), and has continued to see an improvement in her bone density. A gluten-free diet came to her rescue.

This woman's experience is not an anomaly. As far back as 1996, research showed that going on a gluten-free diet would reverse bone-density loss, even in patients who did not show symptoms of malabsorption – the primary reason why osteoporosis occurs among people with coeliac disease.[10] (In cases of malabsorption, the body does not absorb minerals and other nutrients necessary for bone growth. Porosity then results.) In that study of 63 patients, *all* of them improved when they followed a gluten-free diet.

The improvement is not short-term. Authors of a 5-year follow-up study of coeliac patients who had adhered to a gluten-free diet said, "According to our results, bone disease in coeliac patients is cured in most patients during 5 years on a gluten-free diet. The improvement in BMD (bone mineral density) mostly occurred already within the first year after the establishment of a gluten-free diet."[11]

The lesson to be learned: if you have been diagnosed with osteopenia or osteoporosis, and you haven't seen improvement with all you have tried, go gluten-free. The diet may save you from pain and suffering.

OSTEOMALACIA

Soft bones. That's what osteomalacia is. Like osteoporosis, this condition weakens the bones and makes them more susceptible to breaking. In osteoporosis, however, bone breaks down faster than it can be replaced. In osteomalacia, bone forms but does not become dense and hard.[12]

In children, this condition is called rickets. In both children and adults, osteomalacia is a serious condition. It is a metabolic bone disease directly caused by a lack of vitamin D.

People may lack this vitamin because they do not get enough sun exposure or because their diets are deficient and they do not take supplements for it. But the condition is often caused by the lack of absorption of the vitamin into the body's system. That lack of absorption may be caused by gluten sensitivity or coeliac disease.

People who have osteomalacia may experience diffuse bone pain, muscle weakness and bone fractures. Muscles in the upper arms and thighs may become very weak, causing elderly people to have difficulty getting up from chairs or climbing stairs.

Doctors first reported an association between coeliac disease and osteomalacia in 1953[13] (long before today's sensitive testing for gluten intolerance). These cases illustrate the connection:

One constant symptom. A 59-year-old male[14] suffered from 2½ years of osteomalacia caused by severe malabsorption. His doctor finally tested for coeliac disease and found that his malabsorption was the only symptom he had. The doctor wrote, "It seems that patients with gluten-sensitive enteropathy [disease] who undergo little exposure to the sun are at particular risk of developing overt osteomalacia. Unrecognized [gluten sensitivity] should always be considered in the differential diagnosis of osteomalacia."

Many symptoms for 20 years. A 67-year-old woman had a 20-year history of recurrent abdominal pain, diarrhoea and diffuse bone pain.[15] Her doctors had labelled her condition "iron absorption disorder", "osteoporosis", and "hyperparathyroidism". However, none of the treatments for these diseases alleviated her symptoms, and she eventually required constant care.

Finally, her doctor diagnosed her with coeliac disease. She was placed on a gluten-free diet, supplemented with high doses of vitamin

D$_3$ and oral calcium and within 3 months she improved to the point that she could take care of herself again.

Back pain. A 43-year-old pre-menopausal woman complained of pain in her spine and back muscles for more than a year.[16] She was of normal height and weight and did not report any other symptoms.

At first, the doctors thought she might have fibromylagia, but tests discounted that diagnosis. She was then given a test for gluten sensitivity (an anti-endomysial antibody test). It was positive. A biopsy confirmed the diagnosis of gluten intolerance. She went on a gluten-free diet and started taking vitamin D supplements, and her symptoms promptly went away. Her small bowel tissue tested normal after 4 months.

Ah, the power of going gluten-free!

ARTHRITIS

What comes to mind when you think of arthritis? Older people who complain of aches and pains? Middle-aged actors in TV commercials who have difficulty remaining active enough to play with their grand-children? Elderly individuals, especially women, bent over and crippled with a dowager's hump?

Whatever your image, all of them are correct. Arthritis is a term that describes more than 100 rheumatic diseases and conditions affecting more than one in seven adults in the UK.[17] (Rheumatic diseases are those characterized by inflammation or pain in muscles, joints or fibrous tissue.)

Arthritis affects the joints, the tissues that surround the joints, and other connective tissue. It is a painful condition and can limit the life activities of sufferers.

Even worse – some arthritic (rheumatic) conditions can affect a number of internal organs of the body.

Arthritis is often thought to be an inevitable consequence of growing older. This is not true. Many forms of arthritis are associated with old age and extraordinary wear and tear on the joints such as through repetitive motion. However, individuals of any age – even very young children – can come down with arthritis that is caused by a faulty immune system. In fact, in the US, more than 300,000 children between the ages of 6 months and 16 years experience juvenile rheumatoid arthritis,[18] an autoimmune disease.

One type of arthritis triggered by the immune system is rheumatoid arthritis (RA). In its first stages, RA causes swelling of the synovial lining of the joints. (The synovial lining is the membrane that surrounds the joints.) Later, the synovial lining thickens and loses its protective characteristics. And finally, the inflamed cells in the synovial lining release enzymes that may digest bone and cartilage. This causes the involved joint to lose its shape and alignment. It also causes a great deal of pain and loss of movement.[19]

Rheumatoid arthritis is chronic and systemic. Not only does it persist, but it may also affect other organs and glands in the body. For example, RA can affect the glands around the eyes and mouth, causing a decreased production of tears and saliva (Sjögren's syndrome), or it can cause serositis – inflammation of the lining around the heart or lungs.

The disease is treated pharmaceutically, often with the use of glucocorticoids. Unfortunately, the treatment can lead to osteopenia and osteoporosis. *And the treatment may not be necessary.*

A 1995 study found that 68 per cent of people with coeliac disease had joint inflammation.[20] Conversely, coeliac disease was found in 26 per cent of 200 individuals in a study designed to identify the prevalence of coeliac disease in arthritic patients.[21] (Keep in mind: these studies were conducted in the late 1990s. The studies were done on coeliac patients – those who had coeliac sprue of the gut, confirmed by biopsy. The statistics *do not* reflect patients who might have tested positive for gluten sensitivity without overt symptoms of coeliac disease if today's sensitive testing had been available!)

It should not surprise you to learn that going on a gluten-free diet can reduce or eliminate RA symptoms. Doctors have suspected for a long time that diet may affect RA symptoms.

For example: in 2001, one US study confirmed that going gluten-free clinically benefits RA patients.[22] In this study, 66 patients with active rheumatoid arthritis were randomly assigned to either a vegan gluten-free diet (38 patients) or a well-balanced non-vegan diet that included gluten (28 patients). The test subjects participated in the study for 12 months and were assessed at the start of the test, as well as at 3-, 6-, and 12-month intervals. Researchers also measured levels of antibodies against gliadin.

Mind you: these were individuals who had rheumatoid arthritis. *Prior to the study, none of them had been diagnosed with gluten sensitivity.*

The results of the study? Twenty-two individuals in the gluten-free group and 25 in the non-gluten-free group completed 9 months or more on the diet regimes. Of those who completed the study, 40.5 per cent (nine patients) in the gluten-free group experienced significant improvement in their RA symptoms, compared with 4 per cent (one patient) in the non-gluten-free group. And – not to minimize its importance – the anti-gliadin antibody levels decreased in the gluten-free group but not in the other group.

Going gluten-free may also help individuals who have osteoarthritis (OA), the oldest and most common type of arthritis. Osteoarthritis exists as two different types: primary OA and secondary OA.

Primary OA is the "wear and tear" form of osteoarthritis. As each of us gets older, it is likely that we will have some degree of primary OA. Although OA is widespread and can be traced to the dawn of human-kind (Ice Age skeletons showing OA have been found), its causes are not known. It is thought to be genetically linked, and some researchers speculate that it may also be autoimmune in origin.

Secondary OA is arthritis that has an apparent cause, such as injury, heredity, obesity or something else. That "something else" might easily be gluten sensitivity.

Whatever researchers have to say, individuals with osteoarthritis who have tried a gluten-free diet give testament to its effectiveness:

An active life restored. At the age of 66, one woman's OA became insufferable. She could hardly climb stairs, and she had lost the grip in her hands. The OA significantly altered her lifestyle, which had been extremely active. Failing to find relief from the medical community, she decided to try something she had read about – an alkaline diet to neutralize acidity in her body. The alkaline diet helped, she said, but she was still plagued with pain. She then decided to change to a gluten-free diet. Within a short time, her pain subsided. She credits both of these diets with almost completely alleviating her symptoms. Now at age 73, she is able to climb stairs, walk up hills and even jog.[23]

Relief for a nursing mother. A young woman who was nursing her infant son went gluten-free because the child had a wheat allergy. The woman had been suffering with OA for some time. Within a week of going gluten-free, she says her symptoms disappeared.[24]

Although rheumatoid arthritis and osteoarthritis are the most studied rheumatic diseases relative to gluten sensitivity, other rheumatic diseases deserve mention.

Ankylosing spondylitis. This is an arthritis that is similar to rheumatoid arthritis but affects the spinal joints, especially the joints at the pelvis. These disorders are related: both are triggered by an autoimmune response in the body.

Does it not stand to reason that if some of these disorders or their symptoms are actually caused by an intolerance to gluten that others would be, too?

Scleroderma. This is a chronic connective tissue disease, generally classified as one of the autoimmune rheumatic diseases.[25] (This classification connects it to rheumatoid arthritis, which we have seen is linked to gluten sensitivity!)

An uncommon condition, scleroderma is described as a hardening of the skin. The disease affects more than the skin, however. In fact, about 75 to 90 per cent of all patients have their digestive system affected by this disease. All organs of the digestive system can be affected – the oesophagus, stomach, small intestine and large intestine.

Sjögren's syndrome. This autoimmune disease is also an arthritis-related disorder that can affect a number of different organs.[26] Its most common manifestation is in the moisture-producing glands, such as the eyes and the mouth, causing dry eyes and dry mouth. Sjögren's occurs in both primary and secondary forms. It is considered primary when it occurs alone, and secondary when it occurs along with other autoimmune diseases, *such as rheumatoid arthritis or lupus.* The secondary form is most common. This disease has no cure – unless, of course, it is caused by gluten sensitivity. Then, as we have seen, a gluten-free diet will relieve symptoms.

Arthritis, as I have said, manifests itself in more than 100 different ways. Not all types of arthritis are associated with gluten sensitivity, but researchers recommend that when the symptoms cannot be resolved, gluten should be suspected.[27]

DIABETES

Gluten sensitivity is also associated with another common condition – diabetes, especially type 1 diabetes and perhaps type 2 diabetes as well. It is estimated that approximately 2 million people in the UK have diabetes, medically known as diabetes mellitus, and up to another 750,000 people have the condition but don't know it.[28]

Diabetes mellitus refers to a group of diseases characterized by high levels of blood sugar (glucose) because of defects in insulin production, insulin action, or both. Individuals who have diabetes fall into one of several different types:

- **Type 1 diabetes.** Previously called insulin-dependent diabetes mellitus or juvenile-onset diabetes, type 1 diabetes is an autoimmune disease. It develops when the pancreas stops producing insulin, which regulates blood glucose. Type 1 diabetes, accounting for 5 to 10 per cent of all diagnosed cases, most often appears in children and young adults, although its onset can actually occur at any age.

- **Type 2 diabetes.** This type was previously called non-insulin-dependent diabetes mellitus, or adult-onset diabetes. Accounting for about 90 to 95 per cent of all diagnosed cases, it usually begins with insulin resistance, a disorder in which the cells do not use insulin properly. As the body's need for insulin rises, the pancreas (which produces insulin) gradually loses its ability to produce the hormone. Type 2 diabetes was formerly called adult-onset diabetes because it typically began at an older age. It is more likely to affect individuals who are obese, have a family history of diabetes, have a history of gestational diabetes, have impaired glucose metabolism, are physically inactive or are black, Asian or from a minority ethnic group.

- **Gestational diabetes.** This is a form of glucose intolerance that is diagnosed in some women during pregnancy. After pregnancy, 5 to 10 per cent of women who have gestational diabetes develop type 2 diabetes. Women who have had gestational diabetes have a 20 to 50 per cent chance of developing diabetes in the next 5 to 10 years.

- **Other types of diabetes.** Some other types of diabetes can result from genetic conditions, surgery, drugs, malnutrition, infections and other illnesses. These types of diabetes may account for 1 to 5 per cent of all diagnosed cases.

To what extent is gluten sensitivity associated with diabetes? Consider these facts:

- In the US, the prevalence of coeliac disease in people with type 1 diabetes is an astounding 10 to 30 times that found in the normal population![29]

- Studies have shown that about 3 to 8 per cent of individuals who have type 1 diabetes have coeliac disease, and at least 5 per cent of individuals who have coeliac disease have type 1 diabetes.

- About 1 in 20 people with type 1 diabetes have coeliac disease with *no symptoms*[30] – that is, they are gluten sensitive but have not developed CD symptoms of the gut.

What about type 2 diabetes? Recent studies have shown that 5 to 30 per cent of people who were originally diagnosed with type 2 diabetes actually have type 1![31] That may mean that even more people with diabetes potentially have gluten sensitivity.

We could speculate that individuals who have forms of diabetes that fall into the "other" category may also be susceptible to gluten sensitivity, especially those who suffer from malnutrition (a symptom of classic coeliac disease).

Regardless of the type of diabetes, individuals with diabetes who have gluten sensitivity benefit from a gluten-free diet. For example: in one study of children with type 1 diabetes who also had coeliac disease, a gluten-free diet resulted in a significant increase in growth and weight gain. In other words, they became healthier.[32]

Studies are not available concerning the effect of a gluten-free diet on adults with diabetes; however, in some diabetes centres, especially in Europe, doctors routinely screen diabetic patients for coeliac disease and recommend a gluten-free diet when results come back positive.

THYROID DISEASE

The thyroid is a butterfly-shaped gland that wraps itself around the front part of the windpipe, just below the Adam's apple. This small gland has a long reach: it produces hormones that keep the body's metabolism running right and maintains proper organ functioning. The hormones affect virtually every cell in the body – which is why, when the thyroid's production of hormones is out of balance, the body has a serious reaction.

Autoimmune thyroid disease (thyroiditis) does throw hormone production out of kilter. The two most common types of thyroiditis are Hashimoto's disease and Graves' disease. It is important not to ignore the association of these diseases with gluten sensitivity.

Hashimoto's disease is *hypothyroidism* – inflammation of the thyroid, resulting in the thyroid working inefficiently and failing to produce enough thyroid hormones. Hashimoto's disease is characterized by an enlarged thyroid, although the enlargement may not be noticeable to the untrained eye. Individuals who have the disease typically cannot tolerate cold. They gain weight, experience unexplainable fatigue, become constipated, have dry skin and lose their hair or have brittle hair. They may also become depressed and experience difficulty concentrating or thinking. Females have heavy menstrual cycles.

Graves' disease is *hyperthyroidism* – an overactive thyroid that produces too high a level of thyroid hormones. The effect of a hyperactive thyroid is virtually the opposite of an underactive thyroid. The excessive amount of thyroid hormones speeds up the body's metabolism and causes nervousness and increased activity, a fast heartbeat, fatigue, moist skin, increased sensitivity to heat, anxiety, increased appetite, weight loss, shakiness and sleeping disorders. The disease is characterized by an enlarged thyroid (goiter) and bulging eyes.

The association of gluten intolerance to autoimmune diseases has been well established in many different studies. In 1994, one of the earliest studies showed that a significant number of people who have coeliac disease also have autoimmune thyroid disease;[33] 14 per cent of coeliac disease patients had autoimmune thyroid disease. Of that number, 10.3 per cent had Hashimoto's disease (hypothyroid), and 3.7 per cent had Graves' disease (hyperthyroid).

In 2001, scientists wanted to see the prevalence of coeliac disease in people with autoimmune thyroid dysfunction.[34] They tested blood from 200 individuals with autoimmune thyroiditis, 50 who had normal thyroid functioning but had thyroid nodules and 250 blood donors.

The results of their tests: the prevalence of coeliac disease in patients with autoimmune thyroiditis was 3.2 per cent, compared with only 0.4 per cent in blood donors. Because of this high incidence rate, the study's authors concluded that patients with autoimmune thyroiditis should be tested for anti–gliadin antibodies. (Again, a reminder: these researchers tested for *coeliac disease* – gluten sensitivity at its worst! Today, more-sensitive tests can identify gluten sensitivity long before it causes coeliac disease.)

The association between CD and autoimmune disease is well established. But does exposure to gluten *cause* autoimmune disease? Some researchers hypothesize yes. In 1999, a study showed that the longer that children and adolescents ate a diet containing gluten before they were diagnosed with coeliac disease, the more autoimmune diseases they came down with later in life.[35]

Even more important: in this same study, when the children with coeliac disease went on a gluten-free diet, their insulin-related antibodies disappeared, and their antithyroid antibodies decreased.

The same type of results occurred in a 2001 study,[36] which included 241 untreated coeliac patients and 212 controls. The first thing this study found was that thyroid disease was three times more prevalent in coeliac patients than in the controls – 12.9 per cent of coeliac patients and only 4.2 per cent of controls were diagnosed with hypothyroidism. (Again, remember: these were patients who were diagnosed with *classic coeliac disease* – not just gluten sensitivity.)

These individuals were put on a gluten-free diet. Remarkably, *almost all patients* who followed a strict gluten-free diet for 12 months experienced normalization of their thyroid function.

A gluten-free diet works. How much more can we say?

CHAPTER 6

DIGESTIVE DISORDERS

As anybody who has ever had them can attest, diarrhoea, flatulence (wind) and bloating are not "fun" conditions. Fortunately, these conditions are generally mild and short term.

Most diarrhoea, flatulence and bloating can be traced to either food poisoning (caused by bacterial infection) or a "flu" (caused by a viral infection). By their nature, these infections are generally self-limiting and of a short-term duration. So, while you feel bad for perhaps 24 to 72 hours, your body successfully fights the infection, and the symptoms go away. Miraculously, it seems, you wake up and feel like your old self again.

But sometimes that doesn't happen. Sometimes, diarrhoea, flatulence and bloating (among other symptoms) don't go away by themselves. That's when you generally consult a medical doctor to find and treat the causes.

Unfortunately, a number of different diseases can hide behind these symptoms. And the cause of the symptoms is not always known – which means that the doctor can treat only the symptoms. Meanwhile, the condition becomes chronic i.e. something you have to live with.

A cause that doctors *infrequently* consider is gluten sensitivity. To illustrate, in 2001, a study showed that the average length of time that people suffered with the most severe form of gluten intolerance – coeliac disease (CD) – before it was accurately diagnosed was an astounding 11 years![1]

We can hope that that period of time is decreasing, because by removing gluten from your diet, the digestive disease may disappear. Let's consider the various types of digestive problems and the symptoms that may mask gluten sensitivity.

COELIAC DISEASE

It's appropriate for us to begin a discussion about digestive diseases by first learning about coeliac disease – the "ultimate" in gluten sensitivity. I need to emphasize: everyone who has coeliac disease has a sensitivity to gluten, but not everyone who is gluten sensitive has coeliac disease.

Coeliac, a full or partial destruction of the intestinal villi (the tiny vascular projections of the small intestine that absorb nutrients) was once thought to be a rare disease. However, according to the charity Coeliac UK, screening studies indicate that about 1 per cent of the population have coeliac disease,[2] which is also known as coeliac sprue, non-tropical sprue and gluten-sensitive enteropathy. Interestingly, a significant number of these people will be undiagnosed, probably because coeliac disease successfully mimics many other diseases. Also, in the US in particular, the medical community is still unaware of its prevalence and fails to consider it when diagnosing symptoms.

A 2003 study, which screened more than 13,000 individuals in 32 US states, also showed that 1 out of 22 people who have a close relative – a parent or sibling, for example – with the disease also has it.[3] And 1 in 39 people who have a grandparent, cousin, aunt or uncle with coeliac disease has it, too. Furthermore, 1 out of 56 people who have gastrointestinal symptoms also has CD.

When a person who has coeliac disease eats food containing gluten – a protein found in all forms of wheat, rye and barley – the body sets off an autoimmune reaction that damages the small intestine. The result is that the food is not properly digested, and malabsorption occurs. You may not only exhibit symptoms – including diarrhoea, flatulence, bloating – you may also become severely malnourished and anaemic and ultimately suffer from a number of other autoimmune disorders. The disease may also leave you vulnerable to some types of cancer.

Left untreated, coeliac disease causes a greater likelihood of premature death.[4]

With that said, let's look at how full-blown coeliac disease and gluten intolerance often become confused with other digestive diseases.

IRRITABLE BOWEL SYNDROME

If you experience persistent diarrhoea or constipation, flatulence, bloating and general malaise, and you can't trace your sick feelings to the more common sources, your doctor may say that your problem is irritable bowel syndrome (IBS), previously known as colitis or spastic colon.

IBS – which affects between 10 and 20 per cent of people living in Western countries,[5] generally people in their twenties and thirties – is considered a functional bowel disorder. That's because it is an abnormality of a physiological function, rather than being caused by some outside force. IBS is generally characterized by the rapid movement of food through the intestinal tract. This rapid movement occurs because the muscles of the intestine are out of sync. When food passes through too quickly, it does not get digested, and gas, bloating and diarrhoea are produced.

IBS itself is not an *organic* disease. Doctors treat the condition by treating the symptoms. That is, they try to make you comfortable. They may prescribe antispasmodic drugs, to be taken in conjunction with fibre, to reduce uncomfortable spasms. And because stress is sometimes a trigger for IBS, doctors may also prescribe antidepressants.

But are these palliative therapies necessary? The individuals in the following cases would say "no".

A digestive roller-coaster ride. When she was still a teenager, Charlene[6] began to experience extreme bloating and indigestion. It seemed to happen after eating spicy or greasy foods, so she began to avoid them.

After she gave birth to her first son, in her early twenties, the condition worsened. She again avoided foods that seemed to trigger the condition, but she periodically suffered from constipation and diarrhoea.

At age 26, after giving birth to her second son, her condition got worse. This is when her doctor finally gave her a diagnosis of IBS. For a while, as she watched her diet, she was fine. But then she began to experience other symptoms: itchy rashes, fatigue, pain in her joints, irritability and pain in the colon. Tests did not find a cause.

Again, she managed her diet more closely, and the symptoms subsided – until her early thirties. She came down with a case of bronchitis. The antibiotics the doctor prescribed triggered severe, explosive diarrhoea. This time the doctor tested for parasites.

The tests were negative.

Charlene took charge of her condition and began researching on the internet, where she found information on gluten intolerance. Suspecting this might be the cause of her IBS, she asked two doctors to test her for coeliac disease. *They mocked her for her internet research and refused to administer the tests.* She took matters into her own hands, went on a gluten-free diet, and is now symptom-free. Her digestive roller-coaster ride finally came to an end.

Kandee's story. In 1980, Kandee came down with a severe case of hives. After the usual treatments with antihistamines failed to help, an allergist did a blood test for antibodies and found that she was allergic to wheat. She stopped eating wheat (but not other gluten-containing foods) and used daily doses of a prescription antihistamine. After several years, she gradually tried eating some wheat again and found she could tolerate about two slices of bread a week without any reaction.

She lived with this condition for 20 years. Then, one day she suddenly came down with what was later diagnosed as IBS. She began to experiment with different diets and settled on a diet that was wheat-free (but not gluten-free). The diet relieved her symptoms.

A year later, she went in for a checkup. Because she knew she had a wheat allergy, she asked about getting a test to see if she had inherited a gene for coeliac disease from her parents. The doctor ran the blood test and discovered that although she did not have coeliac disease, she *was* gluten-intolerant.

She now eats a gluten-free diet and has no problems.

Anecdotal evidence aside, research proves the close association of irritable bowel syndrome and coeliac disease.

One 2003 study[7] set out to show the association of coeliac disease with IBS. The study included 300 people with IBS and 300 who were healthy. All were given blood tests to determine if they had IgA and IgG anti-gliadin and anti-endomysial antibodies – tests that would prove the existence of coeliac disease. Those who had positive antibody results were offered a biopsy to confirm the possibility of coeliac disease – flattened villi in the intestine. (Remember: the researchers were testing for coeliac disease – not gluten sensitivity. CD is full-blown gluten sensitivity.)

The study found that 66 individuals in the IBS group were gluten sensitive, and 14 of them had coeliac disease as confirmed by biopsy. Only two people in the control group had coeliac disease.

The authors of the study said, "Compared with matched controls, irritable bowel syndrome was significantly associated with coeliac disease...Patients with irritable bowel syndrome...should be investigated routinely for coeliac disease."

In another study, also published in 2003,[8] researchers wanted to find out the prevalence of IBS-type symptoms in adult coeliac patients and then see what would happen if those people went on a gluten-free diet.

They randomly selected 150 patients with confirmed coeliac disease from a computerized database. The control group consisted of 162 individuals with no history of coeliac disease.

Of the 150 coeliac patients reviewed, 30 (20 per cent) met the criteria for having IBS, compared with eight (5 per cent) of the controls. Coeliac patients with IBS-type symptoms reported a lower quality of life than did those without the symptoms. The patients who later adhered to a gluten-free diet improved their quality of life in 50 per cent of the criteria assessed during the study.

Finally, in another interesting project aimed at identifying the frequency of coeliac disease among patients with IBS,[9] researchers enrolled 105 patients with IBS. The control group consisted of 105 siblings who did not have any symptoms of IBS. As in other studies, the individuals underwent testing for coeliac disease, followed by a duodenal biopsy for those who tested positive.

Individuals who were diagnosed with CD were placed on a gluten-free diet and then were retested in 6 months.

Researchers found 12 cases of coeliac disease in the IBS patients and none in the controls. Eleven of the CD cases adhered to a gluten-free diet. After 6 months, all of them had significant improvement of symptoms, and three were totally asymptomatic. Six of these individuals even allowed another biopsy. Five of the six showed improvement in the condition of their intestinal villi.

The researchers concluded that coeliac disease is a common finding among patients labelled as having IBS. *And, significantly, a gluten-free diet leads to improvements in symptoms.*

INFLAMMATORY BOWEL DISEASE

Despite a similarity in names and initials, inflammatory bowel disease (IBD) is not the same as irritable bowel syndrome. Both, of course, affect the digestive system. And many of the symptoms are the same, but the conditions are different.

IBD primarily refers to two chronic diseases affecting around one in 400 people in the UK that cause inflammation of the intestines: ulcerative colitis and Crohn's disease. It may also include other disorders such as ulcerative proctitis.

According to the American College of Gastroenterology,[10] the most common symptoms of both ulcerative colitis and Crohn's are diarrhoea, rectal bleeding, urgency to have bowel movements, abdominal cramps and pain, fever and weight loss. Do these sound familiar? They are symptoms commonly experienced by coeliac patients!

What's the difference between the two IBD diseases? In ulcerative colitis, inflammation occurs only in the large intestine (colon) and is limited to the inner lining of the intestinal wall. The inflammation almost always starts in the lowest part of the colon (the rectum) and then extends upward in a continuous pattern. (When ulcerative colitis affects only the lowest part of the colon – the rectum – it is called ulcerative proctitis. When it affects only the left side of the colon, it is named distal colitis.)

In Crohn's disease, inflammation can occur in any part of the intestinal tract, from the mouth to the anal area. Crohn's commonly affects the lower part of the small intestine (the ileum) and the colon. Whereas ulcerative colitis has a continuous pattern of inflammation, Crohn's may skip sections of the intestine, leaving healthy sections between inflamed areas.

Important to note: the exact cause of IBD (regardless if it is colitis or Crohn's) is unknown. But scientists believe it is caused by a *malfunction of the immune system:* the body's immune system in the digestive tract gets turned on to fight an infection but then does not turn off as it should, thus causing inflammation.

Another important fact to note: IBD has a tendency to run in families (just like gluten sensitivity). About 10 to 20 per cent of IBD patients have one or more family members affected with IBD.

Since symptoms of IBD may be essentially the same as those of gluten sensitivity or coeliac disease, and since IBD and gluten sensitivity involve the immune system, and since IBD and gluten sensitivity seem to run in families, would it not make sense to consider gluten sensitivity in these types of digestive cases?

Actually, doctors *have* observed an association between CD and IBD for many years:

- A 1977 paper[11] reported a case involving a teenage boy with Crohn's disease. The boy was not growing properly, had intractable diarrhoea, and was experiencing a delay in developing secondary sexual characteristics. A biopsy showed he had coeliac disease. He went on a gluten-free diet and gained nearly 8 kg (17.6 lb) in 4 weeks. After 2 years on the diet, his intestinal villi exhibited only minor abnormality.

- A 1982 paper[12] described six people with coeliac disease and IBD. Two of those with CD had dermatitis herpetiformis (now recognized as resulting from gluten sensitivity) and ulcerative colitis. Three had CD and ulcerative colitis, and one had Crohn's. The authors wrote, "There seems to be an association between coeliac disease without dermatitis herpetiformis and ulcerative colitis. The possible combination of coeliac disease and inflammatory bowel disease deserves more attention than it has hitherto received."

- In a 1987 study,[13] researchers studied the association of ulcerative colitis (proctitis) to coeliac disease. The authors wrote, "Proctitis as seen in [the] coeliac patients had no unique features to differentiate it from proctitis caused by other disorders...Proctitis is common in patients with coeliac disease presenting with diarrhoea/steatorrhoea. This study supports the finding of an increased association of coeliac disease and ulcerative colitis and is, to our knowledge, the first rectal biopsy study of a coeliac population."

- In 1990,[14] researchers deduced from a study of 182 people with coeliac disease that the risk of ulcerative colitis is five times greater for first-degree relatives of people with coeliac disease than for the general population. They said, "There is a clear association between coeliac disease and ulcerative colitis, which may point to factors involved in the etiology [cause] of colitis."

As we review and consider the impact of these early studies, we must always remember that these researchers were making conclusions based *only on coeliac disease as confirmed by biopsy*. It was not until 1993 that serological testing was made available to detect gluten antibodies. And it was not until recently that testing for gluten sensitivity (through stools and saliva) was developed. (See Chapter 10, Am I Gluten Sensitive?)

Doctors distinguish between CD and IBD, but they now recognize that the prevalence of coeliac disease is high among people affected by Crohn's disease. A 2005 paper showed that correlation.[15] The authors wrote, "The prevalence of coeliac disease seems to be high among patients affected by [Crohn's], and this finding should be kept in mind at the time of the first diagnosis of [Crohn's]. A gluten-free diet should be promptly started."

When properly diagnosed, individuals with IBD-like symptoms do respond to a gluten-free diet. A 2004 paper[16] described three women who had coeliac disease, as well as IBD symptoms:

- One woman had a 6-month history of abdominal pain and weight loss. Testing showed that she had hypothyroidism, as well as iron-deficiency anaemia. A biopsy revealed lesions consistent with coeliac disease and proctitis. She went on a gluten-free diet and is presently well.

- A second woman suffered for 10 years from ulcerative colitis. She failed to gain weight, despite a good diet and control over her lower gastrointestinal symptoms. Testing showed that she was anaemic. With further endoscopic examination, doctors found that she had coeliac disease. She went on a gluten-free diet and has improved.

- A third woman was not so fortunate, but her misfortune might, in fact, be due to her lack of adherence to a gluten-free diet. This patient had been diagnosed with coeliac disease at the age of 6. She did not experience any problems until the age of 33. Then, she suddenly showed symptoms of colitis, which required surgery. (Severe cases of colitis can be treated with surgery.) After the surgery, the woman was still unable to gain weight. She also continued to have abdominal pain. The doctors discovered that she had *not* followed a gluten-free diet, despite knowing that she was gluten intolerant.

Whether gluten sensitivity masquerades as IBD or whether it occurs concurrently with IBD, the fact remains: if you experience symptoms common to IBD, you and your doctor should consider gluten sensitivity. A gluten-free diet may remove your chronic discomfort – and save your life.

GASTRO-OESOPHAGEAL REFLUX (HEARTBURN)

Almost everyone has had heartburn at some time. It can occur after meals or when the stomach is empty. And it feels like a burning sensation in the chest or throat or around the breastbone. When you have a bout of heartburn, you may even taste bile in the back of your mouth.

Occasional heartburn is nothing to worry about. But when it occurs several times a week, it becomes known as gastro-oesophageal reflux disease (GORD), the term used to describe a chronic backflow of acid from the stomach into the oesophagus, the tube through which food passes from the mouth to the stomach.

GORD can affect anyone – including infants and children, as well as adults. Left untreated, GORD can cause oesophagitis (inflamed oesophagus), which can result in more serious consequences, such as bleeding and oesophageal ulcers.

How many of the millions who regularly experience heartburn have gluten sensitivity, we may never know. But what we have known since 1998[17] is that adults with coeliac disease have a high prevalence of oesophageal symptoms. That early study also showed that a gluten-free diet controlled these symptoms.

A 2003 study along the same lines[18] as the 1998 research came to the same conclusions. The researchers evaluated whether untreated adults with coeliac disease experienced an increased prevalence of reflux oesophagitis, and if they did, whether a gluten-free diet would help alleviate GORD symptoms.

The researchers enrolled 205 coeliac patients and 400 non-coeliac patients who had GORD in the study. Oesophagitis was found in 19 per cent of the coeliac patients and just 8 per cent of the people with GORD only. A gluten-free diet decreased the relapse rate of GORD symptoms in those with coeliac disease.

The authors wrote, "Coeliac patients have a high prevalence of reflux oesophagitis. That a gluten-free diet significantly decreased the relapse rate of [GORD] symptoms suggests that coeliac disease may represent a risk factor for development of reflux oesophagitis."

Frequent and chronic heartburn? Perhaps you ought to think "gluten-free".

ULCERS

Ulcers are open sores that can develop anywhere in the digestive system – in the mouth (aphthous stomatitis), oesophagus (because of GORD, as described earlier), stomach (peptic ulcer) and upper small intestine (duodenal ulcer). All of them are painful. And all of them can be associated with gluten sensitivity.

For years, doctors have been advised to screen for coeliac disease in patients with recurrent bouts of mouth ulcers (aphthous stomatitis)[19, 20] because of the strong association of this disorder with coeliac. Scientists believe that mouth ulcers are caused by an autoimmune disorder. A 2002 study indicated that recurrent and non-healing mouth ulcers were one of the symptoms of coeliac in 31 per cent of 48 patients with coeliac disease.[21]

But mouth ulcers have been associated with gluten sensitivity even when coeliac disease has been ruled out. In 1980, researchers selected 20 people who suffered from recurrent mouth ulcers[22] for a study on the effects of a gluten-free diet on their condition. *None* of these individuals had coeliac disease – but they *were* gluten sensitive. And 25 per cent responded favourably to gluten withdrawal! The researchers concluded that a gluten-free diet helps a significant number of people who have chronic mouth ulcers.

The common thinking until the 1990s was that digestive-tract ulcers were caused by too much stress or hot and spicy foods. Scientists now know that most peptic ulcers (one of the most common types of ulcers) are caused by the *Helicobacter pylori* bacteria and some strong anti-inflammatory medications. But forward-thinking doctors do not rule out coeliac disease or gluten sensitivity, especially when they see patients with the painful symptoms of gastric ulcers.[23]

A 1996 case[24] illustrates:

An obese woman complained of night-time abdominal pain, common to duodenal ulcers. Medication to treat the ulcer was ineffective, so the treating gastroenterologist performed an endoscopy and a biopsy. The doctor expected to find an ulcer but was surprised to find an active case of coeliac disease, although the patient did not have any of the classic symptoms of the disease – just pain identical to that generated by ulcers.

The woman was put on a gluten-free diet. Her ulcerative condition cleared up – and she lost weight. A nice ending for a serious problem.

GIARDIASIS

I am sure you have heard of "Montezuma's revenge". It's the illness world travellers – especially those who visit countries that do not have the high sanitary standards they may be used to at home – pick up. The illness is characterized by acute diarrhoea and nausea.

One form of this illness is caused by bacterial infection. But another form of this traveller's diarrhoea – giardiasis – originates from a single-celled, microscopic parasite called *Giardia lamblia*.[25]

This parasite lives in the intestines of human beings and animals and is passed in their stools. Although people travelling abroad often come down with giardiasis, you don't have to go far from home to get it. The parasite is commonly found in drinking water, as well as in recreational water areas, such as public (and even private) swimming pools, hot tubs, lakes and ponds.

When you go swimming, don't swallow the water! That's one way you pick up this parasite. You can also get it by drinking from seemingly unpolluted mountain streams (infected animals defecate in streams) or eating uncooked food that is contaminated with it. (In some countries, fields are often irrigated with contaminated water. Consequently, eating unwashed fruits and vegetables can be risky. That's why your mother told you to wash your apple before you ate it!) You can even pick up giardiasis from nappy bins or changing tables if you touch the contaminated surface and then touch your mouth!

The symptoms of giardiasis are the *same* as those of coeliac disease: diarrhoea, wind or flatulence, cramp and nausea. This makes diagnosis difficult, as the following cases illustrate:[26]

Giardia and coeliac disease. A 23-year-old woman was diagnosed with malabsorption syndrome. She had iron deficiency anaemia, severe diarrhoea and blood-positive stool samples. She was also underweight.

Doctors performed a number of different tests and found that she had a mild giardia infection. They also discovered elevated levels of anti-gliadin antibodies and the presence of anti-endomysium antibodies – both indications that she had coeliac disease.

They prescribed no treatment for the giardiasis. But they put her on a gluten-free diet. Her diarrhoea resolved, she gained weight and her blood tests were normal after 2 months on the diet.

The doctors wrote, "The significance of giardia duodenalis (GD) in the presence of coeliac disease is not clear. Association of these two pathologic conditions has been described...In this patient, it can be speculated that a mild, self-resolving acute GD infection may have unmasked a poorly symptomatic gluten enteropathy."

A traveller's tale. A young woman who worked for the United Nations[27] had been stationed in East Timor in South East Asia for an extended period. When she returned home, she complained of persistent traveller's diarrhoea and was convinced that she was harbouring a parasite.

Her doctor, however, took a careful history and ordered laboratory tests that showed she had classic coeliac disease. Once she started on a gluten-free diet, her symptoms completed resolved.

The lesson is clear: if you still are experiencing symptoms from a recurring parasitic infection such as GD, the medication you're taking, or the infection itself, may have triggered gluten sensitivity. Try going gluten-free and see what happens.

CHAPTER 7

UNDIAGNOSED DISEASES AND CONDITIONS

Not every disease or condition has a scientifically proven cause, yet the symptoms or syndromes can play havoc with your body. It is possible that gluten sensitivity may be the culprit.

CFS AND FIBROMYALGIA

Are you tired? So tired that you can hardly function? Is your tiredness accompanied by muscle aches and pains and possibly flu-like symptoms, such as headache and perhaps abdominal pain and diarrhoea? And does your fatigue never seem to go away, perhaps even worsening if you exercise?

It's possible that you may have chronic fatigue syndrome (CFS) or fibromyalgia.

CFS and fibromyalgia are similar syndromes. To be diagnosed with CFS (also known as myalgic encephalopathy, or ME), an individual must satisfy two criteria:[1]

- **Severe chronic fatigue that lasts 6 months or more.** The fatigue must not be a result of another known medical condition.

- **Four or more of the following symptoms:** substantial impairment in short-term memory or concentration; sore throat; tender lymph nodes; muscle pain; multiple joint pain without swelling or redness; headaches of a new type, pattern or severity; unrefreshing sleep; and postexertional malaise lasting more than 24 hours.

Doctors can sometimes confuse CFS and fibromyalgia because of their similar symptoms. The dominating symptom of fibromyalgia is

73

widespread pain and tenderness in the soft tissues. The pain is described as "aching, exhausting, and nagging, and the tenderness is readily felt at certain points around the body, particularly the joints and multiple organ regions."[2]

Just as people with CFS must exhibit certain symptoms to be diagnosed, so do those with fibromyalgia. Doctors cannot detect the syndrome with laboratory tests, but the American College of Rheumatology has issued guidelines for diagnosis. The guidelines state that for fibromyalgia to be diagnosed, patients must experience tenderness in 11 or 18 "tender points" on the body.

How does all of this relate to gluten sensitivity? Consider:

Linked to the same conditions. For example, people who have certain rheumatic diseases – rheumatoid arthritis, lupus or ankylosing spondylitis – may be more likely to have fibromyalgia.[3]

Does this sound familiar? In an earlier chapter, we discussed gluten sensitivity's association with these same conditions!

Common symptoms. As we have said many times, people who have gluten sensitivity may – or may not – experience symptoms. And those symptoms may vary. Individuals who have classic coeliac disease (CD), however, generally have one symptom in common: they are "tired all the time".

Researchers decided to investigate the prevalence of coeliac disease among people who visited the doctor because of CFS. They tested the blood from 100 consecutive patients who met the criteria for CFS.[4]

They discovered two cases (2 per cent) of previously undiagnosed coeliac disease among the CFS patients. The researchers wrote, "Given our prevalence of 1 per cent and the fact that there is a treatment for [coeliac disease], we now suggest that screening for [coeliac disease] should be added to the relatively short list of mandatory investigations in suspected cases of CFS."

We should emphasize that this study was done in 2001 and *only* used blood tests. We now know that serum testing misses a significant per-centage of gluten-sensitive individuals. (See Chapter 10, Am I Gluten Sensitive?) Had today's more-sensitive testing been available for this study, in all probability, researchers would have found a much higher rate of CFS sufferers who were gluten sensitive.

Another study, published in 2003,[5] identified a rate of misdiagnosed fibromyalgia in people with coeliac disease. The study found that although 82 per cent of people who ultimately were diagnosed with CD complained of fatigue, doctors initially diagnosed 9 per cent of these patients with fibromyalgia!

Why the confusing or missed diagnoses? Probably because people with gluten sensitivity *are* tired, and that tiredness may well result from iron deficiency anaemia.

ANAEMIA

Iron deficiency anaemia is the most common type of anaemia.[6] Iron is an essential component of haemoglobin, the oxygen-carrying pigment in the blood. Normally, your blood gets iron through the food in your diet and by recycling iron from old red blood cells. When an insufficient amount of iron is absorbed, or there is too little iron in your diet, you become anaemic. And if you are anaemic, you become easily tired, fatigued and prone to other illnesses.

Long before today's sensitive blood tests, which can detect gluten sensitivity, as well as coeliac disease, some astute doctors recognized that iron deficiency anaemia *might* be caused by previously unsuspected coeliac disease. A 1994 case illustrates:[7]

A 40-year-old woman suffered from iron deficiency anaemia for 2 years because her doctors could not pinpoint its cause. A number of endoscopic examinations had not revealed any abnormalities of the gastrointestinal system. She had taken oral iron supplements, with no effect. Her doctor finally performed a biopsy, which revealed that she had coeliac disease. She went on a strict gluten-free diet, and the iron level in her blood increased. Her anaemia went away.

In 2001, researchers reported that coeliac disease was diagnosed in 13.7 per cent (26 out of 190) of people who had iron deficiency anaemia![8] These individuals were put on a gluten-free diet and were tested at 6, 12 and 24 months to see their progress toward health.

At 6 months, 77.8 per cent of the patients recovered from anaemia, although only 27.8 per cent reversed from iron deficiency. At 12 months, all but one patient (94.4 per cent) recovered from anaemia and 50 per cent from iron deficiency. And after 24 months on a gluten-free diet, *only one individual was still anaemic.*

The researchers concluded that screening for coeliac disease should be done in adults with iron deficiency anaemia. A gluten-free diet, they observed, allows the intestine to heal. As a consequence, the anaemia goes away after 6 to 12 months.

A later study, published in 2004, showed a different prevalence rate of coeliac disease – 2.8 per cent of 105 people with iron deficiency anaemia[9] – than the earlier study. But the authors make a similar conclusion, stating that because coeliac disease is treatable, it should be suspect as a cause of unexplained iron deficiency anaemia.

So, are you tired and possibly achy all of the time and can't figure out why? Go gluten-free (GF) and see what will happen.

ASTHMA

Imagine trying to breathe deeply, and the result is coughing and wheezing, with little air taken into your lungs. This is caused by asthma, a chronic inflammatory disorder of the airways. Not only is asthma frightening, it is life threatening. Yet it affects approximately 7 per cent of the population in the UK, and a staggering 12 per cent of the population in Australia[10].

Although scientists have not isolated a gene for asthma, they believe that it is an inherited condition. Children are most affected by asthma, but it may affect adults also. In fact, in the UK approximately 700,000 people over the age of 65 have asthma.[11]

Asthma is typically described as an allergic reaction to environmental factors, such as poor air quality, tobacco smoke, smoke from wood-burning stoves, volatile organic compounds, pollen, moulds, dust mites, cockroaches and pet dandruff.

Gluten sensitivity, however, may also cause asthmatic attacks. A 2001 study showed the prevalence of asthma in children with coeliac disease.[12] The authors wrote, "The cumulative incidence of asthma in children with [coeliac disease] (24.6 per cent)...was significantly higher than in children without CD (3.4 per cent)."

Another study, also published in 2001, showed that people with wheat-dependent, exercise-induced anaphylaxis (a severe form of allergic reaction), reacted after eating wheat.[13] Individuals who followed a gluten-free diet remained free of symptoms.

In a similar case report,[14] a 19-year-old student was plagued with chronic hives (urticaria) and asthma for 5 years. Initially, the outbreaks occurred after major exertion during football matches. However, after a couple of years, he noticed that they occurred daily. Despite treatment, he continued to experience both hives and asthma.

The doctors had the young man complete a food survey, which showed that he had a diet rich in wheat flour. His mother was a chef's assistant, and every day, he ate cakes that she baked.

Doctors tested this patient for wheat allergy through pinprick tests. The tests were negative. Despite this, the doctors put him on a wheat-elimination diet (not gluten-free). His chronic symptoms disappeared.

Clinical studies and reported scientific cases are strong evidence that gluten sensitivity is linked to asthma. But to me, the most compelling proof is in the stories people tell. Here are some:[15]

No more inhalers. Before he went on a gluten-free diet, a child had to use two inhalers in the spring, along with eye drops, nasal spray and an antihistamine. His mother reports that since he went gluten-free, "the decrease in asthma symptoms has been remarkable".

No more medicine. A gluten-free diet eliminated a number of allergy symptoms for a young woman – including her asthma. She had been using 250 milligrams of Advair (an asthma medication) twice a day. Now she uses none.

Lifelong asthma a thing of the past. Joan reported that she had had severe asthma her entire life. "My memories of childhood were the loneliness of being awake in the night with asthma, unable to lie down because that made it worse, unable to sleep and not wanting to call my parents because there was little they could do."

She had asked her doctor to test her for food allergies, but the doctor declined, saying that since she was allergic to so many things, it would not make a difference to eliminate certain foods.

She took matters into her own hands. She went gluten-free 16 months ago because of neurological symptoms. But the unexpected result was that her asthmatic symptoms disappeared. She has been without symptoms – or asthma medication – for more than a year, even during spring and autumn, when pollen is significant.

This lady writes, "My theory is that there is a cumulative effect on your body. My gluten intolerance was stressing my body – causing a heightened response to all allergens. Once the stress was removed, the other allergens have not been able to trigger the allergic reaction."

Is her theory right? Does it matter? What does matter is that because of her gluten-free diet, she now leads a normal life. No more asthma.

UNEXPLAINED WEIGHT LOSS (OR GAIN)

Westerners are obsessed with weight – sometimes to the detriment of their health – and often take delight in announcing that they have lost unwanted pounds. Losing weight intentionally is one thing. Losing weight *unintentionally* is another and should raise a flag that a medical condition may be at fault.

Many different conditions, of course, can account for unintentional weight loss, such as:[16]

- Acute infection
- AIDS
- Chronic diarrhoea
- Chronic infections, such as tuberculosis
- Conditions that prevent the easy consumption of food, such as painful mouth ulcers, newly applied orthodontic appliances or loss of teeth
- Depression
- Drug abuse and smoking
- Hyperthyroidism
- Loss of appetite
- Malignancy
- Malnutrition
- Parasitic infections, such as giardiasis
- Some medications, including over-the-counter drugs
- Undiagnosed anorexia nervosa or bulimia

We should add one more cause to this list of conditions: gluten sensitivity.

We have already seen that classic coeliac disease presents itself with chronic diarrhoea and can be confused with parasitic infection (giardiasis) and hyperthyroidism. Left undetected, CD also leads to malnutrition – and that means loss of weight.

Case studies and research repeatedly point to weight loss as a symptom of gluten sensitivity:

- In Denmark, 44 per cent of 50 coeliac patients indicated that they had had weight loss. This was one of the key symptoms that helped doctors identify the disease.[17]

- Ten out of 15 patients who were diagnosed with coeliac disease after being examined for hypocalcaemia (deficiency of calcium in the blood), skeletal disease or both had experienced unexplained weight loss – a clue that led to the CD diagnosis.[18]

- In a survey of 414 members of the Ottawa Chapter of the Canadian Coeliac Association, 64 per cent said that they had experienced unexplained weight loss prior to their diagnosis.

In many of these cases, the patients did not exhibit any other symptoms – no diarrhoea, no skin eruptions, no bloating, no flatulence – just loss of weight.

These studies clearly show that if you experience unintentional weight loss, the problem could be attributed to gluten sensitivity – especially if it is accompanied by other symptoms.

Check it out.

CARDIOMYOPATHY

Approximately 120,000 people in the UK have a type of heart condition known as cardiomyopathy – a serious disease in which the heart muscle becomes inflamed and does not work as it is designed to do.

Cardiomyopathy occurs in three different forms:[19] dilated, hypertrophic and restrictive. The most common of the three types is dilated cardiomyopathy, a condition in which the heart becomes enlarged, weakened and does not pump normally. People generally develop congestive heart failure if they have dilated cardiomyopathy.

When cardiomyopathy is caused by infection or as a result of autoimmune disorders, it may be known as myocarditis.[20]

Some of the symptoms of cardiomyopathy and myocarditis include shortness of breath, swelling of the ankles, palpitations (fluttering) in the chest and chest pain. Once it is identified, doctors generally treat the condition with drugs.

Dilated cardiomyopathy, a form of congestive heart failure, is a recognized atypical symptom of coeliac disease.[21] In fact, one study found that 5.7 per cent of individuals with idiopathic dilated cardiomyopathy have coeliac disease.[22]

If you are gluten sensitive and have cardiomyopathy, however, it is possible that going on a gluten-free diet may reverse the condition, as the following cases illustrate:

Two winners, one loser (who failed to go GF). Three individuals with idiopathic dilated cardiomyopathy and coeliac disease were instructed to follow a gluten-free diet.[23] Two of the three patients were faithful to the diet. After 28 months on a gluten-free diet, they showed improvement in their echocardiogram tests, as well as in a cardiological questionnaire and the Gastrointestinal Symptom Rating Scale questionnaire. The third patient refused to eat gluten-free. He experienced a worsening of symptoms.

GF wins again. An account published in 2005 described the case of a 70-year-old man who was experiencing symptoms of cardiomyopathy (congestive heart failure).[24] He experienced classic symptoms of non-exertional chest pain. The patient had been diagnosed with dermatitis herpetiformis 20 years before but had not followed a gluten-free diet. When he was examined, he had a dermatitis herpetiformis rash, and, of course, the examination showed cardiomyopathy. The patient was put on a strict gluten-free diet. He also continued with his drug treatment of losartan. After 10 months on a gluten-free diet, he had gained over 8 kg (18 lb), his night sweats had resolved, and he had not experienced further episodes of chest pain.

Another form of cardiomyopathy – myocarditis – also responds to a gluten-free diet. In a study published in 2002,[25] researchers screened the serum of 187 patients with myocarditis and found that 4.4 per cent had coeliac disease. All of the individuals responded to a gluten-free diet. The authors of the study wrote, "Patients with biopsy-proven myocarditis, especially in the presence of clinical findings of malabsorption, should be screened for CD. In fact, if CD is associated with autoimmune myocarditis, a gluten-free diet alone or the diet in combination with immunosuppressive agents can significantly improve the clinical outcome."

CHRONIC INFECTIONS

Do you seem to come down with sinusitis, colds, sore throats, ear infections – even urinary tract infections – more often than others? Do you have a problem shaking them off – they seem to linger long after they should be gone? Those chronic infections may be related to an autoimmune disorder such as gluten sensitivity.

Studies have shown that some people who have gluten intolerance also have a deficiency of the IgA antibody.[26, 27] Researchers have found a clear link between IgA deficiency and coeliac disease, with 2.6 per cent of individuals with IgA deficiency having gluten intolerance.[28] These individuals are clinically undistinguishable from patients with normal IgA levels.

Studies have shown that autoimmunity and recurrent infection are more prevalent in IgA-deficient individuals.[29]

More-recent research presents another theory of the relationship between autoimmune disorders and chronic infection. Researchers at Rice University[30] believe that chronic illnesses may trigger autoimmune responses. They explain that one of the primary functions of the immune system is to generate antibodies when an antigen (bacteria or alien substance) invades the body. Each antibody has a chemical signature that allows it to bind with only one particular sequence of amino acids found on a particular antigen. But sometimes antibodies become cross-reactive and bind with something other than the antigen they evolved to attack. This cross-reactivity, they say, causes some autoimmune diseases.

So, does having an autoimmune disease such as gluten sensitivity cause you to come down with chronic infections? Or does a chronic infection cause you to trigger an autoimmune response when you ingest gluten?

While the scientists decide, you might want to go gluten-free.

CHAPTER 8

A WORD ABOUT FIDO

Poor Fido. He gets blamed for all sorts of things, including passing smelly wind. He's usually oblivious to what he has done. But sometimes, even *he* knows the smell is so noxious that he sulks off, banishing himself from the coveted company of humans.

Some flatulence is normal, both in ourselves and in our pets. But when the condition is chronic and the smell is extremely offensive, it's time to look into its causes.

Veterinarians agree that flatulence can be caused by several different conditions:[1]

- Dietary intolerance
- Eating foods that are high in soyabeans or fibre
- Eating spoiled foods
- Infections
- Overeating
- Swallowing air too quickly – usually from gulping food

The first source of flatulence (dietary intolerance) may also be the cause of other problems. Dietary sensitivity or intolerance in pets is well documented. Most cases show up in dogs and cats as skin or gastrointestinal disorders, with the majority of dietary hypersensitivity reactions caused by proteins.[2] And the most common of offending proteins? The researchers list:

- Beef
- Dairy
- Eggs

- Lactose
- Other meat proteins
- *Gluten*

That's correct. Dogs and cats can suffer from gluten sensitivity, just like you.

This shouldn't come as a surprise. Dogs and cats are closely related to human beings, genetically speaking, and are susceptible to many of the same types of chronic diseases that we get.[3]

Veterinary scientists have actually observed gluten sensitivity in pets for some time. They are alerted to the condition through a variety of symptoms, most often gastrointestinal. For example:

- One study of 22 cats that had diarrhoea and vomiting showed that 4 per cent were gluten sensitive.[4]

- A 1992 study showed that gluten was toxic to dogs that had diarrhoea and other gastrointestinal symptoms.[5] The toxicity was proven by biopsy that showed flattened villi.

- A study of 55 cats with chronic idiopathic (from an unknown cause) gastrointestinal problems showed that 29 per cent were food-sensitive, with wheat, beef and corn gluten pinpointed as the most common "allergens".[6]

Just as it is known that removing gluten from the diet of an individual who is gluten sensitive will mitigate the problem, eliminating gluten from an animal's diet also alleviates the problem. In the same 1992 study previously mentioned, flattened villi showed improvement when the dogs were placed on a gluten-free diet and relapsed when they were tested after feeding them gluten.

In another study, when 11 dogs with idiopathic, chronic colitis were treated for 4 months with a commercial diet containing protein sources limited to chicken and rice (in other words, a gluten-free diet!), within 1 month, 60 per cent of the dogs required either no medication or a reduced dosage.[7] Their condition had cleared up.

As a scientist, I, of course, trust research. But I also place considerable faith in anecdotal evidence when it comes from a credible source.

My friend GC went on a gluten-free diet in 2002 and found relief from the symptoms of Crohn's disease, from which she had been suffering for 18 years. GC had a little Maltese dog that suffered from irritable bowel syndrome. The poor little pooch had wind so bad that the room had to be aired out when he passed it!

Since eliminating gluten had given GC a new lease on life, she wondered if it could have the same effect on her pet. She investigated the dog food she had been feeding her pet for years.

I'm not sure of the brand, but GC cares very much for her pet, and I am sure she had bought a high-quality brand of dry food for him, one touted to have all the nutrients a dog needs for a long and healthy life.

Here is the list of ingredients for one of these dog foods:[8]

"Ground yellow corn, chicken by-product meal, corn gluten meal, *whole wheat flour,* beef tallow preserved with mixed tocopherols (source of Vitamin E), rice flour, beef, soy flour, sugar, sorbitol, tricalcium phosphate, water, animal digest, salt, phosphoric acid, potassium chloride, dicalcium phosphate, sorbic acid (a preservative), L-Lysine monohydrochloride, dried peas, dried carrots, calcium carbonate, calcium propionate (a preservative), choline chloride, vitamin supplements (E, A, B_{12}, D_3), added color (Yellow 5, Red 40, Yellow 6, Blue 2), DL-Methionine, zinc sulfate, glyceryl monostearate, ferrous sulfate, niacin, manganese sulfate, calcium pantothenate, riboflavin supplement, biotin, thiamine mononitrate, garlic oil, copper sulfate, pyridoxine hydrochloride, folic acid, menadione sodium bisulfite complex (source of vitamin K activity), calcium iodate, sodium selenite. F-4090."

Those ingredients are quoted from a top brand that you can buy in any supermarket or pet store. But what if she had bought the pooch a less expensive, supermarket-brand tinned food?

Here are the first six ingredients listed on a tin of supermarket-brand dog food whose label says "no added preservatives, formulated for healthy skin and coat, highly digestible, soy free".[9] The dog food lists "chicken, meat by-products, ground rice, wheat flour, wheat gluten, carrageenan" as its top ingredients. (To learn more about the ill effects of the additive carrageenan, see Chapter 13, What If Going Gluten-Free Doesn't Work?)

Keep in mind: just as in "people food", pet-food ingredients are listed in order of volume. These dog foods are loaded with wheat. (So is cat food.)

After GC discovered that the main portion of her dog's diet had been wheat cereal, GC took him off commercial dog food and began to feed him home-cooked chicken, carrots and rice. She occasionally mixed in other vegetables and even fruit. The Maltese licked his chops after every meal.

The result: no diarrhoea, no bloating, no smelly flatulence. On the dog's final checkup, the vet could not believe how old he was. He died at the ripe old age of 17.

One pet-food manufacturer defends its practice of using wheat in dog and cat foods by saying, "Wheat is a grain used as a high-quality carbohydrate source...It provides energy for daily activity...Iams research has shown that including wheat in a complete and balanced diet resulted in a moderate glycemic response in dogs and cats, lower in general than that observed when a rice-based diet was fed."[10]

The company also states that "gluten...is responsible for wheat-sensitive enteropathy [intestinal disease], occasionally found in Irish setters from the United Kingdom....This condition is very rare, and the reason some dogs develop it is not yet clear."

It's clear why people develop gluten sensitivity. What is the mystery about dogs? And while it is true that much of the study of gluten sensitivity has been done on Irish setters, the studies previously cited show that other dogs, and cats, can also become gluten sensitive.

What's in *your* tin or bag of pet food? Is your pet suffering from arthritis? Passing a lot of wind? Having diarrhoeic accidents on the carpet? Or experiencing any of the symptoms of the disorders discussed in the preceding chapters? Maybe it's time to put him on a gluten-free diet.

It is possible to buy gluten-free pet food. Some are advertised as "all wheat and maize gluten free – perfect for all dogs, especially those with gluten intolerances."

If you can't find a pet food that specifies it is gluten free, you will have to read the labels. But read them carefully. You may find hidden sources of gluten in pet food (even premium food) such as "brewer's yeast", a by-product of the brewing industry. (Unless brewer's yeast is prepared from a sugar molasses base, it contains gluten.)

Your best bet to guarantee a gluten-free diet for your pet is to do what GC does: cook the food yourself.

You'll have a healthy and happy pet. And you probably won't need to air out the house nearly so often.

CHAPTER 9

FROM THE FILES OF HEALTH PROFESSIONALS

Are you still a sceptic? Do you doubt that gluten could be a problem in your life or the life of a friend or family member?

If science is not enough, if anecdotes told by people who have recovered from their symptoms by eliminating gluten from their diets aren't enough – well, I invite you to consider the experiences that four distinguished health-care professionals and I have had with our patients.

AN ANSWER TO SUDDEN-ONSET SYMPTOMS

For many people, gluten sensitivity comes on slowly, perhaps because of a genetic propensity, or perhaps because of a growing intolerance to gluten.

For others, however, the onset is rapid. AC's case demonstrates this.

AC is a 24-year-old woman. In 2004, when she was 22, she was diagnosed with pneumonia. To cure the pneumonia, the doctor prescribed a strong antibiotic – Augmentin – that she took for 10 days, followed by Ciprofloxacin for another 10 days. She took acidophilus supplementation while on the antibiotics as a preventive measure against side effects from the antibiotics.

Immediately upon completing the antibiotic regime, AC suffered bad stomach cramps, nausea, dry heaving and diarrhoea. Trying to find the cause of her problems, the doctor ran numerous blood tests (including one for coeliac disease [CD], which was negative) and a stool test for parasites.

The tests did not reveal the cause of her symptoms.

After she completed this battery of tests but refused a colonoscopy, her doctor suggested that her symptoms were stress-related and that she should "learn how to control her stress and work on her diet". (No one really understood what he meant by that.)

Desperate to get rid of the problem, AC tried numerous products from the healthfood store, including fibre supplements and colon cleansers. None worked.

Approximately 4 months after trying these natural products, she came to me for help. At my recommendation, she went on a gluten-free diet. AC had already eliminated dairy, since she found it made her congested and caused her face to break out. (She is able to use goat- and sheep-milk products, as well as almond, rice and soya milks.)

Within a few weeks, AC started to feel well. She stayed off all gluten for 6 months and experienced no symptoms at all.

AC discovered that when she deviates from a gluten-free diet, she feels the effects almost immediately.

For example: if she eats any gluten in the evening, the next day, she wakes up with nausea and dry heaving. When she eats it during the day, her stomach almost immediately becomes bloated and she experiences diarrhoea.

She remains on a strict gluten-free diet.

DR. BOCK'S MIRACLE CHILDREN

Dr. Kenneth Bock, cofounder and codirector of two New York health centres has been prescribing gluten-free (GF) and casein-free (CF) diets for many years, in particular for children with autism, pervasive developmental delay (PDD), Asperger's syndrome, attention-deficit disorder and attention-deficit hyperactivity disorder.

Because the response of these special-needs patients has frequently been so dramatic and because the frequency of coeliac disease is no greater for them than in normal children, he no longer finds the need to test for anti-gliadin antibodies on a routine basis.

Dr. Bock's comprehensive evaluation for each patient focuses on identifying biochemical and metabolic imbalances, dysbiosis (an imbalance between the good and bad bacteria in the intestinal tract) and/or maldigestion and immune imbalances in order to fine-tune their nutritional programme.

Dr. Bock describes three of his patients who have had these almost-miraculous results:

PDD boy "awakened" – almost overnight. MR is a 2½-year-old boy who was diagnosed with pervasive developmental delay (PDD). Prior to becoming Dr. Bock's patient, he had seen a number of specialists and was being treated with various therapies to improve his speech and address other aspects of his developmental delay.

Characteristic of a child with PDD, MR had problems with fine motor coordination, speech and severe drooling. He had no expressive language and was unable to play appropriately.

He had a history of colic until he was 5 months old but now was experiencing constipation.

Dr. Bock immediately put the boy on a GF/CF diet. After a few days, his astonished parents noted that MR "woke up".

MR's dramatic progress has included improved motor skills, eye contact and awareness of surroundings, as well as elimination of constipation.

Through his nutritional therapy, he also experienced great improvement in language skills and attention. His drooling, which was severe, is almost completely gone, and he is no longer speech-delayed.

His paediatric neurologist, astounded by the results achieved with this young boy, reported that he had never seen anything like this in his entire career. MR's therapists, who work with many PDD and autistic children, also state that they have never seen such dramatic improvement in a child with PDD.

MR is almost back to normal. And perhaps the most miraculous part of this story is that *the turnaround occurred in just a matter of months.*

Dr. Bock commented on the parents' observation that MR "woke up". He said that a fascinating biochemical abnormality occurs with children who have PDD and autism: these children actually experience a withdrawal that can only be described as the same type of withdrawal experienced by drug addicts!

According to Dr. Bock, these children frequently don't just have an immune reactivity to gluten and casein; their condition goes far beyond reactivity. They are unable to digest peptides into amino acids. This inability to digest peptides can cause inflammation and immune reactivity, as well as produce morphine-like compounds. These compounds, called gliadomorphine and caseomorphine, exert effects similar to those of morphine itself! These effects cause an opioid addiction similar to the addiction that occurs from the use of any drug containing morphine.

This opioid addiction explains why these children often have an incredibly high tolerance for pain and why many experience withdrawal symptoms similar to those of drug addicts.

When they come out of the withdrawal, they literally "wake up".

The Autism Research Institute[1] has found more than 65 per cent of children with autism improve with a GF/CF diet. These results are so dramatic that researchers at the University of Rochester School of Medicine in Rochester, New York, are currently conducting a double-blind, placebo-controlled trial to study the effects of this diet restriction with a large group of autistic children.

No more head-banging. SW is a 3½-year-old autistic boy who had a very mild speech delay. That condition changed when he received his vaccinations.

According to his parents, 2 months after receiving vaccinations, he experienced a total loss of speech, loss of eye contact, loss of interest in his surroundings, pica (an abnormal craving or appetite for non-food substances, such as dirt, paint or clay), toe walking and a constant glazed look.

He also started banging his head, showed an increased tolerance to pain, and had corrosive diarrhoea, which was so severe that it caused lesions on his buttocks.

Prior to taking their son to Dr. Bock, his parents researched GF/CF diets and started the boy on them. Convinced that nutrition would play a key role in helping their son, they sought nutritional help from Dr. Bock for SW's problems.

Shortly after putting the boy on the diet, the parents saw a significant improvement in his behaviour. SW completely stopped head-banging and pica. His motor skills, toe walking, speech, pain threshold and diarrhoea all improved – all to the amazement of SW's therapists.

Dr. Bock fine-tuned the boy's nutrition to achieve even greater improvement. He evaluated SW's biochemistry and metabolism and recommended specific dietary supplements that caused further improvement in his interest, eye contact and overall functioning.

SW is left with some expressive language delay, but even that continues to improve as he adheres to his dietary regime.

Setback, then dramatic improvement. BG is a 2½-year-old boy diagnosed with mild autism. He suffered speech delay, self-stimulation (eyes moving in a certain way while following the motion of his own hands), flapping, looking at lights and other signs common to autism.

Like SW's parents, BG's parents also did considerable research about his condition, particularly on the internet, and started BG on a GF/CF diet a few months before their first visit with Dr. Bock.

Within 48 hours of starting the diet, BG experienced severe withdrawal symptoms. Then the child became severely autistic, showing no eye contact and using bizarre behaviour. Because of their research, however, his parents were prepared for these conditions.

The setback was temporary. *Within 2 weeks of beginning the diet, BG spoke his first words.*

Although improvement continued, the parents sought Dr. Bock's guidance to fine-tune their son's nutrition through a biomedical approach.

After starting his nutritional therapy, BG began to socialize and play with other children. He surpassed academic goals and was learning almost normally. His improvements continue.

Dr. Bock, as well as my other colleagues, emphasize that it is important to maintain a gluten-free diet for at least 3 months. He also suggests trying a casein-free diet for at least 3 weeks to experience its benefits.

He explains that he uses these diet restrictions in patients with other autoimmune diseases, such as autistic enterocolitis and Hashimoto's thyroiditis, as well as inflammatory bowel disease (IBD) and other illnesses that do not respond to conventional treatment.

DR. DRISKO'S "MARVELLOUS" ADULTS

Dr. Jeanne Drisko is clinical associate professor at the University of Kansas Medical Center, and a conscientious doctor who does a full and comprehensive check-up on each patient.

Dr. Drisko shares her experiences with three of her adult patients who experienced marvellous recoveries.

The power of gluten. MZ is a 19-year-old woman who for several years had suffered from severe chronic fatigue syndrome, as well as irritable bowel syndrome (IBS). Despite being under the care of a number of different doctors throughout her disability, her condition had not improved.

MZ's condition was so severe that she had been homeschooled because of fainting, severe fatigue, brain fog and an inability to concentrate.

Dr. Drisko's IgG testing showed that MZ had sensitivities to gluten and gliadin. She put MZ on a gluten-free diet.

Within a few months, all of her symptoms (including her IBS) resolved. She was able to attend college and lead a normal, healthy and vibrant life.

Then something unusual happened. MZ invited some friends to her home. They brought wheat products – crisps and bread. She did not eat any of it.

However, she was in the proximity of the opened foodstuffs, most likely breathed in particles from them, and she might have touched them. *She immediately had a moderate relapse.*

She had her friends remove all of these products from her house, and she fully recovered once again.

MZ's extraordinary episode is an excellent demonstration of just how powerful gluten and gliadin can be to someone who is extremely sensitive.

Spontaneous dermatitis herpetiformis. SR is a 21-year-old college student with many food sensitivities and gut disturbances. Prior to becoming Dr. Drisko's patient, she had been seen by many different specialists who had not been able to help her.

Dr. Drisko's testing (IgG test) showed that SR had a hypersensitivity to gluten and gliadin. She went on a gluten-free diet, and her condition cleared up.

One day, she was making loaves of bread (which she had no intention of eating) for a party. As she worked with the flour, she broke out in sores all over her body that looked like poison ivy. Despite Dr. Drisko's medical treatment, the rash continued to spread. Dr. Drisko then correctly diagnosed the skin lesions as dermatitis herpetiformis.

SR immediately cleared her home of all gluten-containing products, and the skin lesions resolved.

This case once again demonstrates how hypersensitive an individual can be without even eating gluten.

A gluten challenge. ML is a 50-year-old businessman who had suffered from IBS and back pain for many years. Despite numerous medical interventions by specialists, his conditions had never improved.

Dr. Drisko found that he had elevated IgG antibodies to gluten and gliadin and put on him on a gluten-free diet. His IBS quickly resolved.

His story does not end here, however. ML found that not only had his IBS resolved, so had his back pain! To see if the back pain was related to gluten, he was given a food challenge in which he ate toast and crackers (lots of wheat!) in the morning.

His back pain immediately came back. Gluten reared its powerful head again.

DR. HOFFMAN'S SUCCESS STORIES

Dr. Ronald Hoffman is the medical director of the Hoffman Center in New York City. His clinic, established in 1985, delivers comprehensive and innovative health care, with a special emphasis on nutrition and metabolism. He and his staff work with patients who have bounced from doctor to doctor without success in dealing with their ailments.

Dr. Hoffman has witnessed the miraculous effect of eliminating gluten from the diets of individuals plagued with a variety of symptoms. Here is just a small sampling of the patients who have responded dramatically to a gluten-free diet.

Multiple problems and overweight condition – resolved. GS was a 40-year-old registered dietitian who complained of wind, bloating, rheumatoid arthritis, multiple allergies (mould, dust, etc.), bad sinusitis and exhaustion. She was also overweight.

Because she worked in a hospital, she had access to various specialists. Consequently, an endocrinologist, rheumatologist and allergist were all prescribing medications for her various ailments – but without any success.

Many people who have symptoms pointing to gluten sensitivity are reluctant to give up their lifestyles and go on a gluten-free diet without "proof" from tests. GS was one of these individuals.

Consequently, Dr. Hoffman ran a blood test – the more sophisticated tests were not available at the time of these particular cases – for anti-gliadin IgA antibodies (AGA), anti-tissue transglutaminase (tTG) and the anti-endomysial antibody (EMA).

He anticipated that she would test positive to AGA (showing gluten sensitivity), but to everyone's surprise, the tests came back positive for all three antibodies, indicating that she had full-blown CD.

What was most unusual about this case was the fact that she had gained around over 22 kg (3½ st) since her symptoms had started about

5 years before diagnosis. With CD, the most common presenting symptom is *weight loss* – not weight gain.

After several months on a gluten-free diet, all her symptoms disappeared. She went off all her medications and has maintained good health using dietary supplements instead. Most surprising (and perhaps rewarding to her) was that she has lost all the weight she had gained. She continues to be gluten-free.

Progressive idiopathic ataxia – stopped. AH, a 45-year-old woman, came to see Dr. Hoffman with severe ataxia. Over the course of 5 years prior to visiting Dr. Hoffman, she had had a full check-up by many well-respected neurologists, who diagnosed that she had a type of idiopathic (of unknown cause) ataxia with symptoms similar to those of Friedreich's ataxia.

Friedreich's ataxia is a slowly progressive disorder of the nervous system and muscles. Named for the doctor who first identified it in the early 1860s, Friedreich's ataxia results in an inability to coordinate voluntary muscle movements (ataxia). This condition is caused by degeneration of nerve tissue in the spinal cord and of nerves that extend to peripheral areas, such as the arms and legs. People with this condition have a drunken, stumbling gait when they walk.

Dr. Hoffman was familiar with the well-known link between idiopathic ataxia and gluten sensitivity and tested the woman for gluten sensitivity. He found AGA and EMA both to be positive through blood tests – tests that her neurologist had never ordered.

Despite the results of the blood tests and the fact that her disorder was progressive and she could end up wheelchair-bound, the woman was highly resistant to going on a gluten-free diet.

She was finally convinced to give the diet a try after she was given a number of articles and research studies to read, many of which are cited in this book.

The gluten-free diet completely halted the progression of her disease. She also experienced some improvement in her muscle coordination. Unfortunately, the gluten had inflicted some permanent damage to her nervous system.

It is sad that her gluten sensitivity had not been discovered earlier.

Chronic conditions and allergies – gone. Dr. Hoffman sees at least 50 patients each year with chronic sinusitis, asthma, wind, bloating and common allergies, such as mould, dust and pollen, who test positive for AGA but negative for all the other antibodies. When these patients are taken off gluten, they are able to wean off all their medications that controlled their symptoms.

Other conditions – improved. Dr. Hoffman has also found that patients with thyroid disorders often respond to a gluten-free diet, as well as those with IBS, who are often on medications to control their illness.

These IBS patients do not have coeliac disease; they simply have gluten sensitivity as the cause of their problem. Dr. Hoffman does not wait for CD (characterized by villous atrophy of the small intestines) to develop. If patients come in with a large-intestine biopsy that even shows inflammation, he puts a patient on a gluten-free diet – even if AGA does not show up positive in a blood test.

Dr. Hoffman recognizes the limits of blood tests to identify gluten sensitivity (see Chapter 10, Am I Gluten Sensitive?), but unfortunately the two laboratories that have developed more-sensitive testing procedures for gluten sensitivity are not recognized to do testing in New York (which restricts testing to those labs licensed under its rules).

DR. WEDMAN–ST. LOUIS'S WONDERS

Dr. Wedman-St. Louis is a nutritionist who provides individual nutritional counselling. The individuals she advises are as likely to come to her on their own as they are to be referred by a medical doctor.

No more tummy aches. In mid-summer 2003, 9-year-old MJ began to suffer stomach aches, bloating and cramping. Every time she consumed her favourite foods, such as cheese on toast and watermelon, she experienced a stomach pain so bad that she escaped to bed to sleep, and would refuse to eat those foods again.

After 6 months of stomach aches (and then refusal to eat the offending foods), MJ's mother took her to see a paediatrician. Her specific complaints included stomach aches, weight loss, dark circles under her eyes and a skin rash.

The paediatrician concentrated on the weight loss and stomach aches, and ordered blood tests. Then he told MJ to go home and try using milk-based weight-gain drinks (these are loaded with sugar, artificial flavour and fat) to regain the weight she had lost from her self-imposed restricted diet.

Two days into consuming these drinks, MJ became extremely ill. She experienced such intense stomach aches that she was admitted to the hospital.

At the hospital, doctors ordered more blood tests, which mistakenly showed that she had diabetes. (The hospital mixed up her laboratory results with another patient's). It took 2 days for the hospital to sort out the mistake, after which she was discharged with no diagnosis for her stomach aches.

One month later, her paediatrician finally ordered a blood test for coeliac disease. It came back negative. Approximately 3 weeks later, because she was still not doing well, her pediatrician ordered an endoscopic exam for CD. It, too, came back negative – no flattened villi.

The doctor then ordered another blood test for CD. This one showed slightly elevated anti-gliadin IgA antibodies at a level of 18.2 (normal is less than 10) with normal tTGA. Even though the anti-gliadin IgA antibodies fell outside the normal range, the paediatrician still insisted the CD panel wasn't specific enough for CD and ignored the results.

He did not consider a diagnosis of gluten intolerance. Instead, he concluded that *MJ required psychological counselling and needed to learn how to eat.*

Fortunately, MJ's mother took her to see Dr. Wedman-St. Louis shortly after the last blood test. Dr. Wedman-St. Louis suggested getting an IgG food antibody profile.

The profile indicated either a severe or moderate reactivity to almost every food MJ had been avoiding. She showed a severe reactivity (+5) to casein, milk, egg, wheat and peanuts and a moderate reactivity (+4) to soya, rye and barley.

As a side note: Immunoreactivity tests are limited in what they can identify. If an individual is not in a good nutritional state and has nutritional depletion, the test may show a sensitivity to something that wouldn't be identified if the patient were adequately nourished.

The test may also show severe reactivity to a food that the patient eats daily, whereas it might not produce that level of severity if the patient were eating a variety of foods.

In MJ's case, the immunoreactivity test showed that MJ had both a gluten and a casein intolerance, as well as a soya reactivity.

Dr. Wedman-St. Louis started MJ on a gluten-free/dairy-free diet (which eliminates casein). She recommended excluding eggs as well.

It didn't take long for the diet to work. Within 2 months, MJ's personality changed, she had regained weight, and she was a happy, normal and active girl who no longer suffered from stomach pain or bloating. The dark circles under her eyes and her skin rash – both of which were ignored by her paediatrician – also completely cleared.

To help MJ achieve optimal health, Dr. Wedman-St. Louis recommended nutritional supplements in addition to changing her diet. These nutrients included a multinutrient formula (providing vitamins, minerals and antioxidants), medium-chain triglyceride oil, fish oil, amino acid capsules and other dietary supplements to improve her immune system and enhance gastrointestinal health.

Dr. Wedman-St. Louis also recommended that MJ take *Primadophilus reuteri* as an acidophilus supplement. MJ preferred having capsules emptied into an almond milk smoothie as an easy way to take the supplement.

MJ is not annoyed that she cannot eat the same foods as other kids. Instead, she dutifully checks all labels, because she knows that if she eats the wrong things, she will get a stomach ache – something she doesn't want again. She is very thankful to Dr. Wedman-St. Louis. Her mother remains completely supportive and is thrilled with the results.

No more myasthenia, despite the doctor. When SW was 63 years old in 2002, she was diagnosed with myasthenia gravis, a neuromuscular disorder.

Prior to the diagnosis, she had experienced a number of medical issues: thyroid disease, diabetes, a partial hysterectomy for fibroid tumours in 1965, surgery for ovarian cancer (followed by chemotherapy) in 1995 and colon cancer, which resulted in the removal of 70 per cent of her large colon in 2002. All of these problems were under control when her diagnosis for myasthenia gravis was made.

The myasthenia was clearly interfering with her life, because it was causing severe and very frequent diarrhoea. After 3 years of planning her life around being near a bathroom, SW went to see Dr. Wedman-St. Louis to see what could be done about her "rapid transit time" (diarrhoea). Because SW refused to have blood tests done, Dr. Wedman-St. Louis put her on a specific nutritional repletion that included acidophilus, alpha-lipoic acid, zinc and folate. She also started SW on an elimination, hypoallergenic diet that excluded all grains, dairy, eggs and soya and emphasized drinking a lot of water.

The "gluten-free+" diet was effective. In 1 month, SW's bowel movements decreased from six per day to three. Even more important, she no longer experienced diarrhoea but had normal stools.

The diet also cleared her sleep disorder, allowing her to sleep through the night. And she no longer had droopy eyelids (a symptom of myasthenia gravis). Some friends accused her of having plastic surgery! She loved the compliments. The diet also gave her more energy, and her chronic fatigue lessened. At this point, SW, who initially did not want to take supplements, agreed to take a multinutrient formula supplement for more nutritional repletion.

Prior to seeing Dr. Wedman-St. Louis, SW had been under the care of a gastroenterologist who wanted to schedule a colon resection for her diarrhoea. After working with Dr. Wedman-St. Louis for a period of time, SW returned to the gastroenterologist for a follow-up visit that she had previously scheduled. She explained to the doctor what she had done and how well she was doing. However, her doctor was of the opinion that she was just having "passing improvement".

The improvement didn't pass; SW continued to get better. Over the next 2 months, her bowel movements decreased to normal at two per day. She continued to feel better, her skin was better hydrated, and she looked great.

She went back to her doctor again, since he had scheduled another 2-month follow-up. She expected him to give her a clean bill of health. Instead, he told her she would need surgery at a future time, since her improvement might not last. However, since she was better now, she wouldn't need the bowel resection at this time. But, if her symptoms returned...

Dr. Wedman-St. Louis discussed the possibility of reintroducing some of the foods SW had eliminated (such as eggs), but SW has no desire to add any of the foods back into her diet, since she is afraid her symptoms might be triggered. Although she used to love the foods she has given up, she doesn't want to risk getting sick again.

TREATMENT PROTOCOLS

All of these doctors (and many of my colleagues) use similar treatment protocols with patients they suspect may have autoimmune diseases, such as gluten sensitivity:

Identification of targeted nutritional needs. Check-up methods vary, but the end result is a comprehensive understanding of the patient's nutritional deficiencies.

Gluten-free diet. Even in the absence of blood tests or other tests that definitively point to gluten sensitivity, they put patients who have been unsuccessful with other treatment protocols on a gluten-free diet. And they keep patients on this diet for at least 3 months to see its results.

Casein-free diet. Depending upon the patient, the doctors frequently recommend a casein-free diet, especially for those individuals suffering from gastrointestinal disorders, such as IBD or IBS.

Paleolithic diet. In addition to having patients go gluten-free, they often put patients with autoimmune disease on a "Paleolithic diet", which is essentially grain-free, with fresh, natural foods as recommended in this book. They believe, as I do, that our ancestors did not eat the way we do today, and genetically, we are not able to adapt to the drastic changes in our diet that have occurred over thousands of years.

Dietary supplementation. All of the doctors use dietary supplementation – either orally or intravenously, or both, to help the patient be restored to health faster.

Detoxification. In addition to providing dietary supplementation, the doctors use supplements specifically selected to help rid the body of toxic elements.

CHAPTER 10

AM I GLUTEN SENSITIVE?

Throughout this book, we've shown that gluten causes problems in a great number of people. If you suspect you may be one of these people, the easiest thing to do is to eliminate gluten from your diet. If your body responds, you will know it. You will feel and be healthier.

Perhaps, though, you want definitive proof to show that you are gluten sensitive. You are in luck. You can get a doctor to test for gluten sensitivity. The key, though, is to get the *right* test.

Before we look at the right tests for gluten sensitivity, let's consider the wrong tests – tests for coeliac disease (CD). Remember that coeliac disease is gluten sensitivity gone awry! The tests that doctors use to tell if you have coeliac disease *cannot* tell them if you are gluten sensitive.

BLOOD TESTS

In the digestive process, if you are gluten sensitive, your body produces antibodies to gluten. The gold standard for confirming a diagnosis of coeliac disease is a positive blood test for anti-gliadin IgA antibodies (AGA) *plus* anti-tissue transglutaminase (tTGA) (two of the three antibodies produced if you are gluten sensitive). Even more definitive – if a blood test is positive for AGA, tTGA, *and* anti-endomysial antibody (EMA) (the third antibody), doctors are almost 100 per cent certain you have coeliac disease.

But blood tests are inadequate to detect gluten sensitivity, for a couple of reasons:

Partial atrophy is ignored. You can *only* be guaranteed to test positive for AGA, tTGA and EMA if *total* villous atrophy has occurred – that is, only if the villi are *completely* flattened.

If you have partial, subtotal or infiltrating villous atrophy, you may *not* test positive for AGA, tTGA or EMA. The atrophy and inflammation of the villi may not be severe enough to allow all these antibodies to easily pass through your intestinal barrier. Only some of them – or even none of them! – may be in your bloodstream, depending upon the condition of your villi and the progression of your gluten sensitivity.

Despite the fact that you have a problem with gluten (that's why the antibodies show up in your bloodstream in the first place), if the other tests are negative, you'll need to wait until *total* villous atrophy has occurred to get a positive test that confirms coeliac disease.

Unfortunately, by the time that total villous atrophy occurs, you are also one sick puppy, with symptoms that could include diarrhoea, wind, bloating, nausea, vomiting, fat in the stool, malabsorption and significant weight loss. You may even experience periods of constipation.

Laboratory tests are incomplete. Another reason why blood tests are not accurate is because typical laboratory tests do not identify all the antibodies in your blood.

When a laboratory tests for antibodies, it first creates a buffer agent and then introduces a blood sample into the agent to see what types of antibodies are produced.

The most common antibody that a gluten-sensitive individual produces is anti-gliadin. The agent laboratories use for this antibody test is wheat mixed into a water solution.

The problem with a wheat-based solution? Gliadin does not dissolve in water. As a result, more than 30 gliadin peptides (molecules) are not evaluated by this test. Your body may be reacting to gliadin peptides that are not picked up by these blood tests.

BIOPSY

Some doctors are not satisfied with the blood tests – or, if the blood tests come back negative for AGA and tTGA but you still have symptoms, they decide to take a look – literally. They do a biopsy through an endoscopic procedure.

But unless significant structural damage has occurred to the villi of the small intestines, doctors rule out coeliac disease and gluten sensitivity.

Without total villous atrophy, doctors consider a biopsy negative – even if early inflammatory changes are seen.

However, research has shown that the brunt of the immune reaction to gluten can affect the function of the intestines and cause symptoms *without* structural damage.

Since the minority of gluten-sensitive individuals actually develop coeliac disease, a biopsy that confirms only significant damage means that the vast majority of those reacting to gluten remain undiagnosed and untreated for years.

GENETIC TESTING

Genetic testing is another way to find out if you may be gluten sensitive. For example, it is estimated that 90 per cent of patients in the US who develop coeliac disease test positive for a gene called HLA-DQ2.[1] Virtually all remaining patients test positive for another gene, HLA-DQ8. Testing for these genes is done by swabbing the inside of the mouth to gather mucosa.

If the mucosa tests positive for one or both of these genes, there is a high probability that you have gluten sensitivity and may develop coeliac disease. But the test is inconclusive because many people who do *not* have CD test positive for these genes. So without positive blood tests, genetic screening cannot tell if you are gluten sensitive. Note: these tests are not widely available outside the US.

Researchers are investigating other genes (such as histocompatibility class 1–related genes) to diagnose more-atypical forms of CD, but these tests are not in use yet.

INVASIVE BUT SENSITIVE TESTING

Earlier, we said that when a gluten-sensitive person ingests food containing gluten, the gluten becomes an antigen that is attacked by antibodies (AGA, tTGA or EMA). If the villi are flattened because of pronounced inflammation, these antibodies escape into the bloodstream. But if the villi are not atrophied or are only partially atrophied, antibodies may not (cannot) get into the bloodstream.

Regardless of whether you have antibodies in your bloodstream, if you are gluten sensitive, you *still* have AGA. Although these antibodies are not in your blood, they *are* in your intestine, according to cutting-edge research conducted in the 1990s.[2]

Researchers measured AGA in blood and intestinal fluid by having people in the study swallow a long tube that migrated into the upper small intestines. The research found that *untreated* CD patients had AGA present in both their blood *and* their small intestine.

CD patients who had followed a gluten-free diet for a year and had substantially healed their villous atrophy no longer had AGA present in their blood. However, they still had mild inflammation, and they had a measurable amount of AGA inside the intestine.

Another study investigating rectal installation of gluten (a gluten enema) found an abnormal immunological reaction in 20 per cent of children with type 1 (insulin dependent) diabetes. But blood tests for antibodies were negative, and their intestinal biopsies were normal.

What was found was substantial infiltration of lymphocytes – a localized inflammatory immune response. When these children were put on a gluten-free diet, they experienced improved growth and better blood-sugar control.

(As a side note: cow's milk consumption before 1 year of age has also been associated with type 1 diabetes in children. If these children had been screened early for gluten and dairy sensitivity or had been started on a gluten-free diet as soon as the symptoms of growth failure and/or poor blood sugar were evident, it is probable that the destruction of the cells that produce insulin could have been avoided.)

The results of these research projects made convincing arguments that more-conclusive tests for gluten sensitivity could be developed, forgoing blood tests and biopsies in favour of tests that examined intestinal fluids.

The late Dr. Anne Ferguson, a researcher from the University of Edinburgh Department of Medicine, pioneered the development of such a test: patients swallowed a tube, through which many gallons of non-absorbable fluid were poured, in order to achieve a complete lavage (emptying) of all their gastrointestinal contents. These contents had to be passed by rectum and collected into a large vat and then analyzed for the presence of AGA and tTGA.

The test was clearly far more sensitive for testing for gluten intolerance than the conventional blood testing, but it was not embraced by the medical community because of the arduous procedure that had to be performed to collect the intestinal contents for analysis. And, as it wasn't exactly non-invasive, it was less than pleasant for patients.

CONCLUSIVE TESTS FOR GLUTEN SENSITIVITY

Fortunately, there are a number of tests that are likely to reveal gluten sensitivity in anyone who has it.

Stool Testing for Antibodies

Two medical researchers, Drs. Kenneth Fine[3] and Aristo Vojdani, are among many current scientists who concur that better tests are needed to assess gluten sensitivity in individuals who do not have villous atrophy.

Because of the shortcomings of blood tests, the inconclusive evidence of biopsies, and the invasive nature of lavage tests, these researchers agree that evidence of immunologic reaction to gluten has to come from a test for antibodies located where the food comes into direct contact with the tissue, such as inside the intestinal tract or the mouth.

Dr. Fine recognized the value of Dr. Ferguson's work and took up where she left off. His cutting-edge research on microscopic colitis led him to the discovery that stool analysis is an excellent and non-invasive way to assess gluten sensitivity. This also means that it would be able to diagnose gluten sensitivity years before coeliac disease develops.

Dr. Fine explained his incredible discovery to me:

Microscopic colitis is a common chronic diarrhoeal syndrome and accounts for 10 per cent of all cases of chronic diarrhoea. It is the most common cause of ongoing chronic diarrhoea in treated coeliac, affecting 4 per cent of all coeliac patients.

However, from his published research, despite the presence of the HLA-DQ2 gene (the gene that suggests gluten sensitivity) in 64 per cent of patients with microscopic colitis, few got positive blood tests or biopsies consistent with coeliac disease, because total villous atrophy had not occurred. The biopsies did, however, reveal varying degrees of inflammation and mild villous blunting in 70 per cent of the patients.

Negative tests for coeliac did not rule out the possibility of gluten sensitivity. He decided to see if the anti-gliadin IgA antibodies were present in the stools of the research subjects.

His initial data was astounding: in people with untreated coeliac disease, stool analysis showed a positive presence of the antibodies in 100 per cent of the patients. The standard blood test showed a positive presence of antibodies in 76 per cent of the patients.[4]

Since that time, Dr. Fine has compared hundreds of tests on people with microscopic colitis. He found that only 7 per cent of these individuals test positive for antibodies in blood tests, while 76 per cent test positive through the stool test.

Also, he has found that 79 per cent of family members of patients with coeliac disease have a positive stool test, 77 per cent of patients with any type of autoimmune disease test positive, and 57 per cent of people with irritable bowel syndrome and similar symptoms test positive.

Fifty per cent of people with chronic diarrhoea of unknown origin test positive, out of which only 10 to 12 per cent test positive on the blood tests – the same as normal volunteers.

From this and other data, it appears that the stool test for AGA is far more sensitive than standard coeliac-panel blood tests. His data has also shown that 29 per cent of the normal population of the US, almost all of whom eat gluten, show an immunological reaction to gluten in their intestines, even with the absence of any illness or symptoms.

This is not so far-fetched, given that 11 per cent of these "normals" still display positive blood tests, and according to more recent analysis, as many as 42 per cent carry the HLA-DQ2 or DQ8 coeliac gene.

Dr. Fine also measures the DQ1 and DQ3 genes, which also predispose many people to gluten sensitivity. Positive tests to any one or more of these genes further raise the probability that an individual is gluten sensitive.

All of these genetic markers are easily evaluated by a simple buccal smear, which is a gentle scraping of the inside of the cheek with a small spatula that collects the cells for analysis.

As a further confirmation that the stool tests conclusively indicate gluten sensitivity, individuals who test positive respond to a gluten-free diet. For example: Dr. Fine has treated 25 patients who had refractory (not improving) or relapsing microscopic colitis with a gluten-free diet. Nineteen resolved completely, and the other five were noticeably improved. He has also added a dairy-free regime, as I do when I suspect gluten sensitivity, and found even greater improvement in some patients.

Dr. Fine continues to study the problem of gluten sensitivity. In the meantime, he has applied his research to a testing facility (www.enterolab.com) which provides stool or genetic testing. The laboratory is in the US but it will send tests to most countries, provided the order is placed with them via their website.

Salivary Testing for Antibodies

Dr. Aristo Vojdani[5] was extremely disappointed with the conventional blood-analysis testing for coeliac and was well aware that it would not reveal sensitivity to gluten unless the intestinal villi were totally destroyed.

He was also familiar with research in animals that demonstrated that when a bacterial oral antigen (from milk or gluten, for example) was orally consumed, AGA and tTG antibodies could not be detected in the blood. However, the antibodies could be detected in the animal's stool and saliva.

He (like Dr. Fine and me) was also aware that a gluten-free diet was therapeutic for a host of illnesses and that an individual could respond to a gluten-free diet for an illness when there were no intestinal symptoms.

Dr. Vojdani determined to prove to sceptics that the positive response to a gluten-free dietary intervention was not a placebo effect. Thus, he developed a sophisticated salivary assay for testing for AGA and tTGA:

- Patients who have AGA in their saliva are considered to have gluten sensitivity.

- A positive test for both AGA and tTGA confirms coeliac disease.

- A positive test for only tTGA, which shows up in type 1 diabetes, for example, demonstrates an autoimmune disease.

Dr. Vojdani feels it is important for someone with a positive salivary tTGA to try a gluten-free and dairy-free diet for several months, since these foods are immunoreactive in many people with autoimmune disease.

Like Dr. Fine, Dr. Vojdani has applied his research to a laboratory setting (www.immuno-sci-lab.com), although at the time of writing, these tests are not yet available outside the US.

PART 3

GOING
GLUTEN-FREE

Life is full of choices. From the moment you get up in the morning, you have a choice:

- Should you get up at 6 a.m., or stay in bed?
- Should you read a book, or watch TV?
- Should you ride your exercise bike or surf the internet?
- Should you order a salad or a burger for lunch?

Even when you think you are making *good* choices – such as eating a diet based on recommended nutrients – you may *not* be making the *right* choices! Not if you are gluten sensitive.

For many years we have been encouraged to obtain at least half the energy in our diets from carbohydrates, mostly starchy carbohydrates. It's hardly surprising then that grains – especially wheat – are a key part of the standard Western diet.

But, as we have seen, grains can make you sick if you are gluten sensitive.

So, if you want to eat healthy foods, you are faced with *new* choices. This part helps you make those decisions.

CHAPTER 11: SETTING YOURSELF FREE. In this chapter, you'll learn how to start and follow a gluten-free lifestyle.

CHAPTER 12: SUPPLEMENTING YOUR HEALTH. Severely gluten-sensitive individuals need an extra boost to make sure they are getting all the nutrients their body needs. This chapter tells what types of supplements you should take – and why.

CHAPTER 13: WHAT IF GOING GLUTEN-FREE DOESN'T WORK? Sometimes going gluten-free is not enough. You'll find out why – and what you can do next.

CHAPTER 11

SETTING YOURSELF FREE

No pills. No medical or surgical solution. The only way to treat gluten sensitivity is to eliminate gluten from your diet.

If you are plagued by the chronic symptoms of conditions we described in Part 2 and suspect you are gluten sensitive, a gluten-free diet may make you well again. You have *nothing* to lose (except your symptoms) by trying it for at least 2 weeks. If your symptoms are severe, however, it may take up to 3 months to feel the positive effects of the diet. Isn't your health worth a 90-day investment?

The decision to go gluten-free may seem formidable because you think, "I won't be able to eat my favourite foods! I won't be able to go out to restaurants any more!"

Not so. Going gluten-free definitely means making changes in your nutritional sources and probably (but not necessarily) doing more cooking at home. But it does not mean living the life of a gourmet hermit.

You will find that by eliminating gluten from your life, you will actually be setting yourself free. You will no longer suffer from the inexplicable symptoms that failed to respond to medication. You *will* feel better.

LABEL READING

In the UK, only foods that meet Codex gluten-free standards can be labelled "gluten-free". Codex is the abbreviated term for Codex Alimentarius, the food code of the World Health Organization. This food code is a collection of international food standards that cover all foods – raw or processed. Codex's goal is to protect the health of consumers and facilitate fair practices in the food trade.[1]

Codex standards state that a gluten-free food is:

- One consisting of or containing such cereals as wheat, triticale (a hybrid form of wheat), rye, barley or oats or their constituents, which have been rendered gluten-free

- One in which any ingredients normally present containing gluten have been substituted by other ingredients not containing gluten

The standard further defines gluten-free to mean "that the total nitrogen content of the gluten-containing cereal grains used in the product does not exceed 0.05 grams per 100 grams of these grains on a dry-matter basis."[2] The standard also dictates how manufacturers should test for gluten.

In Australia and New Zealand food labelling is governed by Food Standards Australia New Zealand (FSANZ). Rather confusingly, its code has two standards regarding the gluten content of foods: gluten free and low gluten. In order for a food to be labelled "gluten free" it must not contain detectable gluten and no oats or malt: food labelled "low gluten" must contain less than 0.02 per cent gluten.

Stringent gluten free labelling laws in the EU also mean that any food that contains gluten has to clearly label it on the pack – either in the nutritional information panel or in the ingredients list.

I therefore recommend that you carefully read food labels. You also need to talk to your pharmacist about your prescriptions to make sure their coatings are gluten-free. Then move on to your cosmetics.

Yes, cosmetics. Cosmetic products – including lipsticks, lotions and shampoo – may also contain gluten. For most people who are gluten sensitive, the gluten content of cosmetics should not pose a problem. But if you have a skin disorder, such as dermatitis herpetiformis, psoriasis, eczema, acne or other type of dermatitis, it may be especially important to read labels, since it may be possible to absorb gluten through open lesions. (Note: No medical research has been done on the effect of gluten absorbed through the skin. But if you have dermatitis herpetiformis, using gluten-free cosmetics and shampoos may be advisable.)

Unsafe Ingredients

Here are some of the obvious (and less than obvious) ingredient terms to look for on food and cosmetic labels:[3, 4]

- Amino peptide complex (from barley)
- Amp-isostearoyl hydrolyzed wheat protein
- Barley (including barley malt)
- Barley extract
- Brewer's yeast (unless prepared with a sugar molasses base)
- Disodium wheatgermamido peg2 sulfosuccinate
- Filler flour (this generally means wheat flour)
- Hordeum vulgare (barley) extract
- Hydrolyzed vegetable protein or hydrolyzed wheat protein
- Hydrolyzed wheat gluten
- Hydrolyzed wheat starch
- Modified wheat starch
- Rye
- Triticum vulgare (wheat)
- Vegetable starch (it could be a mixture of starches, including wheat starch)
- Wheat (all types of wheat, including durum, semolina, spelt, kamut, bulgur and triticale)
- Wheat amino acid
- Wheat bran extract
- Wheat dextrimaltose
- Wheat germ (extracts, glycerides and oil)
- Wheat protein
- Wheat rusk
- Wheat starch

In addition to these wheat-, rye- and barley-based gluten ingredients, I also recommend eliminating products that use oat-derived ingredients (usually found in cosmetics or shampoos) at least initially, especially if you have skin lesions. It's been my clinical experience that many people who are gluten sensitive do not tolerate oats well, even though oats do not contain gluten.

Oat-derived ingredients include:[5]

- Avena sativa (oat) flour
- Oat (avena sativa) extract
- Oat beta glucan
- Oat extract
- Oat flour
- Sodium lauroyl oat amino acids

KITCHEN CUPBOARD PURGING

Now that you know which ingredients to look for (anything with wheat, barley, rye and oats initially), it's time to raid the kitchen.

When my co-author's husband discovered he was gluten sensitive (*because of the research she did for this book*), they made a meticulous foray into the foodstuffs stored in the refrigerator, freezer and kitchen cupboards. While some things (such as flour and pancake mix) were "no-brainers", other items containing gluten surprised them. The lesson they learned: read labels carefully; don't take *anything* for granted.

Forbidden Foods

Here are *some* food items you want to purge from your kitchen:

- Barbecue sauce (check the label for wheat or soy sauce)
- Beer and lager
- Bread, including rolls, pittas and tortillas
- Breadcrumbs
- Breaded products (such as breaded chicken and fish)
- Cakes and biscuits
- Cereal (check even corn- and rice-based cereals; many use malt for flour, and malt is made from barley)
- Chocolate bars (check the label carefully)
- Chicken and beef stock (check to see if they contain wheat; some do not)

- Couscous
- Crackers
- Croutons
- Farina
- Flour
- Frozen vegetables with sauce packets
- Frozen ready meals
- Gravy (packaged and bottled)
- Ice cream cones
- Ice cream (if it contains gluten as a binder or in added ingredients, such as cookie dough; check the label carefully)
- Imitation bacon bits
- Macaroni and spaghetti (and all other types of wheat-based pasta)
- Malt vinegar
- Meat marinades (with soy sauce)
- Noodles and noodle products
- Pastry products
- Pretzels
- Rice dinner mixes
- Salad dressings and meat marinades (if they contain wheat or soy sauce)
- Sausage products (check the label)
- Seitan (imitation meat made from wheat gluten)
- Soba noodles (unless they are 100 per cent buckwheat)
- Soy sauce (unless it is specifically wheat-free or is labelled gluten-free)
- Stuffing mix
- Teriyaki sauce
- Tinned and packet soups (wheat is used as a thickener in most soups)

- Tinned luncheon meat
- Vegetable side dishes that contain sauces or noodles

The list of "forbidden foods" is admittedly extensive. But if you examine it carefully, you'll see that its focus is *processed* foods – that is, foods that have been prepared for convenience.

Safe Foods

Although the list of forbidden foods is long, you won't go hungry. Here are the things that are safe for you to eat or use in food preparation:

Vegetables. All vegetables are safe to eat (unless you have an allergy to them) and are an excellent source of needed vitamins and minerals. None contain gluten.

Best for you are fresh vegetables (preferably organically grown, so that they are not contaminated by pesticides and chemical fertilizers). Organic produce can provide up to six times (that's 600 per cent!) more vitamins, minerals and antioxidants when compared with conventionally grown produce. But, if fresh vegetables are not available, include frozen and even tinned vegetables in your diet. (Always check the label to make sure frozen and tinned vegetables do not have any gluten added to the processing.)

Be sure to include a variety of leafy green vegetables (such as broccoli, cabbage, endive, escarole, kale, pak choi, romaine lettuce, spinach, spring greens and watercress); yellow vegetables (such as carrots, pumpkin, sweet potatoes and squash); pulses (broad beans, chick peas and cannellini beans); root vegetables (such as potatoes, beetroot and swede); and other vegetables (such as asparagus, aubergine, brussels sprouts, cabbage, courgette, cucumbers, green and red peppers, mushrooms, okra, onions, radishes and tomatoes).

Beverages. All types of beverages make it to the "safe list", including coffee, tea and alcoholic products (wine and distilled spirits, but not beer or lager).

My recommendation: Drink water (not tap unless it's run through a filter) and/or sparkling mineral water. It's the best no-calorie, thirst-quenching beverage.

Stay away from sugar-sweetened drinks, especially in the initial stages of going gluten-free. Sugar-sweetened drinks can cause wind, and they are a major culprit in causing obesity and diabetes. I also recommend that you stay away from so-called "diet" beverages, especially those that contain the artificial sweetener aspartame, which can have adverse effects on the body.

Additionally, the use of *any* sweetened beverage will keep you addicted to the taste of sweeteners. And – you may find this surprising – no low- or non-calorie beverage has *ever* been shown to promote weight loss. In fact, numerous studies show that they may cause weight gain.

Dairy products. Provided you are not intolerant of dairy products, milk, yogurt and hard and soft cheeses are okay to eat. I recommend, however, that you stop using dairy products when you first start your gluten-free diet, until your symptoms go away. (For more information on milk intolerance, see Chapter 13, What If Going Gluten-Free Doesn't Work?)

Fruits. Fruits provide needed nutrients and fibre. Fortunately, you can safely eat all fruits. Fresh is best, of course.

Nuts. Unless you have allergies to tree nuts and peanuts (which are actually a legume, not a nut), nuts are not only safe to eat, but they are also good for you, since they may help reduce cholesterol. They have a high fat content (unsaturated), however, so eat them in moderation.

Meats, poultry, eggs and fish. No gluten, but lots of valuable protein in these foods. Grilling is the best way to preserve nutritional content.

Grains. You can eat all grains, *except* wheat, barley and rye, since they contain gluten.

I also advise against consuming oats, at least until your symptoms subside. Although oats do not have known gluten content, they can become contaminated, since they may be grown in former wheat fields. Or contamination may occur during the processing stage of milling.

Snacks. Going on a gluten-free diet does not mean you have to give up snacks. As a nutritionist, I recommend snacking on nuts and fruit. But, realistically, I know how tempting other snack foods can be, especially salty snacks.

Potato crisps and corn chips are okay, but be sure to check ingredients on the bag for gluten. Some flavoured crisps (such as barbecue flavour) contain gluten. Pressed potato crisps that come in a tube may also contain gluten, which is used as a binder. Read the label carefully.

My recommendation: Choose baked snack products over those that are fried. If you eat popcorn, air-popped is a healthy source of fibre; microwave-popped is loaded with fat.

Desserts. Gelatine and similar dessert mixes are generally "safe", as well as most ice creams. (Avoid ice creams that have added ingredients, such as "cookie dough" or "cheesecake".) Although "standard" bakery items are taboo, you can eat baked goods prepared with wheat-flour substitutes. But all desserts other than fruit should be eaten only occasionally.

Oils. A well-balanced diet includes some unsaturated fats. A gluten-free diet can contain vegetable oils (preferably extra-virgin olive oil or coconut oil), butter and margarine (nonhydrogenated, with no trans fats).

Condiments. Ketchup, salsa, herbs, pure spices, mustard, vinegars (except for malt vinegar), salad dressings and marinades are gluten-free. *Exception:* Avoid any dressing or marinade that contains soy sauce.

Sweeteners. Sugar, honey and jams (preferably no-sugar-added and organic) and corn syrup are all safe to consume. Use in moderation, however.

When choosing sweeteners, look for those that have a naturally low glycaemic index (GI). (The glycaemic index is a numeric value given to the rate at which a particular food raises your blood sugar.[6] Refined sugars have a high GI.)

Low-GI sweeteners include sugar alcohols, such as xylitol and maltitol (which are also natural but may cause wind if you have inflammatory bowel disease [IBD]), and fructose. Remember, however, that any sugar can cause wind and loose stools in individuals with IBD.

Sucralose (Splenda) is another alternative. It is derived from sugar through a patented, multistep process that selectively substitutes three chlorine atoms for three hydrogen-oxygen groups on the sugar molecule. It appears to be well tolerated by most people and has a well-documented safety profile.

Do not use artificial sweeteners! As I indicated earlier, they can have adverse effects and should not be used by anyone.

Miscellaneous foodstuffs. Although you may not think of them as part of your diet, a number of ingredients are used in food preparation, either in baking or as thickeners. Arrowroot, bicarbonate of soda, baking powder, cornflour, cream of tartar and yeast can be safely used.

SUBSTITUTES

It should be clear by now that the only foods that do not belong on your well-balanced, gluten-free diet are those containing wheat, barley and rye. Unfortunately, those three grains (especially wheat) are used as breakfast cereals, in side dishes and in baked goods.

Breakfast Cereals

You will be able to purchase online, in health food stores, and even in some mainstream grocery stores and supermarkets, hot and cold breakfast cereals that are similar in taste and texture to the many cereals you currently enjoy. Among the cereals you'll find are:

- Puffed millet
- Puffed rice
- Quinoa flakes
- Real corn flakes (without wheat added)

Side Dishes

Although you can still eat many of the traditional side dishes you have always enjoyed, some will no longer be available to you, such as couscous and spaghetti.

Again, health food stores, supermarkets and online gluten-free shops can provide you with safe alternatives:

- Buckwheat
- Corn spaghetti
- Quinoa noodles
- Rice noodles (various sizes and shapes, many now available in supermarkets)

Flour Substitutes

If you are like most people who have grown up on the soft, gooey texture of white bread, or you have learned to savour the goodness of fresh-baked speciality breads, the one food item you will miss most on your new diet is bread.

Gluten – the protein that causes us so many problems – is the same protein that causes bread to rise and reach its chewy, savoury consistency. You will be able to eat bread made from substitute grains, but regrettably it will not have the texture or consistency of the bread you have come to enjoy.

Nevertheless, you will be able to enjoy bread, buns, cakes, biscuits and other goodies. You will also be able to have crunchy or hot breakfast cereals. And you will be able to prepare side dishes similar to couscous (a forbidden food).

Here is a list of grain substitutes. I've indicated in which forms they are available (such as flour, grain or flakes). Even if you do not bake, you will want to have some of these flour substitutes on hand, to use as thickeners or coatings.[7]

- **Almonds, finely ground.** Made from blanched, ground almonds this "flour" is used in sweet breads, cakes and desserts.

- **Amaranth flour.** This is a flavourful flour that should be used in combination with other flours for added nutrition. In its granular form, amaranth can be added to soups or stews or be cooked for a hot cereal.

- **Besan (chickpea or gram) flour.** This flour is popular in Middle Eastern cooking. It is often combined with broad beans for a blended flour. It is available in most health food stores. You can even make your own by lightly roasting dried chickpeas, then grinding them in a blender or food processor until the mixture reaches the consistency of flour.

- **Broad bean flour.** This is not widely available outside the US (where it is called fava bean flour) but you may be able to find a source on the internet.

- **Buckwheat (soba) flour.** This grain has a unique taste that is especially good in quick and yeast breads. It can be substituted for other types of flours.

- **Buckwheat groats.** Groats are hulled buckwheat seeds that can be steamed, cooked like rice or as a hot cereal, or even milled at home into flour.

- **Buckwheat, roasted (kasha).** Roasted buckwheat kernels can be used as a cereal or a side dish.

- **Corn (masa) flour.** Corn flour is used in many tortilla recipes. You can buy processed corn flour, but you can also make it from cornmeal in your blender.

- **Flaxseed, ground.** This "flour" is high in fibre and fat, as well as nutrients. Add a small amount for a nutty flavour and fibre.

- **Millet.** Hulled millet seed can be cooked as a hot cereal or as a side dish or can be added to bread recipes for a crunchy taste. It can be purchased as a seed, as a dry puffed cereal (similar to puffed rice) or as flour. It is available in health food stores.

- **Potato flour.** Use this flour in bread and pancake recipes or as a thickener for smooth sauces, gravies and soups.

- **Quinoa.** This is one of the oldest cultivated grains. It is high in protein, calcium and iron. You can substitute quinoa flour for half of the all-purpose flour in many recipes or completely replace wheat flour in cakes and biscuit recipes – even some breads. You can also purchase quinoa as cereal flakes (similar to wheat flakes) or as a grain, which can be cooked as a hot cereal or as a side dish.

- **Rice.** As well as its standard form, rice is also available as a flour (white and brown), which is a primary ingredient in many gluten-free bread recipes. Gluten-free puffed rice cereal is also available.

- **Soya flour.** This flour is made from ground soyabeans. It has a slightly nutty flavour and can be used in combination with other wheat-flour substitutes. Soya flour is also used to condition bread dough. Try adding 1 tablespoon for each 140 g (5 oz) of flour for a lighter loaf.

- **Tapioca flour.** This flour is not made from grain but rather from cassava (yucca) root. It is a starchy, slightly sweet, white flour. Use up to 75 g (2½ oz) per recipe to sweeten breads made with rice and millet flour. You should be able to find this flour in health food stores as well as online.

- **Teff.** This is a very fine Ethiopian grain. Cooked, it makes a farina-like cereal. Ground into a very fine flour, it is used to make a traditional spongy flat bread, called injera. Unfortunately it is not yet widely available.

GROCERY SHOPPING

Picture, for a moment, your favourite supermarket. Walk around the outer aisles. Except for the bakery/deli section, the food items you tend to find on the outside aisle of the shop are fresh foods – meats, dairy, fruits and vegetables. Processed foods are shelved on the inside aisles and freezers. (Exception: tinned and frozen vegetables and fruits without extra sauces or processing are generally gluten-free.)

You must carefully read the labels of anything that is packaged, but you have an abundance of delicious fresh food from which to select your menu.

Prepare your shopping list, take a list of forbidden ingredients and foods with you (until you have it burnt into your memory), and read every label before you put an item in your trolley. Food shopping will take longer than usual, but you don't want to take any packaged food for granted.

Unfortunately, you won't be able to find everything you want or need at your local supermarket. This will change in time. But for now, you will have to use other resources:

Health food stores. Health food stores have the foods that you need (especially prepared foods). And their employees are generally knowledgeable and are customer-service oriented. These people know about gluten-free diets! You don't have to explain anything to them. Just tell them you are starting a gluten-free diet and need some help getting started.

Health food departments. Some of the bigger supermarkets are entering the gluten-free market, albeit very slowly, with an aisle or two of health foods, some of which are gluten-free. A few chain stores have sections devoted to special diets or "free from" foods and make it a point to carry products that are labelled gluten-free by food manufacturers.

Online shopping. Once you get "over the hump" in buying your first gluten-free foods in person, you may choose to venture into online shopping. Many resources are available to you – some are direct from food manufacturers, others in virtual stores.

Online shopping has several advantages: you can do it 24/7; you are unlimited in the variety of goods you can purchase; and you may save money, especially if you deal directly with food manufacturers. You will find many online charities for coeliacs have excellent links to specialist producers.

Speciality shops. Some of the grains and flours you may want to try are used extensively by people of other cultures. If you live in an area rich in diversity, you may be able to find speciality shops in which to purchase these grains and flours.

EATING OUT

Going gluten-free does *not* mean you are doomed to eating your own home-cooked foods day after day. Gluten sensitivity is not a handicap – it is a condition. And just as people who have diabetes and food allergies learn to deal with their conditions, so can you.

Asking questions and speaking up about your dietary needs are important. Restaurateurs are generally very accommodating of people with special needs – especially food allergies. Because of the possible legal ramifications involved in serving customers with allergies the wrong food, they take extra care to meet customer needs. The customer just has to make those needs known.

Yes – I know. Gluten sensitivity is *not* an allergy. But when you go to a restaurant for a meal, your goal is to eat a good, healthy meal. Meeting that goal is contingent on communicating your needs. Your waiter and the chef may not understand the term "gluten sensitivity". But they will understand "wheat allergy".

You will find that you can eat in any type of restaurant – even in restaurants you typically associate with gluten-containing foods, such as Italian restaurants. You simply have to choose your foods wisely, ask questions, let your special needs be known and enjoy the food.

Basic Restaurant Rules

Eating in a restaurant calls for "gluten common sense". Here are some tips:

Have a snack before you go. Especially if you are eating late, have a light snack before going to the restaurant. That way, you won't be tempted to reach for the bread.

Tell your waiter you have a "wheat allergy". As I indicated earlier, it's a small fib that will communicate efficiently your need to avoid wheat, barley and rye.

Even better than telling your waiter about your "allergy" – use a restaurant card.

Many gluten-sensitive people carry a "dietary alert card" to give to the waiter when ordering. The card indicates that you have a wheat allergy and need to refrain from eating foods prepared with wheat flour, including any sauces or gravies prepared with flour, croutons, bread or soy sauce.

Ask the waiter to give the card to the chef. Restaurant kitchens are hectic areas. Verbal instructions can get lost in the confusion. The restaurant card helps to minimize this confusion.

You can write and print your own restaurant card, or buy them online. You can purchase cards written in English and in other languages, especially helpful if you are travelling abroad or if you patronize restaurants owned and operated by native speakers.

Bypass fried food. It isn't good for you anyway! But aside from the dubious nutritional value of fried foods, particularly those fried in cheap vegetable oil, these items are often battered. And the batter is almost always wheat-based. Consequently, the oil in which foods are fried may be contaminated with gluten.

Stick to plain protein, potatoes or rice and vegetables. Avoid sauces and gravies. Grilled meat, fish or poultry basted with olive oil and lemon juice is a good choice. If you order rice, ask if it is cooked in chicken stock. Many stocks contain gluten.

Order "naked" salads. No croutons, please. You don't want gluten crumbs in your greens.

Use only oil and vinegar salad dressing. And do it yourself. Although most bottled salad dressings do not contain gluten, you do not know the composition of commercial dressings. And some do have gluten, especially Asian-style dressings, which contain soy sauce. Better to limit your choice to mix-it-yourself oil and vinegar.

Substitute rice, beans, lentils or potatoes for pasta. In Italian restaurants, ask for risotto instead of pasta.

PARTY TIME

Holidays and special gatherings with friends and family can be another trying time for people on a gluten-free diet. All of those delightful morsels, cakes and treats! And meals! What to do?

Here are some tips:

Talk to your host. Before the party, tell your host about your special dietary concerns and find out what will be on the menu. It's not that you expect your host or hostess to cook special items for you. But you want to know what you should avoid.

Volunteer to bring a food item. Make a gluten-free dish and you will have at least one item you can eat with gusto. And if you take a dessert, you can have a worry-free after-dinner sweet.

Snack ahead of time. Or have dinner before you go to the party. Then, if you find nothing (or few items) gluten-free on the buffet table, you won't be tempted to partake of a toxic item.

Eat salad and vegetables. Unless the salad is loaded with croutons, it is a safe alternative for you. Just make sure the salad dressing is gluten-free, too. Plain vegetables are another good option.

Keep in mind what you can eat. Not all party food is forbidden. You can't have beer, but you can have wine, soft drinks and distilled alcoholic beverages.

You can't have crackers, but you can have cheese, plain corn chips (not flavoured, unless you know they're gluten-free) and plain potato crisps (but not flavoured ones, which contain gluten).

You can't have sandwiches, but you can have the luncheon meats (ham, turkey or chicken, for example).

You can't have cakes or biscuits, but you can have gelatine and fruit desserts, sorbets and most ice creams.

You can't have pasta salad, but you can have potato salad.

FIRST STEPS

The only thing that is left for you to do is to start. Don't delay a second longer. I have a few more words of advice to help you on your way to a good life:

Find a friend. That friend may be a nutritionist who can guide you in your choice of foods and supplements. But if you cannot afford to go to a nutritionist, seek support through groups, either in person or at least online. Going gluten-free is an emotional decision that does affect your lifestyle to some extent. Having a gluten-free friend will help you maintain perspective.

Go easy on raw veggies. If you have severe gastrointestinal symptoms, your doctor has probably eliminated raw vegetables from your diet. Go easy on yourself during the initial stages of your healing. You may not be able to tolerate salads or raw or al dente vegetables initially. The goal is to eliminate gastrointestinal inflammation. So, to do this, reintroduce vegetables slowly and judiciously.

Prepare soups, and cook the vegetables until they are soft. Or steam them, and then purée them. These cooking methods help break down the fibre and make the vegetables more digestible.

When you start eating salads, chop the greens into fine pieces. Again, the chopping helps to break down the fibre and assist your digestion.

Don't worry. You won't have to do this forever – just until your symptoms go away. Then you will be able to introduce more-palatable vegetables to your diet.

Make water your beverage of choice. As I indicated earlier, sugary drinks may cause wind, especially if you have severe gastrointestinal symptoms. Drink lots of water, filtered tap or bottled still or sparking mineral water.

Remember: you *always* have a choice. Going gluten-free is a choice – your choice to improve your quality of life and to live symptom-free. Make the right choice for life.

CHAPTER 12

SUPPLEMENTING YOUR HEALTH

Once you have taken control over gluten by eliminating it from your diet – and you have given a gluten-free diet an adequate trial (from 2 weeks up to 3 months if you have severe symptoms) – you will be on your road to recovery.

You can – and should – give your recovery a boost, however, with dietary supplementation. Supplementation is important for improving immune function and detoxification, for decreasing oxidative stress and inflammation and for healing and restoring mucosal integrity and the functioning of the gastrointestinal tract.

Immediately upon beginning your new dietary regime, start taking the supplements listed under Stage 1.

After about 3 weeks, add the supplements in Stage 2. *A word of caution:* If you have inflammatory bowel disease (IBD), irritable bowel syndrome (IBS) or any other gastrointestinal problem as the key manifestation of gluten sensitivity, before you start Stage 2 supplementation, give the gluten-free (and casein-free) diet a fair chance to work their magic. My experience with patients is that when gluten and casein peptides are the culprits of intestinal disorders, and they are totally removed from the diet, the healing process that occurs just from this restriction is nothing short of amazing.

Finally, when you are feeling substantially better, add the supplements in Stage 3.

STAGE 1 SUPPLEMENTATION

The supplements listed under Stage 1 will provide you with all the multinutrients and the major antioxidants your body requires. Begin taking them when you start your gluten-free diet.

Multivitamins and Minerals

I recommend using a full-spectrum multivitamin/mineral supplement that provides the *approximate* amounts (you are unlikely to find this exact combination) of nutrients described below.

These types of multinutrients are available as tablets, capsules and even as powders. Experiment with various delivery systems, because you may find that you have a personal preference for digesting capsules, tablets or powders.

I have listed *optimal* amounts of nutrients, based on my revolutionary ODIs – Optimal Daily Intakes – which are generally more than a 1-per-day multinutrient formula provides.

Remember: these are *guidelines* to make choosing a supplement easier. Since various brands use different formulas, if a brand you choose does not have the amount of a nutrient listed below, consider supplementing with an additional amount of that nutrient.[1]

- **Vitamin A:** 5,000 IU

- **Beta-carotene** (natural only): 11,000 IU

- **Vitamin D_3:** 400 IU

- **Vitamin E** (d-alpha-tocopheryl succinate): 400 IU

- **B complex:** A good-quality B-complex or multivitamin supplement generally will supply at least 25 milligrams each of thiamin (B_1), riboflavin (B_2), niacin (B_3), pyridoxine (B_6), pantothenic acid, PABA, choline, and inositol. It also may contain about 12 to 25 micrograms of vitamin B_{12}, 400 micrograms of folic acid, and 300 micrograms of biotin.

- **Folic acid:** 400 micrograms

- **Cobalamin** (B_{12}): 25 micrograms

- **Boron:** 3 milligrams

- **Calcium:** 500 milligrams

- **Chromium:** 200 micrograms

- **Copper:** 0.5 milligrams (This is in many foods, so it is not critical to take as a supplement.)

- **Iodine:** 150 micrograms (unless you have a known reactivity to iodine)

- **Iron:** Take this only if you have a known iron deficiency and no active IBD. Supplementation can exacerbate inflammation and should be used only under professional guidance.

- **Magnesium:** 250 milligrams

- **Manganese:** 15 milligrams

- **Selenium:** 100 micrograms

- **Phosphorus and potassium:** You can get these easily through food, so supplementation is generally not necessary (though most multivitamins contain them).

- **Calcium and magnesium:** Your aim is an intake of 1,000 to 1,500 milligrams of calcium and 500 to 750 milligrams of magnesium daily *from a combination of supplements and diet*. If your diet does not provide this amount, you may need to add calcium and magnesium supplementation *in addition to your multivitamin/mineral formula*.

- **Vitamin D:** Additional vitamin D supplementation may also be necessary to prevent/treat bone loss. Recent research has shown that if you have very little sun exposure and wear sunscreen, you may be at risk of vitamin D deficiency. A simple blood analysis will show if your levels of vitamin D are too low (though you will probably need to pay for this through a nutritionist, unless you are at obvious risk and your doctor agrees to one). If your levels are low, you may require 2,000 to 4,000 IU of additional vitamin D. You can always seek the advice of an experienced doctor or nutritionist for a more individualized programme.

Fish Oil

Your body needs a number of different types of fatty acids to maintain good health. Among these are omega-3 and omega-6 fatty acids. These fatty acids, however, must be in balance.

Omega-3 essential fatty acids – eicosapentaenoic acid (EPA) and docosahexanoic acid (DHA) – are "good fats" that your body cannot produce on its own. EPA and DHA are used to create hormonal-like compounds known as prostaglandins, which (among other things) can both enhance and inhibit inflammation.

A good source of omega-3 fatty acids is fish oil.

Fish oil has been shown in numerous studies to be therapeutic for IBD and autoimmune disease. Fish oil also protects against heart disease and sudden death. It is important for bone health, and it is protective and potentially therapeutic for cancer, since it may halt the spread of metastasis. It is also essential for healthy skin and hair.

Although you can get omega-3 fatty acids from flax (linseed oil) and walnuts, I recommend fish oil over them. The reason: flax and walnuts first break down into another omega-3 fatty acid – alpha-linolenic acid – before undergoing several more enzymatic steps to become the more active EPA and DHA.

The more work your body has to go through to get to the EPA and DHA, the longer it takes. Fish oil gets faster results. And fish oil has also been studied more extensively than flaxseed oil. Its benefits are well documented.

Omega-6 fatty acids are commonly found in most vegetable oils as linoleic acid and are used by the body to form inflammatory prostaglandins. Arachidonic acid is another omega-6 fatty acid that is found in most meats, especially commercial beef and chicken, which comes from animals that are fed corn products and other foods that are deficient in omega-3 fatty acids but are rich sources of omega-6.

You need to be aware that inflammation is not all bad. We need an inflammatory response to activate our immune system and to heal. Chronic inflammation, of course, is another matter. When inflammation reaches that stage, it becomes an issue.

Chronic inflammation stimulates an overactive immune system and creates the potential for tissue and organ damage. It is a culprit in almost every disease.

We need both omega-3 and omega-6 fatty acids. But we need them in proper balance. Our ancestors consumed a diet with a balance of omega-6 and omega-3 fatty acids of approximately 1:1 to 2:1.

Today, because of the limited sources of omega-3 in our diets, we consume a diet of omega-6 to omega-3 of approximately 30:1! So most of us are walking around in state of chronic inflammation. No wonder there is so much research on EPA and DHA (omega-3 fatty acids) showing their therapeutic benefit on so many illnesses!

With respect to inflammatory bowel disease, EPA- and DHA-rich fish oil works like "natural" cortisone. It can dramatically reduce inflammation without the negative side effects associated with steroids.

Fish oil is safe and natural. You can find fish oil capsules, as well as liquid supplements, that taste reasonably palatable. Fish oil supplements should not have an offensive smell when you open the bottle. (A slight smell is okay.) If they do, the capsules may contain impurities that are causing rancidity.

Fish oil supplements also last longer if you store them in the refrigerator, where the low temperature also decreases the odour. Pharmaceutical-grade fish oil (which I take) has virtually no smell at all.

Many of the research studies conducted on fish oil required subjects to take as many as 9 to 12 capsules per day to overcome the inflammatory influence of omega-6 fatty acids in the diet.

My recommendation: Take a daily dose of four to six capsules (approximately 2 to 3 grams) of fish oil or the equivalent as a liquid. This amount will allow you to maintain a lower-fat diet (not more than 20 per cent) yet reap the benefits of fish oil in controlling inflammation.[1]

If you find that fish oil "repeats" on you, check to make sure the capsules are not rancid. This is a primary cause. Also:

- Buy pharmaceutical-grade fish oil.

- Look for enteric-coated fish oil. The coating stops the supplement from dissolving until it gets to the stomach.

Coenzyme Q_{10}

Coenzyme Q_{10} (CoQ_{10}) is known as ubiquinone because it is ubiquitous: it exists everywhere in the body.

Although CoQ_{10} is not an essential nutrient because we make it in our bodies, chronically ill people do not make enough CoQ_{10} to supply their needs. It is a powerful antioxidant, and a great amount of research has shown that it is important for both the prevention and treatment of many degenerative diseases, including heart disease and cancer.

The most important reason to supplement your diet with CoQ_{10} is that it is crucial to supplying energy to every cell in your body. One of the reasons sick people feel so tired and achy is that illness and certain drugs such as statins deplete CoQ_{10}.

My recommendation: Take at least 100 to 200 milligrams per day of CoQ_{10}.[1]

STAGE 2 SUPPLEMENTATION

Begin taking the two supplements listed here after you have been on your gluten-free diet for 2 to 3 weeks. By that time, you should begin feeling much better, although you won't be completely healed.

The supplements I recommend adding at this stage are additional antioxidants, which are important in regulating the immune function and decreasing inflammation. They are essential in the defence against oxidative stress, which occurs when toxic free radicals are formed at a rate greater than the amount we can handle with our body's antioxidant defense mechanisms.

Imagine rust forming around metal – a great visual for oxidative stress. Antioxidants stop the rust from forming.

Oxidation can occur anywhere in your body. The multinutrient formula you started taking at Stage 1 should provide enough of the *major* antioxidants you need. Additional vitamin C and quercetin will further reduce inflammation and improve antioxidant defence.

My recommendation: Take 1,000 to 4,000 milligrams of vitamin C (buffered, non-acidic) per day, and 500 to 2,000 milligrams of quercetin per day.

STAGE 3 SUPPLEMENTATION

As you continue on your gluten-free diet and the supplements in Stages 1 and 2, your body will continue to get better. Symptoms will go away. And finally, you will be substantially healed.

It is at this time – at least 1 month into your gluten-free diet – that I recommend taking Stage 3 supplements, which aid in the restoration of the intestine. Intestinal restoration is an important part of therapy, especially in those with coeliac disease (CD) or IBD caused by gluten and/ or casein sensitivity.

Stage 3 supplements can dramatically improve the immune function in the gastrointestinal (GI) tract, heal the intestinal villi, increase protective mucin synthesis, and decrease intestinal permeability so that large peptides (such as a gluten) do not enter the bloodstream from the GI tract.

But – you may get a lot of wind from these supplements if your intestine is not completely healed. So, be patient before starting on these supplements.

Here are the additional dietary supplements to consider:

Acidophilus and Other Beneficial Microorganisms

A number of "friendly", or "good", floras inhabit our gastrointestinal tract. These floras keep unfriendly (bad) microorganisms at bay.

Our GI tract is never sterile, nor would we want it to be. But the body struggles to maintain a balance between good and bad microorganisms. We want the beneficial floras to win, but inflammation and immune disruption cause the bad microorganisms to flourish.

Many food products contain beneficial microorganisms, such as:[2]

- *Lactobacillus acidophilus*

- *Lactobacillus bifidus*

- *Lactobacillus brevis*

- *Lactobacillus casei GG*

- *Lactobacillus cellobiosus*

- *Lactobacillus fermenti*

- *Lactobacillus leichmannii*

- *Lactobacillus plantarum*

- *Lactobacillus salivarius*

- *Lactobacillus sporogenes*

- *Saccharomyces boulardii* (This is available only by itself and is discussed below.)

- *Bifidobacterium* spp.

- *Enterococcus faecium*

- *Streptococcus thermophilus*

These beneficial bacteria can be purchased as supplements, either alone, such as *L. acidophilus* or *L. bifidus,* or in combination with the other beneficial flora that are listed.

Saccharomyces boulardii is a beneficial yeast that is sold by itself as a supplement. Research demonstrates that *S. boulardii* is rather specific for those who have been treated heavily with antibiotics and have developed antibiotic-resistant bacteria such as *Clostridium difficile.*

To reestablish the gut's beneficial flora after treatment with antibiotics, I recommend taking a *Lactobacillus* supplement, as well as the *S. boulardii*. A minimum therapeutic dose of *S. boulardii* is 500 milligrams per day. However, if you have developed antibiotic-resistant bacteria (such as *C. difficile*), you may have to take up to 3 grams per day to eradicate the bacteria.

Take *S. boulardii* by itself to minimize wind. Always follow label directions for the best times to take the supplements and whether you should take them with meals or between meals.

The other friendly floras on the list are generally taken as anywhere from 1 billion to 10 billion viable organisms, rather than as milligrams.[2, 3, 4, 5]

A number of companies manufacture excellent dietary supplements containing one or more of these floras, though they are generally based in the US. In my clinical experience, I have found that *L. casei GG* (sold as Culturelle) is an excellent supplement to promote healthy flora. The company supports the product with excellent research. (Culturelle can be bought online and shipped from the US – see Resources.)

Supplements such as *L. casei GG* also have the ability to improve immune function in the GI tract and may protect against bacteria and viral infection by improving mucosal integrity. Since different supplements provide different doses of the beneficial flora, it is best to follow label directions.[2, 3, 4, 5]

My recommendations:

- *L. casei GG* – take 1 or 2 capsules each day.
- *S. boulardii* – take 500 milligrams each day for antibiotic-resistant bacteria such as *C. difficile*. Consider taking 3 grams daily for an active *C. difficile* infection.

Glutamine

Glutamine is an important amino acid in the GI tract because it modulates inflammation and promotes repair mechanisms. While it is not considered essential, because the body can actually produce it, we synthesize large quantities of it to produce from 30 to 35 per cent of our total amino acid pool.

Glutamine is necessary for the synthesis of glucosamine, which, in turn, is necessary for the synthesis of mucin, the protective layer in the gut. (Research has shown that patients with Crohn's disease and ulcerative colitis have diminished amounts of the enzyme responsible for the biosynthesis of mucin.)

Glutamine is important for nourishing and restoring the intestinal villi that have been affected by immune reactivity and inflammation. It also helps prevent bacteria from attaching to the intestinal wall and growing and spreading.

Glutamine is indispensable for the formation of glutathione, a major antioxidant. Glutathione helps the liver detoxify the many toxins that we are exposed to in our environment, as well as those that form internally.

We form more toxins when we are sick and inflamed and when our immune systems are impaired. We are less able to clear these toxins when we do not have enough vitamins, minerals, antioxidants, and other nutrients such as glutamine, which support our body's detoxification mechanisms.

Supplemental doses of glutamine range from 1 gram to 8 grams per day. Some practitioners use higher doses if necessary.[4, 5, 6]

My recommendation: Take 500 to 3,000 milligrams of L-glutamine. Higher doses should be taken only under professional advice.

Phosphatidylcholine

Phosphatidylcholine (PC) may prevent collagen deposition and stricture formation that can occur when colonic tissue is inflamed. In animal studies, it was shown to reduce colitis, decrease permeability and heal the intestinal mucosa.

PC is available in capsule and granule forms. Follow label directions for capsules, since it comes in different strengths. If you are using the granules (which are generally less expensive), take from 1 to 3 tablespoons each day, mixed in juice (or half juice, half water) or just about any cold or room-temperature beverage.[5, 6]

My recommendation: A daily dose of 100 to 300 milligrams. However, PC is generally derived from either soya or chicken yolks, so if you have sensitivity to either of these, try a lower dose first.

Fibre

Fibre is great for keeping the intestines and bowels healthy and regular and for detoxification. Soluble fibre, such as psyllium and ground flaxseeds, is fermented by colonic bacteria and forms the short-chain fatty acids butyrate, acetate and proprionate, which are the primary fuel sources for the colon. Fibre decreases the pH of the intestines, which encourages the growth of beneficial flora and suppresses the growth of the bad bacteria.[5]

If you add fibre to your diet, start with 1 tablespoon per day, added to food or beverages. You can increase the amount as needed, up to 3 tablespoons per day, or as tolerated.

I would not recommend taking a fibre supplement initially unless you are constipated or do *not* have IBD. The reason: fibre can cause excessive wind if the digestive tract is inflamed.

Fibre is available in various forms. I am a fan of flaxseeds, which are a tasty and better alternative than flaxseed oil. Ground flaxseeds give you the beneficial fibre, omega-3 fatty acids and lignans that are superb for promoting hormonal health.

Common sources of supplemental fibre that you should not use are wheat and barley bran, which may contain gluten, or oat bran, which may be contaminated with gluten.

My recommendation: 1 to 2 tablespoons of fibre supplement. Follow the label directions.

Other Anti-Inflammatories

A number of other specific dietary supplements, such as *Boswellia serrata,* bromelain and turmeric[6] may also help decrease inflammation and can be taken if needed.

Additional Dietary Supplements

Many of my professional colleagues and I often recommend more-active forms of specific dietary supplements, depending upon the needs of our patients. A practitioner who specializes in nutritional biochemistry can determine if you should take these types of supplements, which may include:[1]

- **Pyridoxal-5-phosphate** (the active form of vitamin B_6)
- **Methylcobalamin** (the active form of B_{12}, often given sublingually or by injection)
- **Folinic acid** (the active form of folic acid)

Additionally, practitioners sometimes recommend additional supplements to help the body rid itself of toxins. Many of these recommendations are based on laboratory evaluation of toxic metals, detoxification pathways, and even genetic issues that can affect our ability to detoxify.

Based on the results of these evaluations, practitioners well versed in detoxification may recommend:

- N-acetylcysteine
- Glutathione
- Milk thistle (silymarin)
- Garlic
- Artichoke
- Turmeric
- Infrared saunas to assist the body in eliminating toxins

If you have been sick for some time, I would recommend that a more intensive detoxification be done under professional advice.

The Best Ways to Take Your Supplements
1. Always take your supplements with food – unless otherwise instructed on the label of the bottle. For example: it is recommended that some acidophilus supplements be taken between meals.
2. Start slowly – especially with gastrointestinal disorders. If you have IBS, IBD, CD, or any other gastrointestinal disorder, you may want to add the supplements slowly, starting with the lower dose. For example: if you are going to take a six-per-day multivitamin, instead of immediately starting with two at each meal, try one with each meal for a few days.
3. Start with a lower dose. If you have IBS, IBD, CD or any other GI disorder, you may want to start with the lower dose of a particular supplement. For example: you may want to try 500 milligrams of vitamin C for several days before going up to a dose of 1 gram or more each day.
4. Store your supplements in a cool, dry place. You can store fish oil in the refrigerator if you prefer.
5. Always check the expiry dates of your supplements. If they are expired, throw them away and buy new ones. The potency of most supplements will last 6 to 12 months after the container is opened.
6. Find your preference. Experiment with taking tablets, capsules and powders. See which works best for you.

ENZYMES TO THE RESCUE

Supplementation will help heal you and will help keep you healthy. But "gluten slips" happen.

What happens if you are eating out or are travelling and you inadvertently eat some gluten? Are you doomed to suffer the full consequences?

Fortunately, you have a remedy – digestive enzymes.

A study was conducted with 21 CD patients who were in remission.[7] The study involved challenging them with a modest amount of gluten every day over a period of 2 weeks and giving the experimental group an enzyme extract three times a day. (The control group was given a placebo.)

The enzyme therapy significantly reduced symptoms in the experiment group compared with those taking the placebo. The most common symptom reported in these individuals was abdominal pain and bloating, rather than diarrhoea.

This study demonstrates that enzyme therapy can substantially minimize symptoms in people with CD who are exposed to gluten. It would also be effective for gluten-sensitive individuals who experience gastrointestinal symptoms when exposed to gluten.

Unfortunately, the study looked *only* at serum levels of antibodies and intestinal biopsies. It is unlikely that a recovered CD patient would have full-blown villous atrophy in a matter of 2 weeks when exposed to a modest amount of gluten. Therefore, the symptom scores were a better indicator of the benefit of the enzyme therapy.

The enzyme used was a proprietary, patented animal enzyme formula called Glutenon (Glutagen Pty. Ltd., Melbourne, Australia). At the time of publication, this enzyme was not yet available outside Australia. But it may be soon; search for it on the internet.

Although the tested enzyme is currently unavailable, a number of other enteric-coated enzyme preparations are available. One of the most studied enteric-coated enzyme preparations is Wobenzym N (Mucos Pharma, GmbH & Co., Berlin, Germany). It is available through the internet and is backed by more than 25 years of extensive research.

Wobenzym N is a patented multi-enzyme product with a proprietary blend of proteolytic (protein-digesting) enzymes. Enteric coating ensures that the tablet will not be digested by stomach acid and will instead move into your lower intestines before the active enzymes are released to do their job.

This is why an enteric-coated enzyme can help alleviate some of the wind and bloating: it works where the gluten causes the inflammation – in the intestines. Also, protein is digested in the intestines, not in the stomach. Since gluten is a protein, this type of enzyme can help digest it and render it less irritating.

While the enzyme won't completely eliminate the problem, it may help alleviate at least some of the wind and bloating that many gluten-sensitive and CD patients experience when they eat gluten but may not know it until after the fact.

My recommendation: Always carry this type of enzyme with you. Make sure that whichever enteric-coated enzyme preparation you use provides proteolytic enzymes. They are the *only* enzymes that digest protein.

I can also say from clinical experience that some people feel better and digest their food better when they use enteric-coated enzymes. Follow the label directions, since formulation strength varies among brands.

As a preventive measure – when you don't have perfect control over what you're eating – it is best to take enteric-coated enzymes on an empty stomach – at least 30 minutes before a meal. If you miss that opportunity, take them as soon as possible after you eat. Always carry the enzyme with you, so you have it when you need it. But don't take enzymes and think that you can continue eating gluten if it is causing you health problems. *This is not a cure.* Research has shown that the enzymes may simply help the symptoms of wind and bloating.

CHAPTER 13

WHAT IF GOING GLUTEN-FREE DOESN'T WORK?

I learned a long time ago that every problem has *at least* one solution – but sometimes, the solution is not easy or simple. If you experience symptoms that suggest gluten sensitivity, a strict gluten-free diet often brings results in as little as 2 weeks. But sometimes, it doesn't. Be patient. Give it a try (no cheating!) for up to 3 months. Remember that problems a long time in the making take a long time in solving.

CROSS-REACTIVITY

A gluten-free diet is the single, easy solution to one problem – gluten sensitivity. But the human body is a complex mechanism, a sum of our environment, the food we eat – and genetics. Often, all these conditions predispose us to concurrent problems that are similar in nature. This is especially true of autoimmune diseases. If you have an immune reaction to one particular type of food, you may experience cross-reactivity to other foods.

Cross-reactivity is a condition in which the autoimmune antibodies your body generates (such as anti-gliadin IgA antibodies, which cause a reaction to gluten) mistake other food proteins for the ones you cannot tolerate. When you experience a cross-reaction to other foods, the effect on your body is the same as if you had ingested gluten.

If going on a gluten-free diet fails to bring the results you anticipate, I recommend eliminating the following foods (one at a time, in the order given), because you may be experiencing cross-reactivity:

Dairy products. As you have already read throughout this book, my colleagues and I advocate eliminating *all* dairy products (from cows) from your diet – and I advise doing this concurrent with going on a gluten-free diet if you have severe digestive problems.

Drs. Fine and Vojdani, researchers who have developed methods of testing for gluten (See Chapter 10, Am I Gluten Sensitive?), have found that patients with gluten sensitivity have a high frequency of cross-reactivity to milk – most notably the milk protein casein (sodium caseinate and calcium caseinate) and whey.

Do not confuse immunoreactivity to milk with lactose intolerance. They are completely different! Lactose intolerance is an inability to digest lactose (milk sugar) because of limited production of the lactase enzyme in the intestines. Virtually all babies are born with lactase, but around the age of 2, a lactase deficiency develops in most people.

Diet is the only way to control the symptoms of lactose intolerance. Individuals who react to small amounts of lactose can take lactase enzymes, which are available without a prescription. The tablets must be taken with the first bite of dairy food.

But I want to reiterate: lactose intolerance is *not* the same as immuno-reactivity to milk.

Immunoreactivity to casein and whey is similar to the immune response your body has to gluten if you are gluten sensitive. The only treatment for this condition is a diet free of casein and whey – eliminating not only milk but also cheese, yogurt and ice cream – *anything* that has milk in it, even soups and soya burgers that have cheese added to them – and protein drinks that have casein added.

(Some people who cannot tolerate milk products turn to soya products as an alternative. However, if you think that soya products are safe, think again! Some of these products have casein added to them – so read the label carefully.)

Suggestion: Remain on a dual gluten-free/casein-free diet for 3 weeks after all symptoms have gone away. Then try reintroducing goat, sheep or rice milk products in a limited amount to see if you can tolerate them. If not, remain casein-free.

Nightshades. Nightshades – tomatoes, white potatoes, aubergine, peppers and tobacco – are a class of plants that have a protein called lectin, which is similar to gluten and which has been associated with coeliac disease.[1] When you eat these foods, antibodies you have formed against gluten react to the nightshade lectin, resulting in the same type of immune reaction you have to gluten.

Dr. Norman Childers, professor emeritus at the University of Florida, discovered a significant link between nightshades and autoimmunity. When Dr. Childers, who is now in his late nineties, was 50 years old, he was diagnosed with diverticulitis – a condition involving inflammation of the microscopic pockets that line the intestine.

When he stopped eating foods in the nightshade family, all of his colon problems, as well as his arthritic problems, disappeared. This spurred him to study the relationships between nightshades and autoimmune disorders, especially arthritis. In surveys of patients with arthritis, he found that 94 per cent had complete or substantial relief from symptoms when they adhered to a nightshade-free diet.[2] Dr. Childers admits that it is difficult to adhere to a nightshade-free regime because of the prevalence of these foods in our diet. However, he writes that allowing even some nightshades in your diet can jeopardize recovery.

The recommendation, therefore, is to avoid all nightshades if you continue to have symptoms despite being on a strict gluten-free diet.

Peanuts and soya. Not only are these known to cause allergic reactions, they may also cause autoimmune reactions because of their high lectin content. Peanuts and soya are among the allergens that food manufacturers are required to list on labels.

However, when you eliminate these foods, take care when you eat out. Soya is one of those hidden ingredients in foods and is included in such benign-looking foods as margarine.

OTHER DIETARY CHANGES

Although cross-reactivity is the most common reason that some people fail to respond to a strict gluten-free diet, there are others.

I spoke with a colleague, Dr. Melvyn Grovit, who is an appointed member of the New York State Board for Dietetics/Nutrition.

Although Dr. Grovit was a successful podiatrist, his passion has always been nutrition. That passion was sparked when he had Crohn's disease as a teenager and had 18 feet of his intestine surgically removed in order to save his life. He now specializes in helping people who have severe forms of inflammatory bowel disease (IBD).

Dr. Grovit says that in the food chain, a number of specific foods and additives may cause inflammation and severe immune reactions. In addition to the recommendations we've already discussed, he advises:

Avoid foods that contain carrageenan. Carrageenan is a food additive and thickening agent derived from red algae that gained prominence during the low-fat craze that swept the Western world several years ago. Food manufacturers use this additive in many different foods because it adds softness and smoothness to products.

Among the different types of products that contain carrageenan are some types of chocolate pudding, soya milk, chewable vitamins and minerals, turkey and other processed meats, cottage cheese and soya products that are made to look and taste like deli items.

Although it is generally not found in powdered baby formulas, carrageenan is an overlooked ingredient in liquid infant formulas. Because carrageenan is in so many liquid infant formulas, Dr. Grovit speculates that this additive may influence the statistics that show that breast-fed babies have a lower incidence of IBD.

The extensive use of carrageenan means that you may be eating a significant amount of it. Like gluten, it has been introduced into our food chain at levels that were never before available in whole foods.

Limit consumption of *all* high-fibre grains. Dr. Grovit also suggests limiting the consumption of *all* high-fibre grains (and pulses) while the intestinal tract is inflamed and in trouble.

Eating a high-fibre diet is healthy and good for most people. But in his experience, and mine, most people with IBD have some degree of carbohydrate intolerance and fare better on a lower-fibre diet.

After the intestinal tract is substantially healed, you may again be able to tolerate high-fibre foods.

Eliminate suspect foods. Dr. Grovit is a firm believer, as I am, in paying attention to anything you eat that you believe makes you sick. You should eliminate any food you suspect causes you to feel ill and see if you feel better for it. If you do feel better, stay away from that food.

Avoid corn. While corn products are generally used as a substitute grain for those with coeliac disease and gluten sensitivity, Dr. Grovit has found that corn in the setting of inflammatory bowel disease is a food best not eaten. It is too difficult to digest.

In particular, avoid corn grown in the United States as a large proportion of it has genetically modified DNA.[3] Much of the alteration has come about through cross-pollination from fields of genetically modified strains to nonmodified crops.[4] This is less of a problem in Europe, where genetically modified crops are not as widespread.

Food engineers have theoretically modified these grains to improve specific qualities and to improve their resistance to insects and disease. However, the effect these genetically modified plants have on human beings (or animals) is largely unknown for the long term.

Use an enzyme-based anti-wind food supplement. Consider taking an 'antiwind' food enzyme such as Beano when you eat nutrient-dense foods, such as broccoli, cabbage, cauliflower, pulses, grains, cereals, nuts, seeds and many other foods, if you have IBD. The supplement helps break down the natural sugars in these foods and makes digestion easier.

TO A BETTER LIFE

Gluten sensitivity is a cunning and powerful condition affecting a significant number of people. It is cunning because it masquerades itself as symptoms of other diseases. It is powerful because it alters the lifestyle and health of anyone who has it. *But it is easily treatable.*

If this book has raised your level of awareness, and you now suspect you may be gluten sensitive, take the next step: go gluten-free.

It's really not that difficult:

1. **Eliminate all gluten from your diet.** Read labels, ask questions of food manufacturers and restaurants when eating out, and be careful. In other words: be diligent about what you eat.

2. **Supplement.** Take appropriate supplements (see Chapter 12, Supplementing Your Health) to speed your recovery and ensure wellness.

3. **Remove other offending foods.** If your gluten-free diet has not given you the results you seek, don't give up. Eliminate dairy products, then (if necessary) nightshades, peanuts and soya.

4. **Be patient!** The chances are excellent that you will feel better within 2 weeks. But if you don't, give yourself 3 months. Your symptoms didn't become severe overnight nor will recovery happen overnight.

Gluten is not an essential protein for your good health. You do not need wheat, barley, rye or oats to live a happy, healthy life.

In fact, if you *don't* eat them, you will have a *better* life. What do you have to lose?

PART 4
COPING WITH COOKING

Some people love to cook. Others hate it. Most people are somewhere in between but opt for easy-to-prepare foods because cooking takes time. And time (at least discretionary time) is in short supply for most of us. That, of course, is why the food-processing industry has prospered.

Cooking is a skill. And although you can master a skill, that doesn't mean you *like* to use it. So, we have written this section to accommodate different levels of skills and interests. You'll find ideas, tips, menus and recipes in several chapters.

CHAPTER 14: A SUBSTITUTE FOR ALL REASONS. This chapter provides you with the substitutes you'll need for gluten-free cooking, including common dairy-free substitutes.

CHAPTER 15: GLUTEN-FREE COOKING. In this chapter, you'll find plenty of recipes – from those that need the minimum of effort to those that require you to spend just that little bit longer in the kitchen.

CHAPTER 16: GIVE ME BREAD! Bread is the one food type that almost everyone on a gluten-free diet misses – even if you weren't a big bread eater before going on the diet. So, we'll give you some proven bread options.

CHAPTER 17: A 14-DAY GF DIET. The previous chapters gave you recipes. In this chapter, you'll put a healthy 14-day menu together. Plus, you'll get ideas on how to stay on your GF diet while eating out.

Before you turn to the next chapter, a caveat: *"Tryer beware!"*

Being a nutritionist does not make me a cook or a baker. I've spent time in the kitchen, but I do not intend to pass myself off as an expert in the recipe department. On the scale of "I hate to cook" to "I'm an expert cook," I fall somewhere in between.

So does my co-author. She is a writer and a researcher. Like me, she knows her way around the kitchen quite well, but she is not a cook or a baker. Like most people, she tries to keep things simple in the kitchen.

So, mind the caveat. We have tried many of these recipes but not all. So we have relied on the veracity and enthusiasm of those who have shared them with us.

Bon appetit!

CHAPTER 14

A SUBSTITUTE FOR ALL REASONS

One of our goals in writing this section of the book is to prove to you that cooking – and living – gluten-free is not hard. You will find that you can take almost any recipe you enjoyed in your "gluten-eating" days and adapt it to gluten-free cooking.

But some of these recipes will require making key substitutions. So, listen up! Here are some basics to take to heart.

FLOUR SUBSTITUTES

We have adapted many of the following recipes to accommodate the special needs of a GF diet. You'll see that some call for flour.

Most of us, in our pre-GF days, never thought much about flour. Recipes most often called for plain flour or self-raising flour. Once in a while, perhaps, we purchased a speciality flour – but not often. Wheat was our friend.

Not any more.

Since wheat is off-limits, you have a wide variety of flours from which to choose. We told you about many of these flours in Chapter 11, such as almond, amaranth, buckwheat, corn, millet, quinoa, potato, rice, sorghum, soya, tapioca and teff. Most of these flours are not used by themselves; they are mixed in various proportions and with rising agents, such as xanthan or guar gum, to make them taste and act more like wheat.

When you bake (especially bread), you will find that experimenting with a variety of flours will be fun (if not sometimes disastrous!). In general cooking, however, I recommend keeping things simple. Try either of these two choices:

A premixed plain flour. Look for a flour that is made of a combination of assorted wheat-flour substitutes: for example, gram flour, potato starch, tapioca flour and sorghum flour. You should try a few before deciding which works best for you.

Bette Hagman's featherlight rice flour mix.[1] In the US, Bette Hagman has become known in coeliac circles as the bread goddess. Her bread flour mixture (minus the rising agents) makes the perfect plain flour to keep on your kitchen worktop.

Here's how to mix it:

Bette's Featherlight Rice Flour Mix

INGREDIENTS

375 g (13 oz) rice flour

250 g (9 oz) tapioca flour

375 g (13 oz) cornflour

3 tablespoons potato flour (This is potato flour, not potato starch!)

DIRECTIONS

Thoroughly sift all the ingredients and keep in a dry place.

Tip: You can adjust the recipe up or down; just keep the proportions the same. (For the potato flour, use 1 teaspoon per 140 g/5 oz of flour mix.)

DAIRY SUBSTITUTES

Throughout this book, I have recommended that when you begin a gluten-free lifestyle, you also go dairy-free, at least for 2 to 3 weeks, because of the possibility of cross-reactivity. This is especially true if your gluten sensitivity has exhibited itself in gastric problems. Until your body heals, it may fool itself into thinking that casein is gluten. Obviously, that would mean a continuation of the same problems you had while eating gluten.

That's why I recommend going dairy-free.

Patients who accept GF often baulk at going dairy-free. How, they wonder, can they do that? So much of cooking and baking calls for milk or cheese.

Do not despair. Going dairy-free is possible. There is lots of helpful advice on the internet. One of the best sources of information and recipes is the US site Go Dairy Free, www.godairyfree.org.

This website tells you about substitutes – and even guides you into preparing many of them. I've listed a few of the recipes from the website if you wish to prepare some of the milk substitutes at home.

I suggest that you experiment with the different milk substitutes. They all have different tastes that subtly lend themselves to recipes. When you go dairy-free milk shopping, please read labels closely. Some milk substitutes use sugar to sweeten them. Instead of buying a pre-sweetened (with sugar) milk substitute, buy the product unsweetened and add vanilla extract or the sweetener of your choice.

You will find many dairy substitutes for milk, including almond milk, cashew milk, rice milk, coconut milk and soya milk. Oat milk may work well for some people as well – but be sure that it is certified GF to avoid possible reactivity problems from contamination.

Goat's Milk and Sheep's Milk

Many people who are sensitive to the casein in cow's milk find that they can tolerate goat's milk and sheep's milk – and milk products made from these animals. Goat's milk is available in health food stores and many supermarkets. Sheep's milk may be more difficult to find; look in health food stores.

Soya Milk

I'm sure you have seen soya milk in the supermarket. It has become a very popular drink, in "regular", as well as vanilla and even chocolate.

Soya has a distinctive taste. It is made from ground soyabeans, filtered water and a small amount of brown rice sweetener. Usually it is fortified with calcium to match that of milk. Note: if you are reactive to soya (and many people are – it is one of the top food allergens), use another milk substitute!

You can prepare soya milk from scratch at home, although you may find it easier to buy it, since it is readily available at the supermarket.

Soya Milk[2]

INGREDIENTS

170 g (6 oz) dried soyabeans

Your choice of sweetener, as desired

1½ teaspoons vanilla or almond extract (optional)

DIRECTIONS

1. Soak the soyabeans in 1.2 litres (2 pints) water for 12 to 14 hours.
2. Heat another 1.2 litres (2 pints) water in a large saucepan over medium heat.
3. Drain the beans.
4. Add the beans and 350 ml (12 fl oz) lukewarm water to a blender and blend on high for 1 minute.
5. Immediately transfer the soyabean blend to your heated water in the saucepan.
6. Repeat this process with the remaining soyabeans, a ladle at a time.
7. As soon as you have added all the beans to the saucepan, bring it slowly to the boil, stirring constantly.
8. Reduce the heat and simmer, stirring constantly, for 15 minutes. Be careful not to scorch the milk while cooking.
9. Remove from the heat. Strain the milk through cheesecloth or a tea towel.
10. Press any remaining milk through with a large spoon.
11. You may pour another 120 ml (4 fl oz) water through, in order to get it all.
12. Your soya milk is now complete and can be sweetened and flavoured if it is intended for drinking purposes.

Rice Milk

This "milk" is made from brown rice, water and brown rice sweetener. You can find it in most supermarkets.

You will find it a little pricier than soya milk, though. So, if it better suits your budget, you might want to try making it at home – it's quick and cheap to do.

Rice Milk

INGREDIENTS

170 g (6 oz) warm/hot rice (cooked)

1 litre (1¾ pt) hot water

1 teaspoon vanilla extract (omit the vanilla if using the rice milk for
savoury dishes)

Your sweetener of choice (optional)

DIRECTIONS

1. Put the rice, water, vanilla extract and sweetener, if using, in a
blender and purée for 3 to 5 minutes until smooth.
2. Let it stand for 30 minutes or more, up to several hours.
3. Then, without shaking, pour the rice milk into another container, being careful not to let the sediment at the bottom pour
into the new container.
4. Alternatively, if you are in a hurry, strain the rice milk through
cheesecloth.
5. This makes about 1 litre (1¾ pt).

Almond Milk

Almond milk, prepared from ground almonds, is a wonderful substitute
for dairy milk, especially if you do not like the taste of rice or soya
milk. It is my personal favourite. My favourite is an unsweetened brand
flavoured with natural vanilla for my cappuccino. You can make
almond milk at home, but it may be more expensive than just buying it
ready-made. Almond milk is also a little more expensive than rice or
soya milk.

However, almond milk can be substituted for cow's milk in any
recipe.

Potato Milk

This was new to me, too! But potatoes can be made into a milk substitute just as easily as you can make rice milk. And if you want to try
potato milk, you actually may have to prepare it yourself, since it is so
new that it is difficult to find.

Go Dairy Free says it is still in the "conceptual stages", which means that it hasn't been tested in all types of cooking. But if you want to experiment, you may find this to be a cooking substitute that works for you.

Potato Milk

INGREDIENTS

1 large potato, peeled

725 ml (26 fl oz) hot/warm water

Salt

1 teaspoon vanilla extract

30 g (1 oz) slivered almonds (for calcium)

2 tablespoons honey or maple syrup, to sweeten

DIRECTIONS

1. Boil the potato in the water with a little salt.
2. Reserve the cooking water and add enough warm water to make 1 litre (1¾ pt).
3. In a blender, add the water, potato, vanilla extract, slivered almonds and honey, and blend for approximately 5 minutes.
4. Strain through a tea towel or cheesecloth.

Cheese

Try goat's or sheep's cheese as a cheese substitute. Tofu makes a good soft-cheese substitute. And you will find some hard and soft soya "cheeses" in the health food store.

Here are recipes from Go Dairy Free for preparing noncheese substitutes for two popular cheeses: Parmesan and cream cheese.

Parmesan Substitute

INGREDIENTS

145 g (5 oz) raw almonds, blanched and peeled

8 tablespoons nutritional yeast flakes (available in health food stores)

½ teaspoon sea salt

DIRECTIONS

1. To blanch and peel the almonds yourself, soak them in boiling water for 5 minutes. The skins should pop off easily.
2. Pat the almonds dry to remove excess moisture.
3. Place the almonds, yeast flakes and sea salt in a food processor or blender and reduce to a fine powder.
4. Store in the refrigerator for a fairly long shelf life.

Cream Cheese Alternative

INGREDIENTS

145 g (5 oz) firm silken tofu

2 tablespoons olive oil

3 tablespoons lemon juice or 2 tablespoons vinegar

1 tablespoon sugar

½ teaspoon sea salt

DIRECTIONS

1. Combine the tofu, oil, lemon juice, sugar and salt in a blender and process until smooth.
2. Pour into a bowl and chill.

Butter

Butter is a dairy product. If you cannot tolerate dairy, I do *not* recommend using margarine because of trans fats. One alternative is to use coconut oil, which is an excellent fat to replace butter in recipes. It has the same characteristics of butter, margarine or vegetable fat.

You can also use extra-virgin olive oil (which is extremely healthy), a lighter tasting olive oil (which has a milder taste) or a soya-based substitute. (Did you know that you can even bake with olive oil instead of solid vegetable fat? You will have to use less oil than you would vegetable fat, however; otherwise the baked goods may be too oily.)

My top recommendation for a butter substitute, however, is coconut oil. It is solid at room temperature and can be exchanged 1:1 for butter or margarine. It is also much healthier as it contains no trans fat and *lowers* cholesterol levels.

Soured Cream

If you want a dairy-free substitute for soured cream, blend silken tofu until it is smooth. For an even more soured cream-like taste, try this:[3]

Soured Tofu Cream

INGREDIENTS

> 230 g (8 oz) silken tofu
>
> 3 tablespoons lemon juice or 1½ tablespoons vinegar
>
> 2 tablespoons olive oil
>
> 1½ teaspoons maple syrup, honey or sugar
>
> ⅛ teaspoon sea salt
>
> 1 tablespoon unsweetened or plain soya milk, plus additional for consistency

DIRECTIONS

1. Combine the tofu, lemon juice, oil, maple syrup, salt and soya milk in a blender and purée until smooth.
2. You may add the soya milk 1 tablespoon at a time, until your desired consistency is reached.

Sugar Substitutes

In Chapter 11, Setting Yourself Free, I told you about a number of sugar substitutes that are on the market. These include:

- Fructose
- Honey
- Maltitol
- Maple syrup
- Xylitol

Sucralose (Splenda) is another alternative, along with some newer products that incorporate sucralose as part of their formulas. It appears to be well tolerated by most people.

CHAPTER 15

GLUTEN-FREE COOKING

Do you wake up in the morning too rushed to prepare and eat a proper breakfast? And when you come home at night, are you too tired and have too little interest in the kitchen to cook anything that requires more than a quick warming?

Perhaps your kitchen is in pristine condition because you almost never have to wash a pot, let alone a dish or a glass!

If this describes you, then you'll be glad to know that you *can* survive on a gluten-free diet without doing much cooking.

However, this will come at a price. But it's a price that you are probably already paying: quality of food. Not that processed gluten-free food is bad, but home-cooked meals are so much better!

Another price you will pay is the cost of processed gluten-free foodstuffs. Prepared gluten-free food costs considerably more than its non-gluten-free equivalents.

However, if *nothing* I say can convince you to dust off (literally) your dishes and pans and learn the fine art of cooking you can still find some useful ideas and recipes in this chapter.

For those who enjoy cooking, we provide plenty of delicious dishes for you to prepare. Most are relatively simple and, although you'll need to spend some time in the kitchen, I think you'll be happy with the results.

I'd like to emphasize that I always encourage using fresh ingredients, preferably organic, whenever they are available and affordable. You may not be able to taste the difference, but your body will definitely feel the effect of not ingesting residual pesticides, herbicides and chemical fertilizers that are used on mass-produced fruits and vegetables.

We've adapted many of the following recipes to accommodate the special needs of a GF diet. However, bear in mind the following when shopping: always, *always* check labels! And read them carefully. The EU food-allergens labelling law specifies that 12 common allergens, including wheat, rye and barley, must be clearly stated on the label. Many manufacturers note these allergens in bold letters in a separate statement from the rest of the ingredients.

Others, however, do not make a separate statement and merely list the allergens (such as wheat) within the list of ingredients, which may be printed in very fine print. So, take your time and read carefully.

Keep in mind, too, that manufacturers may change processing methods and ingredients. A product you purchased last month that did not contain gluten could have changed formulation! So, it's always wise to read first, eat later.

Although some food processors reveal, on their websites or by request, which of their foods are gluten-free, others will not commit to saying their products do not contain gluten, probably because of liability issues. And others print a disclaimer on their labels, stating that the product "may be manufactured in a plant that processes wheat" or other allergens.

In other words: be prudent in all your purchases but especially in those that involve any type of processed foods.

GF FOODS IN YOUR LOCAL SUPERMARKET

In an earlier chapter, we discussed things that you should avoid eating and how to spot gluten-containing foods. Let's take a "walk" through your local supermarket and see the different gluten-free foods that are "ripe" for picking. Just be careful with your choices. Just because something is gluten-free doesn't mean it's healthy!

Fresh fruits. All fresh fruits are gluten-free. Buy whatever is in season, and enjoy the nutrients and refreshment they offer. Fresh fruits make a perfect dessert or a light snack.

Tinned, jarred and frozen fruits. Peaches, pears, oranges, grapefruit – all tinned fruits – are gluten-free, although they are not as nutritious as fresh fruits. Select "in juice" varieties for healthier eating. Frozen fruits are more nutritious and better tasting than tinned.

Juices. Do you enjoy a glass of orange juice in the morning? Apple juice? Or how about mango and peach? Juices are gluten-free. Enjoy.

(But stay away from "super juices" or "green" juices, which contain many nutrients but include wheat and barley grass.)

Fresh vegetables. Like fruits, all vegetables are gluten-free. All can be prepared easily – even if you don't like to cook! Watch out for pre-prepared vegetable mixes that contain small packets of sauces – many will contain gluten.

Tinned, jarred and frozen vegetables. What's your preference? Peas, carrots, beans, asparagus, artichokes, mushrooms, parsnips, spinach – tinned, jarred and frozen vegetables are all gluten-free. The only obvious thing you have to stay clear of is anything breaded.

Salads. Leafy salads sold in bags are gluten-free. *Tip:* For the most nutrients, avoid salads made primarily of iceberg lettuce, which has the fewest nutrients of all types of lettuce. As a rule of thumb, lettuce that is a darker green is more nutritious. For example, romaine or watercress have seven to eight times as much beta-carotene, two to four times the calcium, and twice the amount of potassium as iceberg lettuce.[1]

Delicatessen counter. If you are not on a dairy-free diet, cheese is a good choice. It is naturally gluten-free. Many cold meats are also GF, such as roasted turkey, chicken and ham, but do ask. I recommend selecting brands that have lower fat and lower salt contents, prepared without nitrates and nitrites. I also highly recommend organic cheeses, which you can now find at many supermarkets.

Dairy products. Milk, soured cream, soft and hard cheeses (such as cream cheese, ricotta, mozzarella, Cheddar, Edam and Swiss, to name a few), and yogurt are all naturally gluten-free. The healthiest products are low-fat and low-salt, as well as low-fat and fat-free unsweetened yogurts. (*Caution:* If you are considering a processed cheese or a low-fat yogurt or one that has flavouring added to it, check the label carefully. These products may have gluten added to them.)

Are you dairy-free, too? The dairy aisle still contains products that you can buy ready-to-eat, such as milk substitutes (soya, almond or rice milk) and tofu. Keep in mind: soya is one of the foods that many food-sensitive people react to. If you are one of those individuals, you still have alternatives, although you may have to find them in a health food store instead of your supermarket.

Eggs. Eggs are a great source of protein. They are naturally gluten-free. Egg substitutes (such as No Egg) are also gluten-free. I personally love organic eggs, which are high in omega-3 fatty acids – great for your heart!

Shelf-stable foods. These are foods that can be stored and transported without refrigeration and are easy to take with you when you are on the go. Products such as GF fruit and nut bars, biscuits and crispbreads are now widely available but a more diverse choice is usually found on the websites of small specialist producers.

Meats, fish and poultry. Excellent choices! I recommend selecting organic when these meats, fish and poultry are available and affordable. These can be easily transformed into nutritious main courses that provide you with necessary protein.

What to be wary of? Meatless meats, fish and poultry. Vegetarian counterfeits are not appropriate substitutes for gluten-sensitive individuals. Gluten is a primary ingredient in these protein alternatives.

Condiments. Spices add zest and taste to prepared foods. Always check labels, but spices and herbs are naturally gluten-free. Mustard, ketchup and salsa are also gluten-free. I've checked the labels on many different brands of mayonnaise and have not yet found one that contains gluten.

Cereals. With the exception of oatmeal – which is technically gluten-free – the cereals you find in the cereal aisle of most supermarkets contain a hidden source of gluten – malt, which is made from barley.

I do not recommend eating oats because of the risk of cross-contamination. The exception is gluten-free oats, which you may be able to purchase online (this product is readily available in the US but is more difficult to source elsewhere). The oats are not guaranteed to be GF, but they are processed in a dedicated mill, and according to one producer "the level of non-oat grains [is] less than 0.05 per cent."[2]

Many supermarkets are beginning to carry a few varieties of gluten-free cereals, which may be found in an "organic" or "free-from" section of the store. I have purchased corn flakes, quinoa flakes, rice crispies, puffed rice, puffed millet and puffed corn in the local supermarket.

Snack foods. Popcorn is okay; check the label for gluten on popcorn that contains flavourings. Some varieties of corn tortilla chips have no gluten. Nor do unflavoured potato crisps. Before you reach for flavoured crisps, such as barbecue or Cheddar cheese, look at the ingredients. As a nutritionist, I urge you to eat these snacks sparingly and to select baked varieties over fried. (Fresh fruit, nuts and baby carrots make great GF snacks!)

A word of caution: Although many brands of snacks are gluten-free, the ingredients may note that they are made in facilities that process wheat. Cross-contamination may be an issue, especially if you are extremely sensitive to gluten.

Desserts. If you are not dairy-intolerant, ice cream and sorbets are almost always gluten-free, unless they include ingredients such as "cookies", "cheesecake" or "brownies". Virtually all brands, even pre-mium brands, of ice cream use carrageenan to improve texture. If you want to reduce your intake of this additive, stick to making your own ice cream at home.

Beverages. Coffee, tea, natural fruit juices and fruit squashes are all gluten-free. Check the label on hot chocolate mixes.

Now on to cooking!

GF COOKING: BREAKFASTS

On the run? Don't skimp on breakfast. It's the most important meal of the day. Breakfast helps regulate your metabolism, so it's important to eat the right foods – foods that are not too high in sugar – so the fact that a gluten-free diet excludes chocolate muffins is a good thing!

Although you can't stop at the corner coffee shop, if you are in a hurry you can still have breakfast on the go. Simply select the range of eat-any-where GF foods available in the supermarket and on-line, such as:

- Corn cakes
- Fruit and nut bars
- Hot cross buns
- Muffins (available in several flavours)
- Pancakes

If you have time to sit down, enjoy a bowl of cereal (but not "regu-lar" cereal, which is flavoured with malt, a derivative of barley). You will find gluten-free cereals in a number of varieties, including:

- Buckwheat flakes
- Corn flakes (look for brands marked GF)

- Indian corn, flax and amaranth
- Muesli (look for brands marked GF)
- Porridge flakes (not oats but a mix of rice and millet flakes)
- Puffed millet (very similar to old-fashioned puffed oats)
- Puffed rice

Before you rush out the door, however, ensure good nutrition by supplementing your on-the-go breakfast item with a glass of juice – or better – a piece of fresh fruit or milk or dairy-free milk. You can, of course, have a cup of coffee or tea; I recommend decaffeinated.

Breakfast bars, muffins and cereal can become boring – and although there are more and more gluten-free choices, many are still high in carbohydrates and simple sugars. A more nutritious beginning to your day would come from a breakfast high in protein.

Try the following GF breakfasts. There are some simple ideas to get you started and more complex recipes for when you have a little more time. You'll enjoy variety and will kick-start your day in a healthy way.

Tropical Breakfast Shake[3]

Here's a quick and easy GF and dairy-free on-the-go breakfast. It will take about 5 minutes to prepare and will serve two. (Or, if you prefer – drink one and save one for tomorrow!)

The hardest part of this recipe is cutting up the fruit for the drink.

INGREDIENTS

90 g (3 oz) GF soft tofu, silken style

2 tablespoons honey

120 ml (4 fl oz) orange juice

2 teaspoons lemon juice

170 g (6 oz) pineapple, chopped

1 small banana, sliced

6 ice cubes

DIRECTIONS

1. Combine the tofu, honey, orange juice, lemon juice, pineapple, banana and ice cubes in a blender.
2. Purée for about 30 seconds, or until well blended and frothy.

Optional: Garnish with cubed fruits such as mango, kiwi fruit and raspberries on skewers.

Peanut Butter Pancakes

Who doesn't enjoy a good pancake every once in a while? They are high in carbohydrates, but you can "offset" those carbs by avoiding butter to top them off. Instead, try this:

INGREDIENTS

2 GF frozen pancakes

2 tablespoons unsweetened peanut butter

DIRECTIONS

1. Pop the pancakes into a toaster, toasting both sides until crisp, or reheat them in a medium oven.
2. Spread your favourite peanut butter on them for a flavourful boost of protein and energy.
3. For an even tastier treat, add some all-fruit jam over the peanut butter.

Turkey on Toast

Turkey on toast? Whoever heard of eating turkey for breakfast? Well, why not? Turkey is lean and is all protein. It takes your body longer to digest protein, so a breakfast of turkey on toast will keep you satisfied longer into the day.

INGREDIENTS

1 slice GF bread

Mustard or mayonnaise, to taste

1 slice turkey

1 slice tomato

DIRECTIONS

1. Toast the bread and spread with the mustard.
2. Place the turkey and tomato on the bread.
3. Enjoy your lunch-for-breakfast treat.

Cream Cheese and Salmon Roll

Soft GF rolls are best for this simple but nutritious breakfast.

INGREDIENTS

1 GF white roll, fresh or thawed
1 tablespoon cream cheese or cheese substitute
2 small slices smoked salmon

DIRECTIONS

1. Cut the roll in two and lightly toast the outside.
2. Top with the cream cheese and salmon.

Orange Pink-Grapefruit Smoothie [4]

This is a delicious sweet-and-sour breakfast treat.

INGREDIENTS

2 oranges
1 pink grapefruit
8 ice cubes
Honey, to taste

DIRECTIONS

1. Cut the oranges and grapefruit into pieces, carefully removing all the membranes and seeds.
2. Chill the fruits in the freezer for a while for smoother consistency.
3. Combine the fruits in a blender with the ice and as much honey as you like – at least 1 teaspoon. Adjust to taste.

Almond Butter and Banana Toast

Ready-made gluten-free bread tends to be crumbly, dries out easily and does not toast as well as wheat bread. The nut butter hides the texture and provides nutrition. Almond butter makes a nice change from peanut butter and is readily available in health food stores.

INGREDIENTS

2–3 slices GF bread

4 tablespoons almond butter

1 banana

DIRECTIONS

1. Toast the bread (both sides). (*Note:* GF bread does not usually turn to a toasted colour, like wheat bread does.)
2. Spread the almond butter on each slice of toast.
3. Slice the banana crosswise, and add a layer of banana slices on top of the peanut butter.
4. Eat as is – or for a treat, put the toast under a grill for a minute to warm the almond butter.

Optional: Add honey on top of the banana and pop under the grill until it starts to sizzle.

Hot Honey Spread[5]

As long as you have bread, pancakes, muffins or other GF bread stuffed in your refrigerator or freezer, spice them up with different types of spreads for an easy breakfast. Okay, it will take you a few minutes to prepare this spread – but once done, it's *done* and ready to use.

This unusual honey spread is hot to the taste – peppers make it that way.

INGREDIENTS

340 ml (12 oz) honey

1 teaspoon crushed red pepper flakes

DIRECTIONS

1. Combine the honey and pepper flakes in a heavy saucepan.
2. Warm over low heat for 10 minutes.
3. Cover and turn off the heat.
4. Let the mixture stand for 1 to 2 hours. Don't rush this step! This is when the heat and flavour of the red peppers permeates the honey.
5. Strain the mixture through a fine sieve, and pour into sterilized jars with tightly fitting lids.
6. Store at room temperature.

Tip: You can easily adjust this recipe (up or down). Just keep the ratios the same.

Breakfast Tortilla

Corn tortillas are a great base for eggs and cheese. This recipe may not be standard breakfast fare but it makes a good brunch at weekends. Just make sure the corn tortilla is gluten free.

INGREDIENTS

1 large egg

Grated Cheddar cheese or cheese substitute

1 GF corn tortilla

Salsa, hot sauce or taco sauce, to taste

DIRECTIONS

1. Scramble the egg.
2. As the egg begins to set in the pan, sprinkle on the cheese.
3. Meanwhile, warm the tortilla in a medium oven.
4. Fill the centre of the tortilla with the egg mixture. Add salsa or sauce, to taste. Fold in the ends and overlap the sides.

Variations: If your culinary creativity becomes stimulated (and you have time), fry some chopped green peppers, a few thin slices of potato and onion until lightly browned. Build the tortilla beginning with the potato mixture, and then add the scrambled eggs. Top with salsa. Wrap in foil. You can make several of these and keep them in your refrigerator until you are ready to eat them.

Classic Omelette[6]

An omelette can be dressed up in many different ways. Start with this basic recipe, then use your imagination with additional ingredients – whatever you have on hand or whatever suits your breakfast whims.

INGREDIENTS

60–90 g (2–4 oz) filling, such as apples, potatoes, onions, peppers, leeks, meat or cheese

2 eggs

1 tablespoon milk, milk substitute or water

Salt and ground pepper to taste

Herbs such as basil, dill, coriander, rosemary and parsley, finely chopped (optional)

1 teaspoon butter (or 2 teaspoons if cooking filling)

DIRECTIONS

1. Cook the filling ingredients as needed. Set aside.
2. If you are making a cheese omelette, thinly slice the cheese (so that it will melt easily) or grate it. Set aside.
3. Crack the eggs into a small mixing bowl, and whisk until well beaten.
4. Add the milk, salt, ground pepper and herbs, if using. Stir to mix. Set aside.
5. Heat a small omelette pan or frying pan over high heat until very hot (approximately 30 seconds).
6. Add the butter, making sure it coats the bottom of the pan. As soon as the butter stops bubbling and sizzling (and before it starts to brown), slowly pour in the egg mixture. Tilt the pan to spread the egg mixture evenly.
7. Let the eggs cook and firm up for about 10 seconds. Then shake the pan and use a spatula to gently direct the mixture away from the sides and into the middle. Allow the remaining liquid to flow into the space left at the sides of the pan. Cook for 1 minute longer, or until the egg mixture holds together.

8. Add the filling. Put in the vegetables or fruit or meat first, then any cheese. (The middle will still be runny.)
9. Tilt the pan and use the spatula to fold one-third of the omelette toward the middle.
10. Shake the pan to slide the omelette to the edge of the pan.
11. Hold the pan above the serving plate, then tip it so that the omelette rolls off and folds itself onto the plate. The two edges will be tucked underneath.

Goat's Cheese Omelette[7]

Most omelettes are prepared with cheese made from cow's milk. If you cannot tolerate cow's milk but find goat's milk digestible (or just want a change of taste), try this omelette, which serves two.

INGREDIENTS

3 eggs
2 teaspoons water
⅛ teaspoon salt
60 g (2 oz) plain goat's cheese

DIRECTIONS

1. Beat the eggs in a small mixing bowl.
2. Add the water and salt and beat well.
3. Coat a frying pan with drizzled olive oil or coat with a GF nonstick cooking spray.
4. Add half the egg mixture, swirling over the pan evenly.
5. Cook for 30 seconds, or until the mixture starts to firm up.
6. With a spatula, push the sides of the omelette to the centre and tip the pan for the uncooked egg to cover.
7. Sprinkle half of the goat's cheese over half of the omelette.
8. Fold the omelette in half. Continue cooking until the bottom is lightly browned.
9. Turn over and cook for 30 seconds longer.
10. Slide onto a plate.
11. Repeat with the second half of the egg mixture.

Baked Herb Cheese Omelette[8]

We usually think of omelettes as being prepared in a frying pan. Here is one that is easily whipped together and is baked in the oven. It will serve four.

INGREDIENTS

4 eggs

100 g (3½ oz) GF flour

480 ml (16 fl oz) milk or milk substitute, such as soya, rice or almond milk

60 g (2 oz) grated cheese or cheese substitute

2–3 tablespoons fresh basil, chopped

DIRECTIONS

1. Preheat the oven to 200°C/400°F/gas 6.
2. Break the eggs into a medium mixing bowl.
3. Whisk the eggs and gradually add the flour until mixed well.
4. Add the milk and whisk until well combined.
5. Coat a 20–30 cm (10–12 in) ceramic or heavy glass baking dish with a GF nonstick cooking spray.
6. Sprinkle the cheese and basil into the dish.
7. Pour the egg mixture over the cheese.
8. Bake for 30 minutes, or until puffed and brown on top.
9. Cut into sections and serve warm.

Tip: To make a heartier baked omelette, add a little cubed ham.

Hot Buckwheat Breakfast Cereal

Buckwheat makes a tasty breakfast cereal and is especially good with dried fruit.

INGREDIENTS

¼ teaspoon salt

600 ml (1 pint) water, milk or milk substitute

75 g (2½ oz) roasted buckwheat

75 g (2½ oz) raisins, chopped dried apricots or prunes (or a combination)

DIRECTIONS

1. In a medium saucepan, stir the salt into the water, milk or milk substitute.
2. Bring to the boil.
3. Stir in the buckwheat, as well as any dried fruit you would like to add.
4. Cook, uncovered, stirring frequently, while maintaining a gentle boil, for 8 to 11 minutes, or until it reaches the consistency you prefer.
5. Serve plain or with milk or milk substitute and a favourite sweetener, such as honey.

Quinoa Flakes Hot Cereal

Hot quinoa flakes make a delicious, hearty breakfast. The taste is slightly nutty, and it takes only 90 seconds to prepare.

INGREDIENTS

240 ml (8 fl oz) water (for thicker cereal, use less water; for thinner, use more)
30 g (1 oz) quinoa flakes
Dash of salt (optional)

DIRECTIONS

1. In a small pot, bring the water to a rapid boil.
2. Add quinoa flakes and salt, if using, to the boiling water.
3. Bring the mixture back to the boil and cook for 90 seconds, stirring frequently.
4. Remove from the heat and allow to cool. (The cereal will thicken slightly as it cools.)
5. Sweeten to taste.

Pancakes

This recipe has been adapted from a basic pancake recipe. As you experiment, you'll find that you can substitute GF flour with a little xantham gum to help the "gluing" process along.

Once you are comfortable with a recipe such as this, prepare a larger quantity of the dry ingredients, label the container and store it in a dry cupboard. It'll be ready for you when you want to make a batch.

INGREDIENTS

1 large egg

145 g (5 oz) GF flour

180 ml (6 fl oz) milk or milk substitute

1 tablespoon brown sugar

2 tablespoons olive oil

3 teaspoons baking powder

½ teaspoon xanthan gum

¼ teaspoon salt

Butter or nonstick cooking spray

DIRECTIONS

1. Break the egg into a medium bowl and beat it or whisk it by hand until it is fluffy.
2. Beat in the flour, milk, brown sugar, oil, baking powder, xantham gum and salt until the batter is smooth. For thinner pancakes, add more milk.
3. Heat the griddle or a frying pan over medium heat. Test the temperature is correct by sprinkling with a few drops of water. If bubbles jump around, the heat is just right.
4. If necessary, grease the griddle or pan with the butter.
5. For each pancake, pour about 4 tablespoons of batter.
6. Cook the pancakes until they are puffed and dry around the edges.
7. Turn over and cook the other side until golden brown.

Tips: Make the pancakes extra special by stirring in fresh or frozen (but thawed and drained) blueberries or blackberries. Mmm!

Did you prepare too much batter? Finish cooking the pancakes and freeze them. Pop them into your toaster for a quick on-the-go breakfast.

Breakfast Apple-Citrus Compote[9]

Fruit provides essential vitamins and minerals. The best way to eat fruit is fresh. But occasionally, you may want a change of pace. Here is a good way to start your day.

INGREDIENTS

2 medium tart apples, peeled and sliced
250 g (9 oz) pitted prunes
350 ml (12 fl oz) orange juice
2 tablespoons honey
1 tablespoon lemon juice
½ teaspoon ground cinnamon
2 navel oranges, peeled and cut into segments
2 pink grapefruits, peeled and cut into segments
Mint sprigs (optional)

DIRECTIONS

1. In a large saucepan, combine the apples, prunes and orange juice and bring to the boil.
2. Reduce the heat and simmer for about 10 minutes, or until the apples are tender but not soft.
3. Remove from the heat and stir in the honey, lemon juice and cinnamon.
4. Cool, cover and chill.
5. Stir in the oranges and grapefruits.
6. To serve, spoon the fruits with their liquid into serving dishes. Garnish with the mint sprigs, if using.

Broccoli Frittata[10]

Broccoli for breakfast? Why not? Who says breakfast has to consist of toast, cereal and eggs? Give this a try – at least for a weekend breakfast.

INGREDIENTS

2½ tablespoons finely chopped onion

2 teaspoons butter

285 g (10 oz) frozen broccoli, cooked and drained

½ small clove garlic, crushed (optional)

170 g (6 oz) cooked rice

2½ tablespoons grated Parmesan cheese or cheese substitute

2 eggs, slightly beaten

60 ml (2 fl oz) milk

½ teaspoon salt (optional)

Dash of ground black pepper

40 g (1¼ oz) grated mozzarella cheese or cheese substitute

DIRECTIONS

1. Sauté the onion in the butter, until tender but not brown.
2. Add the broccoli, garlic (if using), rice and Parmesan and mix well.
3. Combine the eggs, milk, salt and pepper.
4. Stir the egg mixture into the rice mixture.
5. Turn into a well-buttered, shallow casserole dish.
6. Top with the mozzarella.
7. Bake at 180°C/350°F/gas 4 for 20 to 25 minutes, or until set.

Breakfast Hash[11]

Do you have leftover pork in your refrigerator? Use it, along with bacon, in this breakfast hash. Serve with GF toast. This recipe serves six.

INGREDIENTS

6 slices lean back bacon, chopped

1 bunch spring onions, sliced

1 small green pepper, chopped

425 g (15 oz) cooked, chopped potatoes

2 teaspoons GF Worcestershire sauce

¼ teaspoon salt

⅛ teaspoon ground pepper

425 g (15 oz) chopped cooked pork

170 g (6 oz) drained, chopped pickled beetroot

DIRECTIONS

1. Cook the bacon until crisp in a large non-stick frying pan.
2. Add the onions and pepper. Cook over medium-high heat for 1 minute.
3. Stir in the potatoes, Worcestershire sauce, salt and ground pepper. Cook for 5 minutes, stirring occasionally.
4. Stir in the pork and beetroot. Cook until heated through.

Blueberry Sauce

If your breakfast plans include pancakes (page 171) or French toast (made with GF bread, of course), then treat yourself to this blueberry sauce to dress them up.

INGREDIENTS

285 g (10 oz) fresh or frozen blueberries

60 ml (2 fl oz) water

240 ml (8 fl oz) orange juice

150 g (5½ oz) sugar (A healthier choice: instead of sugar, use xylitol, a natural sweetener. Follow directions on the packet for substitution ratios.)

60 ml (2 fl oz) cold water

3 tablespoons cornflour

½ teaspoon almond extract

⅛ teaspoon ground cinnamon

DIRECTIONS

1. In a saucepan over medium heat, combine the blueberries, 60 ml (2 fl oz) water, orange juice and sugar.
2. Stir gently and bring to the boil.
3. In a cup or small bowl, mix together the cold water and cornflour.
4. Gently stir the cornflour mixture into the blueberries. Do not mash the berries.
5. Simmer gently for 3 to 4 minutes, or until thick enough to coat the back of a metal spoon.
6. Remove from the heat and stir in the almond extract and cinnamon.
7. Thin the sauce with water if it is too thick for your liking.

Amaranth Pancakes[12]

Here's a GF pancake recipe that uses amaranth flour, which you may have to order online or buy at a health food store. This makes 6 servings.

INGREDIENTS

145 g (5 oz) amaranth flour

75 g (2½ oz) arrowroot powder

45 g (1½ oz) ground almonds

1 teaspoon bicarbonate of soda

1 teaspoon ground cinnamon

300 ml (10 fl oz) water

2 tablespoons lemon juice

2 tablespoons vegetable oil

2 tablespoons honey

DIRECTIONS

1. In a large bowl, combine the amaranth flour, arrowroot, almonds, bicarbonate of soda and cinnamon.
2. In a separate bowl, combine the water, lemon juice, oil and honey and mix well.
3. Stir the liquid mixture into the flour mixture and mix well.
4. Heat a lightly oiled griddle or frying pan over medium-high heat.
5. Drop the batter by spoonfuls onto the griddle or pan, using approximately 2 tablespoons for each pancake.
6. Brown on both sides and serve hot.

Cooked Rice Cereal

This cooked rice cereal is actually easy to prepare. To add additional zest, add fresh blueberries or other fruit.

INGREDIENTS

300 g (10½ oz) white rice (uncooked)

480 ml (16 fl oz) semi-skimmed milk or milk substitute

50 g (1¾ oz) sugar

1½ teaspoons ground cinnamon

DIRECTIONS

1. Prepare the rice according to the package directions.
2. Combine the warm cooked rice, milk, sugar and cinnamon.
3. Stir and serve.

Spinach Soufflé[13]

Have you ever prepared a soufflé? This one is easy.

INGREDIENTS

1 large egg

80 ml (3 fl oz) semi-skimmed milk or milk substitute

40 g (1¼ oz) grated Parmesan cheese (or substitute)

1 teaspoon crushed garlic

Salt and pepper, to taste

500 g (1 lb 2 oz) frozen leaf spinach, thawed

DIRECTIONS

1. Preheat the oven to 180°C/350°F/gas 4.
2. Whisk together the egg, milk, cheese, garlic, salt and pepper.
3. Fold in the spinach.
4. Place in a small casserole dish.
5. Bake for 20 minutes, or until lightly set.

GF COOKING: LUNCHES

What do you like to eat for lunch? Sandwiches? Salads? Soup? You can have all of these items on a gluten-free diet.

Tip: For some satisfying "crunch", add a few GF corn tortilla chips (baked is better for you than fried), along with salsa, to your lunch box. With some fruit and perhaps some raw vegetables (broccoli, cauliflower, mushrooms or carrots, for example), you will have a satisfying lunch.

When you get tired of grab-and-go lunches, try the following gluten-free recipes.

Turkey and Bacon Lettuce Wrap

Instead of a traditional BLT sandwich, try this bread-free turkey and bacon lettuce wrap.

INGREDIENTS

3 leaves romaine lettuce

3 thin slices roast turkey

3 thin slices back bacon, chopped

Mayonnaise to taste

Tomatoes, sliced lengthwise

DIRECTIONS

1. Wash the lettuce and pat dry.
2. Grill the bacon until crisp.
3. Spread the mayonnaise, to taste, on each lettuce leaf.
4. Place 1 slice of turkey and as many slices of tomato as desired in the centre of each lettuce leaf and sprinkle with the bacon.
5. Wrap lengthwise. Enjoy!

Chef's Salad to Go

Some supermarkets have salad bars but many of the choices are made with wheat pasta or are covered in croutons. Picking croutons off the salad is not an option for anyone who is gluten-sensitive, because crumbs may contaminate the salad. Instead, prepare your own salad.

INGREDIENTS

Bagged salad (Italian blend or garden blend with a variety of lettuces)

1 hard-boiled egg

Leftover ham, chicken or turkey

GF salad dressing

GF corn chips or crisps

DIRECTIONS

1. Place a lunch-size serving of the salad in a plastic container.
2. Slice the egg and place on top of the salad greens.
3. Slice the ham, chicken or turkey and place on top of the greens and egg.
4. When you are ready for lunch, add the salad dressing. The corn chips or crisps? They make a nice "side" in place of crackers.

Tip: If you do not have leftover ham, chicken or turkey, you can use tinned or deli meats.

Open-Faced Toasted Tuna Salad with Cheese

This is an easy recipe if you have access to a grill. One tin of tuna will make at least two, possibly three, open-faced sandwiches.

INGREDIENTS

1 small tin tuna chunks (preferably packed in water)

1 stick celery, finely chopped

¼ medium onion, finely chopped

Small handful white or red seedless grapes (optional)

30 g (1 oz) finely chopped walnuts or pecans (optional)

2 tablespoons mayonnaise

3 slices GF bread

3 slices Swiss or Cheddar cheese or cheese made from goat, sheep, rice or soya milk

Salt and pepper, to taste

DIRECTIONS

1. Drain the tuna and place in a medium-size bowl.
2. Add the celery, onion, grapes (if using), nuts (if using) and mayonnaise. Mix thoroughly.
3. Spread the mixture on the bread.
4. Place a slice of cheese on top of the sandwich.
5. Toast the sandwiches until the cheese melts. Add salt and pepper, to taste.
6. Remove and eat!

Tuna-Salad Lettuce Wrap[14]

Tuna is an excellent source of protein. It is low in fat and high in energy. And it mixes into great salads that can be used in a number of ways. Here is another tuna salad for lunch at home or on the go.

INGREDIENTS

4 baby carrots

6 olives

1 plum tomato

1 small tin tuna chunks, drained

1 teaspoon garlic granules

1 teaspoon salt

1 teaspoon ground black pepper

2 tablespoons GF Caesar salad dressing

4 lettuce leaves

DIRECTIONS

1. Finely chop the carrots and olives. (*Tip:* Use a food processor. It's quick and easy.)
2. By hand, dice the tomato into small chunks.
3. Combine the tuna, carrots, olives and tomato in a mixing bowl.
4. Add the garlic granules, salt, pepper and salad dressing. Mix thoroughly to combine all ingredients.
5. Place ¼ of the mixture in the centre of a large lettuce leaf. Fold the bottom up, and then fold in the sides to wrap the mixture.

Egg Salad[15]

Hard-boiled eggs are easy to prepare, can be eaten "as is", or used in many different recipes. Serve on GF bread as a sandwich or over crisp lettuce as a salad. Here is a simple egg salad that will make 4 servings.

INGREDIENTS

8 eggs

1 tablespoon mayonnaise

2 tablespoons prepared Dijon-style mustard

1 teaspoon dried dillweed

1 teaspoon ground paprika

½ medium red onion, chopped

Salt and pepper, to taste

DIRECTIONS

1. Place the eggs in a saucepan and cover with cold water.
2. Bring the water to the boil. Cover, remove from the heat and let the eggs stand in the water for 10 to 12 minutes.
3. Remove the eggs from the water. Cool under cold water, peel and chop.
4. In a large bowl, combine the eggs, mayonnaise, mustard, dill-weed, paprika, onion and salt and pepper, to taste. Mix well.

Busy-Day Lunch

Want something really easy? This will take minutes to prepare. It's light, healthy and full of flavour.

INGREDIENTS

1 tin sliced carrots

Cheese (Cheddar, Edam or other hard cheeses)

1 onion, chopped

1 apple, chopped

1 individual serving box raisins

½ green pepper, chopped

Italian dressing

DIRECTIONS

1. Drain the carrots well.
2. Cut the cheese into small cubes. (For variety, include several types of cheese.)
3. Mix together the carrots, cheese, onion, apple, raisins and chopped pepper.
4. Pour the dressing on the ingredients, to taste, and toss.
5. Store in a spill-proof plastic container.
6. This lunch travels well in an unrefrigerated lunch bag.

Spinach Salad

Spinach is a good source of vitamins and minerals. This spinach salad takes a little preparation but does not require you to make a dressing from scratch – just make sure your dressing is gluten-free (honey and mustard is good and is usually gluten free).

INGREDIENTS

60 g (2 oz) fresh spinach
¼ medium red onion or sweet onion
1 hard-boiled egg, shelled and sliced
2 medium fresh mushrooms, sliced
1 slice bacon, fried crisp and crumbled
Honey and mustard dressing with poppyseed, to taste

DIRECTIONS

1. Wash and tear the spinach leaves into bite-size pieces.
2. Place the spinach in a large bowl.
3. Slice the onion into rings, adding to the salad as you slice.
4. Add the egg, mushrooms and bacon to the salad.
5. Pour on the dressing and toss – or use it on the side.

Tip: If you take this salad to work or school in a plastic container, do not add the dressing until you are ready to eat.

Chicken Lettuce Wrap Lunch

INGREDIENTS

455 g (1 lb) boneless chicken breast (organic is best)

1 teaspoon garlic granules

1 teaspoon chilli powder

½ teaspoon ground paprika

2 tablespoons GF flour

1 tablespoon olive oil

2 tablespoons hot sauce

1 small red onion, sliced

¼ cucumber, sliced

120 ml (4 fl oz) GF garlic and herb dressing

Large lettuce leaves, washed

4 tablespoons blue cheese, crumbled

DIRECTIONS

1. Cut chicken breast into bite-size chunks.
2. In a plastic bag, mix the garlic granules, chilli powder, paprika and flour.
3. Add the chicken and shake to coat.
4. Heat the oil in a frying pan over medium-high heat.
5. Add the chicken. Turn it frequently to brown and cook on all sides. This will take about 7 minutes.
6. Drizzle hot sauce over the chicken, toss to coat and set aside.
7. In a medium bowl, mix the onion and cucumber with the dressing.
8. On each lettuce leaf, place one-quarter of the chicken mixture.
9. Top with the dressing, and sprinkle with the blue cheese.
10. This can be eaten either hot or cold.

Chicken Salad Sandwich

The next time you roast a chicken or a turkey and have leftovers, mix up a batch of this salad. No leftovers? Buy a rotisserie chicken from the deli counter. Chill and slice off white or dark meat to make the salad.

INGREDIENTS

200 g (7 oz) cooked chicken or turkey, finely chopped

1 stick celery, chopped

2 spring onions, finely chopped

1 tablespoon lemon juice

80 ml (3 fl oz) GF mayonnaise

75 g (2½ oz) sliced seedless grapes, sliced

30 g (1 oz) chopped walnuts

Salt and pepper, to taste

GF bread

Lettuce and tomato

DIRECTIONS

1. Mix the chicken, celery, onions, lemon juice, mayonnaise, grapes and nuts in a mixing bowl.
2. Season with the salt and pepper, to taste.
3. Spread the chicken salad on the bread.
4. Garnish with the lettuce and tomato.

Tip: Go bread-free! Serve the chicken salad in the centre of a large lettuce leaf. Or scoop out tomatoes and fill the centres with the salad.

Asian Salad and Dressing

In my pre-GF days, one of the salad dressings I enjoyed most was an Asian dressing. I found, however, that the commercial brands all contain gluten, probably in the soy sauce used in the dressing.

Here is an Asian salad and dressing to complement your lunch menus.

INGREDIENTS

ASIAN SALAD DRESSING

8 tablespoons rice vinegar (preferred) or white vinegar

6 tablespoons GF soy sauce

4 tablespoons sugar or sweetener substitute (such as xylitol)

2 tablespoons sesame oil

1½ teaspoons grated fresh ginger

2 tablespoons chopped coriander

A few drops of hot chilli oil (optional)

SALAD

50 g (1¾ oz) mangetout

Bagged lettuce leaves

1 small tin mandarin orange slices

1 large tomato, sliced in half and quartered

Small piece cucumber, thinly sliced

3 spring onions, sliced

1 small tin sliced water chestnuts

DIRECTIONS

1. To make the dressing: combine the vinegar, soy sauce, sugar, sesame oil, ginger, coriander, and chilli oil, if using, in a container that you can shake to thoroughly mix.
2. Refrigerate for at least 1 hour to blend the seasonings. This will keep in the refrigerator.
3. Snip the ends from the mangetout. Blanch the mangetout in boiling water for about 45 seconds. (Do not overcook.)
4. Remove from the boiling water and immediately transfer to an ice bath to stop the cooking.
5. Combine the mangetout, lettuce leaves, orange slices, tomato, cucumber, onions and water chestnuts and toss.
6. Just before serving, toss with the Asian salad dressing.

Tip: For a more filling lunch, add leftover pork, chicken or turkey, cut into strips.

Cream of Mushroom Soup

You can find many different types of tinned GF soups in your super-market or online. But one type of soup you may not be able to find is cream of mushroom.

Here is a recipe for a quick cream of mushroom soup that you can make for lunch or for use in other recipes.

INGREDIENTS

455 g (1 lb) mushrooms (any type; using a variety gives a nicer flavour)

2–3 tablespoons butter or coconut oil

½ teaspoon salt

3 tablespoons GF flour

240 ml (8 fl oz) milk, light evaporated milk or milk substitute

400 ml (14 fl oz) GF chicken stock

60 ml (2 fl oz) sherry (optional)

Freshly ground pepper

DIRECTIONS

1. Wipe the mushrooms to clean them and chop coarsely.
2. Melt the butter or coconut oil in a large saucepan over medium heat.
3. Add the mushrooms and cook for about 10 minutes, or until they are nicely browned.
4. Mix the salt into the flour.
5. Sprinkle the browned mushrooms with the flour and salt mixture.
6. Cook, stirring constantly, until the mixture thickens.
7. Gradually stir in the milk and stock. Stir to thoroughly mix and avoid lumps.
8. Heat. Stir in the sherry, if using.
9. Sprinkle with the pepper, to taste, and serve.

Best Fresh Turkey Sandwiches

To make this sandwich extra special I recommend using organic vegetables – tomatoes, lettuce and avocado.

INGREDIENTS

2 slices GF bread

1 tablespoon GF mayonnaise

Fresh deli turkey slices

1 avocado, sliced

1 tomato, sliced

1 romaine lettuce leaf

Sea salt and pepper, to taste

DIRECTIONS

1. Toast the bread lightly.
2. Spread with the mayonnaise, and add the turkey, avocado, tomato, lettuce, salt and pepper.
3. Serve with fresh fruit.

Tofu Salad[16]

This vegetarian lunch for four is similar to egg salad.

INGREDIENTS

455 g (1 lb) firm tofu, mashed or crumbled

1 small onion, chopped

2 sticks celery, chopped

1 clove garlic, crushed

1 tablespoon chopped parsley

Salt to taste

3 tablespoons soya mayonnaise or regular GF mayonnaise

2 tablespoons sweet relish (optional)

½ red pepper, chopped (optional)

Small piece red cabbage, finely chopped (optional)

1 teaspoon mustard or mustard powder (optional)

DIRECTIONS

1. Mix the tofu, onion, celery, garlic, parsley, salt and mayonnaise together. Add the relish, pepper, cabbage and mustard, if using.
2. Serve on GF bread with your favourite garnish, such as lettuce, tomato or alfalfa sprouts. Or serve on a lettuce leaf.

Veggie, Almond and Feta Sandwich or Salad[17]

You can make this to use as a sandwich filling on your favourite GF bread, as lettuce wrap, or as a salad. It will serve four.

INGREDIENTS

2 small courgettes, chopped

2 vine tomatoes, diced

10 chopped kalamata olives

1 red or green pepper, chopped

½ onion, preferably sweet, chopped

¼ cucumber, chopped

50 g (1¾ oz) feta cheese

30 g (1 oz) sliced toasted almonds

2 tablespoons fresh basil, finely chopped

1 teaspoon fresh thyme

2 tablespoons olive oil

2 tablespoons balsamic vinegar

Salt and freshly ground pepper, to taste

DIRECTIONS

1. Mix the first six ingredients in a bowl.
2. Crumble the feta into the bowl, add the almonds, basil and thyme and mix.
3. Mix together the oil and vinegar.
4. Pour the oil and vinegar mixture over the vegetable mixture and toss well. Add the salt and ground pepper, to taste.

Mexican Chicken Soup[18]

Chef Sara Mouton created a "one size fits all" chicken soup, which she adapted to become Italian, Mexican, Asian and Greek. Here is the GF Mexican version. This recipe will make about 650 ml (22 fl oz).

INGREDIENTS

1 large corn tortilla

400 ml (14 fl oz) low-sodium GF chicken stock

75 g (2½ oz) cooked chopped chicken

90 g (3 oz) rinsed, drained black beans

90 g (3 oz) defrosted frozen corn

Small tin chopped tomatoes

Salt to taste

30 g (1 oz) grated mild Cheddar cheese or cheese substitute

DIRECTIONS

1. Preheat the oven to 180°C/350°F/gas 4.
2. Prepare oven-baked tortilla chips by spraying a baking sheet with nonstick cooking spray and placing the tortilla on it.
3. Cut the tortilla into 8 wedges. Bake for 10 minutes.
4. While the tortilla is baking, combine the chicken stock, chicken, beans, corn and tomatoes (with juice) and heat until hot.
5. Add the salt, to taste.
6. Crumble the tortilla chips into the soup.
7. Sprinkle with the cheese.

Tuna Crepes

Crepes look exotic but are not difficult to make. And – more important – you can prepare them GF. Here's a nice recipe featuring tuna.

INGREDIENTS

> 3 eggs or egg substitute
>
> 145 g (5 oz) brown rice flour
>
> 1–2 tablespoons olive oil
>
> 60–120 ml (2–4 fl oz) water (The amount is determined by consistency. Add enough water to make a smooth and runny crepe batter.)
>
> 1 tablespoon vanilla extract
>
> Butter (or substitute) to oil the crepe pan
>
> 1 medium tin light meat tuna in water
>
> 2 tablespoons mayonnaise (regular GF or soya mayo)
>
> 2 tablespoons pickle relish
>
> 1 tablespoon curry powder
>
> Goat's cheese, to taste

DIRECTIONS

1. In a medium bowl, beat the eggs.
2. Gradually add the flour, oil and water, alternating a little of each, until all are incorporated and the proper crepe consistency is achieved.
3. Add the vanilla extract and stir to mix thoroughly.
4. Wipe the crepe pan with enough butter to allow the crepes to slide easily.
5. Use a ladle to pour a small amount of the batter into the hot crepe pan.
6. Pick the pan up, roll the batter around until it covers the pan, then cook until light golden brown.
7. Flip and cook until golden brown on both sides. Do not overcook. Repeat to make remaining crepes.
8. Drain the tuna well.

9. Add the mayonnaise, relish and curry powder and mix well.
10. Place the tuna mixture into the crepes and roll.
11. Top with the goat's cheese.
12. Place under the grill until the cheese melts, then serve with rice or roasted buckwheat and pineapple slices or other fresh fruit.

Avocado and Tomato Salsa

Eat this as a healthy snack with GF rice crackers or blue corn tortilla chips or as an open-faced sandwich on GF millet bread (or your favourite GF bread). Use organic tomatoes and avocados if they are within your budget.

INGREDIENTS

1 avocado
1 tomato
Juice from ½ fresh lemon
Sea salt and fresh pepper, to taste

DIRECTIONS

1. Peel the avocado, remove the stone and chop the flesh into small pieces.
2. Slice and dice the tomato into small pieces. (You can put the tomato and avocado into a food processor and pulse until chopped into small pieces. Be careful not to overprocess.)
3. In a small bowl, mix the avocado and tomato with the lemon juice, and add the salt and pepper.

Dave's Aubergine Caviar

If you don't tell people this is aubergine, they won't know it. Use this as a salsa or as a spread on GF bread, or just eat it as a salad.

INGREDIENTS

2 aubergines
120 ml (4 fl oz) olive oil
2 onions
4 large cloves garlic, crushed
2 green peppers
4–6 finely chopped fresh jalapeño peppers (optional)
2 × 400 g (14 oz) tins chopped plum tomatoes
1 small tin tomato purée
3 tablespoons coarsely ground fresh black pepper
Salt to taste

DIRECTIONS

1. Preheat the oven to 180°C/350°F/gas 4.
2. Prick the aubergines repeatedly with a fork. Bake them for 1 hour.
3. Remove the skin from the aubergines and finely chop the flesh. Set aside.
4. Heat the oil to medium heat and sauté the onions and garlic until the onions are translucent.
5. Add the green peppers, jalapeño peppers (if using), tomatoes with juice, tomato purée and chopped aubergine. Add the ground pepper and salt.
6. Bring to the boil and simmer for 30 minutes.
7. Cool and serve.

BLT and P (Bacon, Leek, Tomato and Potato) Soup[19]

This soup has a number of ingredients, but none requires much prep work. And the cooking time for the soup is less than 15 minutes. Enjoy!

INGREDIENTS

Extra-virgin olive oil, for drizzling

6 slices lean, smoked good-quality bacon, chopped

3 small sticks celery from the heart of the stalk, finely chopped

2 small to medium carrots, peeled

3 leeks, trimmed of tops and roots

1 bay leaf

Salt and pepper, to taste

3 medium starchy potatoes, peeled

2.2 litres (4 pt) GF chicken stock

400 g (14 oz) tin cherry tomatoes, drained

Handful of flat-leaf parsley, finely chopped

GF bread, for dunking

DIRECTIONS

1. Heat a large pan over medium-high heat.
2. Drizzle the oil in the pan and add the bacon.
3. Cook the bacon until brown and crisp. Remove from the pan and set aside.
4. Add the celery to the pan.
5. Lay the carrots flat on a cutting board. Hold each carrot at the root end and use the vegetable peeler to make long, thin strips.
6. Chop the thin slices into small carrot bits or carrot chips, 1 cm (½ in) wide.
7. Add the carrot chips to the celery in the pan and stir.
8. Cut the leeks lengthwise and then into half moons.
9. Place the leeks into a colander and run under cold running water, separating the layers to wash away all the trapped grit.

10. When the leeks are separated and clean, shake off the water and add to the celery and carrots.

11. Stir the vegetables together, add the bay leaf, and season with the salt and pepper.

12. Cook the leeks until wilted (3 to 4 minutes).

13. Meanwhile, cut each potato across into thirds. Stand each piece of potato upright and thinly slice it. The pieces should look like raw potato chips.

14. Add the stock to the vegetables and bring to the boil.

15. Reduce the heat and add the potatoes and tomatoes. Cook for 8 to 10 minutes, or until the potatoes are tender and starting to break up a bit.

16. Add the bacon and parsley and stir.

17. Adjust the seasonings, if necessary. Remove the bay leaf. Serve immediately with GF bread.

Halibut with Lime and Ginger[20]

Fish is an excellent source of protein. It is quick to prepare and delicious to eat. Here is a recipe using halibut fillets, a fish that has a mild, sweet taste. It can be prepared for either lunch or dinner.

INGREDIENTS

4 teaspoons olive oil

4 × 170 g (6 oz) halibut fillets

Salt and pepper, to taste

2 tablespoons GF soy sauce

2 tablespoons freshly squeezed lime juice

3 tablespoons freshly grated ginger

Papaya or Mango Salsa (opposite)

Baking parchment

DIRECTIONS

1. Preheat the oven to 220°C/425°F/gas 7.

2. Cut 4 pieces of baking parchment into oval shapes large enough to enclose the fillets. Drizzle 1 tablespoon of the olive oil over

each piece of parchment, and rub with your hand until the parchment has absorbed the oil.

3. Rinse the fillets and pat dry. Season both sides with salt and pepper.
4. In a small bowl, mix the soy sauce, lime juice and ginger.
5. Place each fillet flat to one side of the oval and spoon one-quarter of the soy-lime-ginger mixture over each of the fillets.
6. Fold the parchment over and tightly crimp to seal shut.
7. Bake on a baking tray for 10 minutes.
8. To serve, peel back the paper to expose the fish, then spoon the salsa over the top.

Tip: You can use thawed halibut fillets. If fresh fish is available, you can substitute sea bass, mullet or monkfish.

Papaya or Mango Salsa[21]

This easy salsa is a good accompaniment to the halibut recipe and can be used to complement other fish, chicken or pork recipes.

INGREDIENTS

2 ripe papayas, skinned, seeded and chopped into 5 mm (¼ in) cubes.
   (If papayas are unavailable, replace with one or two mangoes.)
4 spring onions, trimmed, then very finely chopped
Small handful coriander leaves, chopped
4 tablespoons freshly squeezed lime juice
4 tablespoons finely chopped red pepper
2 chilli peppers, seeds and membranes removed, chopped

DIRECTIONS

1. Combine the papayas, spring onions, coriander, lime juice, pepper and chilli peppers in a medium bowl.
2. Mix thoroughly.
3. Use immediately, or store, covered, in the refrigerator. Flavours will blend together.

GF COOKING: DINNERS

These days you can find lots of "instant" gluten-free dinners online or through large health food stores. Many of the meals on offer are tasty (though often expensive) but they are no substitute for a bit of home cooking now and then.

Pad Thai with Vegetables

Don't be put off by the number of ingredients in this recipe – most are readily available. It's deliciously tasty, too!

INGREDIENTS

2 portions rice noodles

3 tablespoons vegetable oil

1 egg

115 g (4 oz) chopped chicken, whole prawns or cubed tofu

115 g (4 oz) vegetables (Try flash-frozen mixed vegetables. Use what you want and store the rest in the freezer.)

1 tablespoon sugar

2 teaspoons fish sauce

Juice of ½ lime

1 clove garlic, crushed

1 tablespoon tamarind

¼ teaspoon chilli powder

50 g (1¾ oz) fresh beansprouts

50 g (1¾ oz) peanuts, crushed

Lime wedges, fresh chillies and coriander (optional)

DIRECTIONS

1. Place the noodles in a bowl, cover with boiling water and leave to soak for 4 minutes.
2. Drain the noodles well and rinse under cold water for 30 seconds. Set aside.
3. In a wok or large frying pan, heat 1 tablespoon of the oil.
4. Add the egg and scramble.

5. Remove the egg and set aside.
6. In the wok or frying pan, heat the remaining oil.
7. Add the chicken, prawns or tofu and vegetables and cook until done. The chicken or prawns will turn white in colour, and the vegetables should be crisp-tender.
8. Mix the sugar, fish sauce, lime juice, garlic, tamarind and chilli powder in a small bowl and add to the pan, along with the noodles.
9. Cook for 3 to 4 minutes, or until the sauce is absorbed into the noodles.
10. Add the beansprouts and egg.
11. Mix well to combine.
12. Sprinkle with the peanuts and garnish with the lime wedges, chillies and coriander, if using.

Variation: Serve with steamed or boiled white rice. Season to taste with GF soy sauce and chilli sauce.

Easy Spaghetti Dinner

Before you went on a gluten-free diet, how did you prepare spaghetti? Did you open a jar of spaghetti sauce, heat it and pour it over your pasta?

Homemade spaghetti sauce is better (you'll find a recipe for it on the next page). But when you are in a hurry, you can still enjoy an easy-to-prepare Italian meal.

INGREDIENTS

100 g (3½ oz) GF spaghetti pasta (I prefer quinoa. But you may find rice or corn pasta is more readily available.)
½ jar tomato and basil pasta sauce (Just check to make sure it does not contain gluten.)
Garlic granules, basil and thyme (optional)
GF bread
Trans fat-free margarine
Green salad and salad dressing

DIRECTIONS

1. Cook the pasta according to directions. Be careful not to over-cook it! GF pasta can easily turn to mush if overcooked.
2. Place the pasta sauce in a saucepan and heat. For extra flavour, season it with garlic granules, basil, thyme (or other herbs), to taste.
3. While the sauce is heating, slice the bread and spread with the margarine. Sprinkle with garlic granules, to taste.
4. Place the bread under a grill until toasted. (Remember: GF bread does not get to a toasty colour like its wheat counterparts.)
5. When all ingredients are ready, spoon the sauce over a helping of pasta, and serve with the green salad and garlic toast.

Fresh Tomato and Basil Pasta

Prepare this pasta dish using GF pasta, invite your friends over and watch them rave over the dish, unaware that they are eating GF. It takes a little more effort than the previous recipe – but it's well worth it.

INGREDIENTS

5–10 plum tomatoes, diced

5–7 fresh basil leaves

2 large cloves garlic, crushed

5 tablespoons extra-virgin olive oil

Sea salt and pepper, to taste

1 packet GF pasta

Fresh Parmesan cheese or cheese substitute

DIRECTIONS

1. Mix the tomatoes, basil and garlic together.
2. Let it stand at room temperature for at least 1 hour. (This allows the flavours to blend.)
3. Add the oil, and salt and pepper, to taste, and mix.
4. Cook the pasta according to the packet directions. Do not rinse.
5. Combine the pasta with the tomatoes.
6. Grate the cheese over the top.

Pecan-Coated Fish[22]

Pecans add a delicious nutty flavour to the coating. You will find guidance on preparing GF breadcrumbs on the next page.

INGREDIENTS

455 g (1 lb) fresh or frozen white fish fillets, thawed, 1–2 cm (½–¾ in) thick

30 g (1 oz) fine GF dried breadcrumbs

2 tablespoons cornmeal

2 tablespoons grated Parmesan cheese or other cheese (such as a hard goat's cheese)

2 tablespoons ground pecans

¼ teaspoon salt

¼ teaspoon pepper

30 g (1 oz) GF flour

60 ml (2 fl oz) milk or milk substitute

2–3 tablespoons olive oil or coconut oil

40 g (1¼ oz) pecans, finely chopped

DIRECTIONS

1. Rinse the fish and pat dry.
2. Cut into serving-size pieces. Set aside.
3. In a shallow bowl, mix the breadcrumbs, cornmeal, cheese, chopped pecans, salt and pepper.
4. Coat each portion of the fish with flour, dip into the milk, then coat evenly with the breadcrumb mixture. (Note: dipping the fish with flour first helps the crumb mixture stick to it during the cooking process.)
5. Heat the oil in a large frying pan. When the oil is hot, place the fish in the oil and cook for 4 to 6 minutes on each side, or until golden and the fish flakes easily with a fork. Keep warm.
6. Remove excess crumbs from the pan. Add chopped pecans.
7. Cook and stir for about 2 minutes, or until toasted.
8. Sprinkle the pecans over the fish.

GF Breadcrumbs

To prepare GF breadcrumbs, save slices of GF bread that have dried out. Freeze them, if necessary, until you have enough to make the breadcrumbs.

1. Break the bread into small pieces.
2. Arrange in a single depth on a baking sheet and place in the oven on low heat (120°C/250°F/gas ½).
3. Bake until the bread is completely dry but not toasted. Remove from the oven.
4. Cool, then place the bread in a food processor or a blender and process it into crumbs.
5. Use the crumbs in recipes calling for breadcrumbs.

Grilled Salmon with Mustard Sauce[23]

Salmon is an excellent choice of fish. It is high in omega-3, low in saturated fat and low in calories. And it is easy to prepare, as this recipe demonstrates.

INGREDIENTS

240 ml (8 fl oz) soured cream
2 finely chopped spring onions
1½ tablespoons Dijon mustard
1 tablespoon chopped parsley
½ teaspoon salt
½ teaspoon thyme
Dash of pepper
4 salmon steaks, about 2.5 cm (1 in) thick
Salt and pepper, to taste

DIRECTIONS

1. Preheat the grill.
2. Stir together the soured cream, onion, mustard, parsley, salt, thyme and the dash of pepper. Set aside.

3. Sprinkle the salmon steaks lightly with salt and pepper.

4. To grill, line a shallow dish with foil, arrange the steaks on the foil, and grill 15 cm (6 in) from the heat for 7 minutes.

5. Remove the dish from the grill.

6. Spread the soured cream mix generously on top of each steak.

7. Return the salmon to the grill for about 5 minutes longer, or until the fish flakes easily with a fork.

Spicy Cornmeal Cod[24]

This makes a nice change from wheat flour breading typically used for fish. In this recipe the fish is oven-baked to give a crispy crust.

INGREDIENTS

685 g (1½ lb) cod or other lean fish fillets, about 1 cm (½ in) thick

90 g (3 oz) cornmeal (pure cornmeal – not a cornmeal mix)

30 g (1 oz) plain GF flour

½ teaspoon salt

½ teaspoon garlic granules

½ teaspoon dried oregano

½ teaspoon ground chilli powder

½ teaspoon ground black pepper

2 large eggs, beaten

3 tablespoons butter, melted, or olive oil or butter substitute

DIRECTIONS

1. Preheat the oven to 260°C/500°F/highest gas setting.

2. Cut the fish fillets into 10 × 5 cm (4 × 2 in) pieces.

3. Mix the cornmeal, flour, salt, garlic granules, oregano, chilli powder and black pepper.

4. Dip the fish into the eggs, then coat with the cornmeal mixture.

5. Place the fish on an ungreased baking sheet.

6. Drizzle the butter over the fish.

7. Bake for 10 to 12 minutes, turning the fish once, or until golden brown.

Roasted Chicken and Buckwheat Pilaf

Who doesn't like hot roasted chicken? Many supermarkets now sell them from the rotisserie, freshly cooked and ready to eat. Keep the chicken warm while you prepare the buckwheat pilaf.

Not familiar with buckwheat? It is available at your local health food store and is a great alternative to rice or couscous, even without added ingredients. This recipe makes about 4 servings.

INGREDIENTS

2 tablespoons butter

1 small onion, chopped

1 stick celery, chopped

2 large mushrooms, sliced

¼–½ teaspoon salt

⅛ teaspoon pepper

480 ml (16 fl oz) GF chicken stock

1 egg or egg white

170 g (6 oz) roasted buckwheat

1 precooked roasted rotisserie chicken

DIRECTIONS

1. Melt the butter in a medium saucepan and heat until sizzling.
2. Add the onions, celery and mushrooms and cook until tender. Remove to a bowl.
3. In a small saucepan, add the salt and pepper to the chicken stock and heat to boiling.
4. Lightly beat the egg in a bowl with a whisk or fork.
5. Add the buckwheat to the egg and stir to coat all kernels.
6. In the medium saucepan, add the buckwheat. Cook over high heat for 2 to 3 minutes, stirring constantly until the egg dries on the buckwheat and the kernels separate. Reduce the heat to low.
7. Quickly stir in the boiling stock and add the sautéed vegetables. Cover tightly and simmer for 7 to 10 minutes, or until the kasha kernels are tender and the liquid is absorbed.
8. Slice the chicken and serve with the buckwheat pilaf.

Potatoes with Chorizo and Onions[25]

Rachael Ray, a Food TV personality, specializes in 30-minute meals. She suggests this recipe as a side dish, but it makes a hearty dinner, provided you accompany it with a salad and a vegetable.

Check the list on the packet to make sure the chorizo is gluten-free.

INGREDIENTS

2 tablespoons extra-virgin olive oil

340 g (12 oz) chorizo sausage, very thinly sliced on an angle (peel away any loose casings)

6 small potatoes, very thinly sliced

1 medium onion, very thinly sliced

Salt and pepper, to taste

2 teaspoons sweet ground paprika

1 or 2 handfuls chopped flat-leaf parsley

DIRECTIONS

1. Heat a medium frying pan over medium–high heat.
2. Add enough of the oil to coat the pan in two turns. Add the sausage.
3. Cook for 2 minutes.
4. Flip the sausage and cook for 1 minute longer.
5. Add the potatoes and onion to the pan in an even layer, covering the sausage.
6. Season the potatoes and onion with the salt, pepper and paprika.
7. With a spatula, turn sections of the potatoes so that the chorizo is on top and the potatoes and onion are on the bottom.
8. Place a smaller frying pan on top and press down. Weight the frying pan down with a few heavy tins. This will help the potatoes cook more quickly and brown nicely.
9. Cook for 10 to 12 minutes.
10. Remove the weight and turn again to combine all ingredients.
11. Cook for 3 to 4 minutes longer, and add the parsley.
12. Remove from the heat and serve.

Turkey Skewers with Mango Salsa[26]

Do you like to barbecue? You can prepare this on a mini grill as well as outside on a charcoal or gas barbecue. It makes four or five servings.

INGREDIENTS

1.15 kg (2½ lb) turkey breasts

1 teaspoon crushed garlic

1 teaspoon finely chopped fresh ginger

80 ml (3 fl oz) GF soy sauce

60 ml (2 fl oz) rice vinegar

2 teaspoons sugar

Salt and pepper, to taste

Lime juice

Mango Salsa (page 195)

DIRECTIONS

1. Soak wooden skewers for about 10 minutes so that they will not catch fire on the barbecue.
2. Slice the turkey breasts lengthwise into 5 cm (2 in) slices. Thread the turkey onto the skewers. Set aside.
3. Combine the garlic, ginger, soy sauce, vinegar, sugar, and salt and pepper to taste, in a shallow baking dish.
4. Place the turkey skewers in the marinade and refrigerate, covered, for 60 minutes or overnight. (If you prefer, you can marinate the turkey before skewering it.)
5. Prepare the barbecue.
6. Grill over hot coals for 10 minutes per side, or until done, brushing with the marinade occasionally.
7. Sprinkle with the lime juice before serving.
8. Serve with the mango salsa.

Spicy Sesame Chicken Fajitas[27]

Many Mexican or Tex-Mex dishes call for flour fajitas. An easy substitute is corn tortillas, available in most supermarkets.

The chicken (or turkey, if you prefer) in this recipe can be grilled or fried in a little olive oil. This recipe makes 4 to 6 servings.

INGREDIENTS

1.15 kg (2½ lb) skinless, boneless chicken or turkey breasts

30 g (1 oz) sesame seeds

¼ teaspoon ground chilli powder

Salt to taste

2 tablespoons olive oil (if you prefer to cook the chicken in a frying pan instead of grilling it)

18 corn tortillas

340 g (12 oz) chopped avocado

1 large lettuce, shredded

Mango Salsa (page 195)

480 ml (16 fl oz) soured cream

DIRECTIONS

1. Pound the chicken breasts between two pieces of foil to a thickness of 3 mm (⅛ in). (You want the pieces very thin to cook quickly.)
2. Sprinkle with the sesame seeds, chilli powder and salt before cooking. Press into the meat.
3. Grill for about 1½ minutes on each side, until the pink is just gone from the meat but the meat is still moist. (Or cook in a frying pan with the olive oil.)
4. While the chicken is cooking, warm the tortillas on a baking sheet in a 200°C/400°F/gas 6 oven for about 3 minutes.
5. Remove the cooked chicken from the grill or pan.
6. Cut the chicken into strips.
7. Assemble the fajitas: place about 2 tablespoons of the chicken in the centre of a tortilla. Top with the avocado, lettuce, salsa and soured cream. Fold and serve.

Vegetable and Beef Salad

What do you do with leftover meat from a beef or pork roast? Use the leftovers in this salad, which makes a better cold-served main course than it does a side dish. It can be prepared ahead of time.

INGREDIENTS

90 g (3 oz) GF macaroni

115 g (4 oz) fresh broccoli, cut up

285 g (10 oz) bite-size pieces cooked beef or pork

1 medium carrot, grated

60 g (2 oz) sliced fresh mushrooms

180 ml (6 fl oz) Creamy Cucumber Dressing (below)

75 g (2½ oz) cherry tomato halves or quartered medium tomato

DIRECTIONS

1. Cook the macaroni according to package directions. Do not overcook!
2. Drain the macaroni well in a colander.
3. In a large bowl, combine the macaroni, broccoli, beef or pork, carrot and mushrooms. Toss to mix.
4. Add the dressing. Toss to coat all ingredients.
5. Chill for 30 minutes or overnight.
6. Add the tomatoes when you serve it.

Tip: No beef or pork? Use chicken, turkey or prawns.

Creamy Cucumber Dressing[28]

This simple salad dressing will taste great on just about any salad.

INGREDIENTS

230 g (8 oz) natural or goat's yogurt

½ cucumber, peeled and finely chopped

1 teaspoon fresh lemon juice

1 clove garlic, crushed

½ teaspoon salt

½ teaspoon ground white pepper

DIRECTIONS

1. In a blender, combine the yogurt, cucumber, lemon juice, garlic, salt and pepper.
2. Blend until smooth.
3. Refrigerate until chilled.

White Bean Soup with Ham and Greens[29]

This soup does not take long to prepare, but if you are pressed for time, you can make it a day or two ahead of time; it will keep well in the refrigerator. Serve it with a GF bread and a green salad for an easy, light supper.

INGREDIENTS

2 tablespoons extra-virgin olive oil

230 g (8 oz) chopped country ham or honey-baked ham

1 large onion, finely chopped

2 cloves garlic, crushed

½ teaspoon dried thyme

400 g (14 oz) tin cannellini beans, rinsed and drained

1 litre (1¾ pt) GF chicken stock

2 handfuls chopped, trimmed greens or spinach

Salt and freshly ground black pepper, to taste

DIRECTIONS

1. Heat the oil in a heavy saucepan over medium-high heat.
2. Add the ham, onion, garlic and thyme.
3. Stir well to combine and cook for about 7 minutes, or until the onion is tender and translucent but not browned.
4. Add the beans and chicken stock.
5. Simmer for about 20 minutes.
6. Add the greens and simmer for 8 to 12 minutes, or until the greens are tender and wilted.
7. Season with the salt and pepper to taste. Serve with freshly baked GF bread.

Chicken with Sesame Mangetout in Apricot Sauce[30]

Chicken is a healthy source of protein but if you prepare it often, it could become a little boring. Try this dish to give your healthy dinner new life.

INGREDIENTS

2 teaspoons olive oil

3 cloves garlic, crushed

455 g (1 lb) chicken or 1 medium packet tofu, cubed

1 tablespoon sesame seeds

1 jar (285 g/10 oz) all-fruit apricot preserves

1 tablespoon GF soy sauce

1 tablespoon Dijon mustard or regular mustard

½ teaspoon grated fresh ginger

230 g (8 oz) mangetout, with ends trimmed

DIRECTIONS

1. In a large frying pan, over medium heat, warm the oil.
2. Add the garlic and cook for 1 minute.
3. Add the chicken and cook until no longer pink. (Or add cubed tofu and cook for 2 minutes.)
4. Add the sesame seeds and cook for 2 minutes.
5. Add the apricot preserves, soy sauce, mustard and ginger. Bring to the boil.
6. Reduce the heat to low and simmer for 5 minutes.
7. Add the mangetout and simmer until tender-crisp, about 5 minutes.
8. Serve with rice.

Sautéed Pork over Pasta

Here is another Italian dish to add to your recipe list. It is delicious, and although it looks great when you serve it, it is not terribly difficult to prepare.

INGREDIENTS

455 g (1 lb) lean pork tenderloin

Rice flour (enough to coat the meat)

1 tablespoon olive oil and 4 tablespoons butter (You may use 5 tablespoons of olive oil instead of the olive oil and butter, if you prefer.)

8–10 large mushrooms

120 ml (4 fl oz) Marsala wine

Salt and pepper, to taste

GF penne pasta

Freshly grated Parmesan cheese or cheese substitute

DIRECTIONS

1. Cut the pork into strips.
2. Coat the pork with the rice flour.
3. Pour the oil and butter into a frying pan and heat on medium to high heat.
4. Place the pork in the pan and cook.
5. Add the mushrooms, turning frequently to brown on all sides.
6. When the pork and mushrooms are cooked, turn up the heat and add the wine.
7. Let the alcohol in the wine cook down.
8. Add the salt and pepper, to taste.
9. Cook the pasta. Do not rinse.
10. Place the pasta in the pan with the pork and mushroom mixture.
11. Sprinkle with the cheese.
12. Serve with fresh steamed broccoli.

Wild Rice with Walnuts and Dates[31]

Grill your favourite fish (or a chicken breast), and serve this pilaf-style dish alongside it. It will take time to prepare – approximately 90 minutes total, because wild rice requires more cooking time than white rice does – but the results will be worth it. This makes 6 to 8 side-dish servings.

INGREDIENTS

4 sticks celery, chopped

1 small onion, chopped

1 tablespoon butter or butter substitute

150 g (5½ oz) uncooked wild rice, rinsed and drained

400 ml (14 fl oz) GF chicken or beef stock

240 ml (8 fl oz) water

50 g (1¾ oz) pitted whole dates, chopped

30 g (1 oz) chopped walnuts, toasted

DIRECTIONS

1. In a large frying pan, cook the celery and onion in the butter for 10 minutes, or until tender but not brown.
2. Add the rice. Cook and stir for 3 minutes.
3. Add the stock and water and bring to the boil.
4. Reduce the heat. Cover and simmer for 50 to 60 minutes, or until the rice is tender and most of the liquid is absorbed.
5. Stir in the dates and walnuts.
6. Cook, uncovered, for 3 to 4 minutes, or until the mixture is thoroughly heated and the remaining liquid is absorbed.

Chicken Pepper Steak

If possible, use organic chicken for this colourful dish.

INGREDIENTS

4 tablespoons olive oil

2 large boneless, skinless chicken breasts, cut into chunks

2–3 large red, yellow and green peppers, cut into thick strips

Freshly ground black pepper, to taste

1 tablespoon GF Worcestershire sauce

Jasmine rice

1 large clove garlic, crushed

1 teaspoon sea salt

DIRECTIONS

1. Pour 3 tablespoons of the olive oil into a large frying pan to coat the bottom of the pan.
2. Over medium to high heat, combine the chicken, peppers, ground pepper and Worcestershire sauce and cook for 20 to 30 minutes, or until the chicken is done.
3. Prepare the rice. Follow the packet directions, and add the remaining 1 tablespoon olive oil, the garlic and the salt.
4. Serve the chicken pepper steak over the rice.

Grilled Vegetables[32]

They look and taste gourmet, but they are easy to prepare. The "trick" is to baste the veggies with olive oil and to watch the cooking time. You can use a barbecue or oven grill.

HERE ARE SOME VEGETABLES THAT LEND THEMSELVES TO GRILLING:

- Asparagus spears, whole
- Aubergine, cut into 5 mm (¼ in) slices
- Broccoli spears, cut lengthwise in half
- Carrots, boiled until crisp-tender before grilling

- Cauliflower florets, cut lengthwise in half
- Cherry tomatoes
- Corn on the cob, husked and soaked in water before putting on the grill
- Courgettes, cut into 2 cm (¾ in) pieces
- Mushrooms, whole
- Onions, cut into 1 cm (½ in) slices
- Peppers, cut into large strips
- Potatoes, cut into 2.5 cm (1 in) wedges, partially cooked for 5 to 10 minutes before putting on the grill

DIRECTIONS

1. Heat the coals or oven grill.
2. Grill the vegetables 10–15 cm (4–5 in) from the heat.
3. Brush with olive oil or your favourite homemade salad dressing to add flavour and to keep them from drying out.
4. Cook for 10 to 15 minutes, depending upon the level of doneness you prefer.

GF DESSERTS AND SWEET TREATS

The best desserts are the ones that come straight from Mother Nature – fruits. They are sweet, nonprocessed, ready-to-eat and delicious.

That said, I realize that *once in a while,* you will want to have something other than fruit for dessert. But before you indulge, realize that there is just as much gluten-free junk food available to tempt you as there is non-gluten-free. Please don't substitute one type of junk for another! Prepare and eat snacks and desserts sparingly.

Here are a few sweet treats to show you that you won't be *deprived* living a GF way of life. And for many recipes, you don't have to do anything special – just substitute your favourite GF flour.

These are recipes that were modified to be gluten-free. Remember, though: you can substitute coconut oil in equal amounts for butter in any recipe that calls for butter, if you want to use a healthier fat or are avoiding dairy. And there are many healthier, low-glycaemic index sugar substitutes on the market that are preferable to refined sugar, so you do not have to use sugar in a recipe (see Chapter 14).

Chocolate-Chip Cookies

Who doesn't like chocolate chip cookies? I've discovered that baking them usually only requires a slight adaptation of the recipe: use a plain GF flour mixture and add a teaspoon of xanthan or guar gum. I think you'll be quite pleased with the result.

INGREDIENTS

325 g (11 oz) GF plain flour

1 teaspoon bicarbonate of soda

1 teaspoon xanthan or guar gum

1 teaspoon salt

230 g (8 oz) butter, softened

150 g (5½ oz) granulated sugar

150 g (5½ oz) brown sugar

1 teaspoon vanilla extract

2 eggs

340 g (12 oz) chocolate chips

145 g (5 oz) chopped nuts (optional)

DIRECTIONS

1. Preheat the oven to 190°C/375°F/gas 5.
2. Combine the flour, bicarbonate of soda, xanthan or guar gum, and salt in a small bowl. Set aside.
3. Beat the butter, granulated sugar, brown sugar and vanilla extract in a large mixing bowl.
4. Add the eggs one at a time, beating well after each addition.
5. Gradually add the flour mixture into the butter mixture.
6. Stir in the chocolate chips and nuts, if using.
7. Drop by rounded tablespoonsful onto an ungreased baking sheet. (The cookies will spread out. Smaller dollops are better than large ones.)
8. Bake for 9 to 11 minutes.
9. Let stand for 2 minutes, then remove to a rack to cool completely.
10. Serve with milk or milk substitute.

Yellow Cake [33]

Just because you have gone gluten-free doesn't mean that you have to give your cookbooks away! In most cases, you can follow standard recipes, with minor modifications: for this recipe, I substituted the quinoa featherlight flour mixture for wheat flour, and I added xanthan gum to help the baked goods "stick" together better. I also used soya milk instead of cow's milk.

The quinoa flour and soya milk give the cake a slightly nutty (but delicious!) flavour. Once you find the all-purpose GF flour you like best, try substituting it for "regular" flour in your favourite recipes.

INGREDIENTS

325 g (11 oz) GF plain flour

300 g (10½ oz) sugar

3½ teaspoons baking powder

1 teaspoon salt

3 large eggs

115 g (4 oz) solid vegetable fat, diced

300 ml (10 fl oz) milk or milk substitute

1 teaspoon vanilla extract

Topping of your choice

DIRECTIONS

1. Preheat the oven to 180°C/350°F/gas 4. Grease the bottom and sides of a 32 × 22 cm (13 × 9 in) cake tin or two 22 × 4 cm (9 × 1½ in) round tins, and lightly flour.
2. Mix the flour, sugar, baking powder and salt together in a large bowl. Set aside.
3. Beat the eggs and fat until fluffy.
4. Alternate adding the flour mixture and the milk and vanilla extract to the eggs until all are incorporated.
5. Beat with an electric mixer for 3 minutes, scraping the side of the bowl occasionally.
6. Pour into the cake tin(s).

7. Bake the rectangular tin for 45 to 50 minutes, the round tins for 30 to 35 minutes. Check doneness with a skewer.
8. Remove from the oven and cool on a rack.
9. Ice, if desired. (*Note:* Some prepared icings from the supermarket contain wheat!)

Quinoa Apple Sauce Cake[34]

If you have trouble finding the unsweetened apple sauce used in this recipe try the organic or baby food aisles.

INGREDIENTS

230 g (8 oz) quinoa flour
115 g (4 oz) currants
50 g (1¾ oz) chopped pecans
½ teaspoon bicarbonate of soda
½ teaspoon baking powder
½ teaspoon salt
½ teaspoon ground cloves
115 g (4 oz) unsalted butter
200 g (7 oz) demerara sugar
1 large egg
480 g (17 oz) unsweetened apple sauce or apple purée

DIRECTIONS

1. Preheat the oven to 180°C/350°F/gas 4.
2. Sprinkle 30 g (1 oz) of the flour over the currants and pecans and set aside.
3. Blend the bicarbonate of soda, baking powder, salt and cloves with the remaining flour.
4. In another bowl, mix together the butter, sugar and egg.
5. Combine the flour mixture, the butter mixture and the apple sauce, and add the currants and nuts last.
6. Spoon into a greased 20 cm (8 in) square cake pan and bake for 40 to 45 minutes, or until a skewer inserted into the centre comes out clean.

Traveller's Cereal Snack[35]

When you are travelling, it's almost a necessity to take a snack with you. Here's a gluten-free treat that is healthy, too.

INGREDIENTS

115 g (4 oz) gluten-free crispy corn puff cereal

150 g (5½ oz) peanuts

150 g (5½ oz) raisins

75 g (2½ oz) dried banana chips

3 tablespoons butter or coconut oil

3 tablespoons honey

¾ teaspoon ground cinnamon

½ teaspoon salt

90 g (3 oz) flaked coconut

DIRECTIONS

1. Preheat the oven to 160°C/350°F/gas 3.
2. Mix the cereal, peanuts, raisins and banana chips and place in a large ungreased rectangular baking tray. Set aside.
3. Heat the butter and honey in a saucepan over low heat, until the butter is melted.
4. Stir in the cinnamon and salt.
5. Pour over the cereal mixture, tossing until evenly coated.
6. Bake for 15 minutes, stirring once.
7. Stir in the coconut.
8. Let stand for 5 minutes and loosen from the tray.

Macadamia "Biscuit" Base[36]

Some puddings call for a digestive biscuit base, which is off-limits to gluten-sensitive individuals. But this "biscuit" base is a great substitute. The recipe makes enough for one 22 cm (9 in) base. The best part: it's quick (it takes approximately 5 minutes to prepare and 5 minutes to bake).

INGREDIENTS

170 g (6 oz) macadamia nuts

2 eggs

125 g (4½ oz) soya flour

DIRECTIONS

1. Preheat the oven to 180°C/350°F/gas 4.
2. Place the nuts in a food processor and blend until they reach a peanut butter-like consistency.
3. Scrape into a bowl and stir in the eggs and flour until well blended.
4. Place the dough between two pieces of greaseproof paper.
5. Roll out into a 30 cm (12 in) circle.
6. Remove the top piece of greaseproof paper and invert the dough into a 22 cm (9 in) pie dish or springform cake tin.
7. Press into the bottom and up the side of the plate. Remove any overhanging dough.
8. Bake for 5 minutes, or until light golden brown.
9. Fill with your chosen topping or filling.

GF Sweet Pastry Case[37]

Would you like to have a fruit pie with Sunday dinner? Here's a recipe for a pastry case. Just fill with your favourite fruit filling and bake.

INGREDIENTS

230 g (8 oz) butter or coconut oil

250 g (9 oz) sugar

4 eggs

250 g (9 oz) rice flour

75 g (2½ oz) sweet rice flour (from an Oriental market or use rice flour)

1 teaspoon xanthan gum

1½ teaspoons baking powder

¼ teaspoon salt

1 teaspoon vanilla extract

DIRECTIONS

1. Cream together the butter, sugar and eggs.
2. Add the flours, xanthan gum, baking powder, salt and vanilla extract.
3. Mix well and spread about 5 mm (¼ in) deep on the bottom and sides of an 20 cm (8 in) pie dish. A deep dish is best, because this crust takes a little more room than regular pastry cases.
4. Fill shell immediately with your chosen fruit filling, and bake according to the fruit pie recipe you're using.

Lime Sherbet

If you have an ice cream maker, you can prepare this sherbet using milk or a milk substitute.

INGREDIENTS

725 ml (26 fl oz) milk or milk substitute

240 ml (8 fl oz) lime juice cordial

3 tablespoons sweetener of your choice

DIRECTIONS

1. Combine the milk, lime juice and sweetener in a blender or food processor.
2. Pour the mixture into the ice cream maker, following manufacturer's instructions.
3. Mix until iced.
4. You can eat this immediately, or you can "age" it for a deeper flavour.

Tip: Substitute orange juice or lemonade for a variety of flavours.

CHAPTER 16

GIVE ME BREAD!

If I were to take a poll that asked gluten-sensitive people, "What do you miss on a gluten-free diet?" the answer would come back unanimously: *bread*.

We know that "man cannot live by bread *alone*". But it's hard to live *without* bread. You can take gluten out of almost all food and not miss it – except for bread. Bread as we have grown to know it and love it has a taste and texture unique to wheat flour. (Even speciality breads, such as potato, rye and pumpernickel use wheat flour as a base.)

If you have purchased GF bread at the health food store, you have probably been disappointed. It is often dry or crumbly and lacks much taste.

The alternative is to bake your own bread. You may still hunger for the taste of wheat bread, but the bread you bake will tantalize you as it comes out of the oven or bread-making machine.

Many people avoid baking (regular) bread from scratch because of the time and effort. Bread-making machines have made baking bread simple – especially when packet mixes are used.

The good news for GF bread bakers is that baking GF bread is actually easier than baking wheat bread. The easiest – but rather pricey – way to bake is to use a packet bread mix (available in health food stores or online). A better alternative: bake your bread from scratch.

If you have a bread-making machine, use it! But if you don't have one, you can still bake bread without a lot of effort.

So, what are you waiting for? Gather your ingredients and get to work. In a couple of hours, your mouth will start watering as the scent of baking bread fills your kitchen.

FLOUR MIXES

If bread baking becomes a weekly routine, I recommend mixing large batches of all-purpose baking flour.

Most bakers agree that a mixture of several different types of flours produces the best results. Here are three different flour mixtures:

Bette's Featherlight Rice Flour Mix[1]

This rice flour mix produces bread that has a nice light texture. The rice flour gives the lightness; the tapioca flour and cornflour help bind, and the potato flour helps keep moisture in the baked goods. This recipe makes approximately 1.5 kg (3 lb 5 oz) of flour.

INGREDIENTS

500 g (1 lb 2 oz) rice flour

320 g (11 oz) tapioca flour

500 g (1 lb 2 oz) cornflour

4 tablespoons potato flour (This is potato flour, not potato starch!)

DIRECTIONS

Thoroughly mix or sift all ingredients and keep in a dry area.

Quinoa Featherlight Flour Mix

I especially like this flour mix, because of quinoa's slightly nutty flavour. If you can't source quinoa flour you can grind your own in a blender from whole quinoa.

INGREDIENTS

500 g (1 lb 2 oz) quinoa flour

320 g (11 oz) tapioca flour

500 g (1 lb 2 oz) cornflour

4 tablespoons potato flour

DIRECTIONS

Mix or sift all ingredients and store in a dry container.

Cole's Flour Blend[2]

This flour blend can be used in any bread recipe. It combines a number of different flours – rice, sweet rice, garfava, tapioca, amaranth, buckwheat, sorghum and quinoa. A number of these flours – namely the garfava and sorghum – are very difficult to find outside the US, but you can make up for their absence by increasing the amount of one (or more) of the other flours.

INGREDIENTS

200 g (7 oz) brown rice flour

100 g (3½ oz) potato starch (not potato flour)

50 g (1¾ oz) white rice flour

50 g (1¾ oz) sweet rice flour

30 g (1 oz) garfava flour

30 g (1 oz) tapioca flour (same as tapioca starch or tapioca starch flour)

30 g (1 oz) amaranth flour

30 g (1 oz) white buckwheat flour

30 g (1 oz) sorghum flour

30 g (1 oz) quinoa flour

4 teaspoons xanthan gum or guar gum

DIRECTIONS

Sift each flour several times to reduce sticking. Mix all ingredients and store in a dry container.

Tip: You may wish to omit the xanthan gum or guar gum until you are ready to bake your bread, then add in the amount that the recipe calls for (in proportion to the amount of flour). By omitting this ingredient, the flour mixture can be used as a plain flour for other baked goods.

BREAD RECIPES

Although we usually think of "bread" as a loaf that we slice up to use in sandwiches, bread includes rolls, crusty loaves and even pizza crust!

Baking GF bread requires some experimentation – mainly with the flour mixture. When you find a flour mixture that you like, substitute it for the ones in the following recipes.

Here are recipes for several types of breads.

Basic Featherlight Rice or Quinoa Bread[3]

This recipe will make a medium-size loaf.

INGREDIENTS

340 g (12 oz) featherlight rice flour mix or quinoa flour mix (page 220)

2¼ teaspoons xanthan gum

1½ teaspoons unflavoured gelatine

1½ teaspoons egg substitute

¾ teaspoon salt

3 tablespoons sugar

40 g (1¼ oz) dried milk powder or nondairy substitute

2¼ teaspoons dry yeast granules

1 egg plus 2 whites

4½ tablespoons butter, cut into chunks, or coconut oil

¾ teaspoon cider vinegar or white wine vinegar

3 teaspoons honey or molasses

350 ml (12 fl oz) water

DIRECTIONS

1. Grease the bread tin(s) and dust with rice flour.
2. Combine the dry ingredients in a medium bowl and set aside.
3. In another bowl, or the bowl of your mixer, whisk the egg and egg whites, butter, vinegar and honey until blended.
4. Add most of the water to the egg mixture. Add the remaining water, as needed, after you start mixing the bread.
5. For hand mixing, turn the mixer on low and add the dry ingredients a little at a time and mix well.

6. Check to make sure the dough is the consistency of cake batter. Add more water, as necessary.
7. Turn the mixer to high and beat for 3½ minutes.
8. Spoon into the prepared tin(s), cover, and let rise in a warm place for about 35 minutes for rapid-rising yeast, or 60 or more minutes for regular yeast, until the dough reaches the top of the tin.
9. Preheat the oven to 200°C/400°F/gas 6. Bake for 50 to 60 minutes, covering with foil after 10 minutes.
10. For a bread machine: place the ingredients in the machine in the order suggested in the manual.
11. Use the setting for medium crust.

Tip: This basic featherlight recipe is excellent. But if you find it is a little bland, increase the salt to 1 teaspoon. And for even more flavour, add 1 teaspoon coconut or almond extract.

Basic GF Bread[4]

This recipe does not specify the type of GF flour mixture to use – select one that appeals to you. I suggest that you try various bread recipes to find the one that you like best.

INGREDIENTS

3 eggs
1 teaspoon vinegar
60 ml (2 fl oz) olive oil
270 ml (9 fl oz) water
455 g (1 lb) GF flour mix
3 tablespoons sugar
1½ teaspoons salt
75 g (2½ oz) dried milk powder or milk substitute
2¼ teaspoons active dry yeast

DIRECTIONS

1. Combine the eggs, vinegar, oil and water in a mixing bowl. Mix well and set aside.
2. Combine the flour mix, sugar, salt, dried milk powder and yeast in another bowl and mix well.

3. Slowly add the flour mixture to the egg mixture, stirring constantly.

4. Beat for 5 to 7 minutes with a mixer or vigorously by hand to ensure complete mixing. The dough will be the consistency of very thick cake batter.

5. Place the dough in a lightly greased bowl, cover and set in a warm place.

6. Allow the dough to rise until it's about double in size. Punch the dough down and fold into a bread tin coated with nonstick cooking spray.

7. Smooth out any bumps on top of the dough ball.

8. Cover and allow to rise until it's about double.

9. Preheat the oven to 190°C/375°F/gas 5. Bake for 35 minutes.

10. Cover the top of the bread with foil and bake for 20 minutes longer.

Tips: This recipe also works well in bread machines. Set to normal cycle, large loaf size, and follow the directions for your machine.

Egg Bread Loaf[5]

This is not a sandwich bread (it's too crumbly), but it tastes great and makes wonderful toast or can be eaten fresh out of the oven with your dinner. It is fairly fast and easy to prepare.

INGREDIENTS

50 g (1¾ oz) solid vegetable fat or coconut oil

3 tablespoons honey

2 eggs

230 g (8 oz) natural yogurt or soured cream

1 teaspoon vinegar

1 packet yeast (about 1 tablespoon)

75 g (2½ oz) potato starch

190 g (6½ oz) cornflour

½ teaspoon bicarbonate of soda

1 tablespoon baking powder

2 teaspoons xanthan gum

¼ teaspoon salt

DIRECTIONS

1. Preheat the oven to 180°C/350°F/gas 4.
2. Grease a loaf tin and set aside.
3. In a large bowl, combine the oil, honey, eggs, yogurt and vinegar. With an electric mixer, combine well to remove all lumps.
4. Gradually add the yeast, potato starch, cornflour, bicarbonate of soda, baking powder, xanthan gum and salt. Mix by hand. The dough will be quite wet.
5. Place the dough in the prepared tin, and smooth the top with your wet hands.
6. Bake for 40 to 45 minutes, or until the loaf is lightly browned and a wooden pick inserted in the middle comes out clean.

Dinner Rolls[6]

INGREDIENTS

2 large eggs

¾ teaspoon cider vinegar

3 tablespoons olive oil

240 ml (8 fl oz) very warm water

200 g (7 oz) white rice flour

50 g (1¾ oz) potato starch

40 g (1¼ oz) tapioca flour

30 g (1 oz) cornflour

2 tablespoons sugar

2 teaspoons xanthan gum

1 teaspoon salt

60 g (2 oz) dried milk powder

2¼ teaspoons dry yeast

DIRECTIONS

1. In a large bowl, mix the eggs, vinegar, oil and water.
2. In a separate bowl, combine the rice flour, potato starch, tapioca flour, cornflour, sugar, xanthan gum, salt, dried milk powder and yeast.

3. Add the flour mixture to the egg mixture a little at a time and mix well. The dough should be stiffer than a cake batter.
4. If the dough appears to be too dry, add water, 1 tablespoon at a time.
5. Spoon the dough into a 12-hole muffin tin coated with non-stick cooking spray.
6. Preheat the oven to 180°C/350°F/gas 4.
7. Let the dough rise approximately 30 minutes on top of the warm oven, or until the dough doubles in size.
8. Bake for 20 to 25 minutes.

Pizza Crust[7]

This crispy pizza crust tastes delicious and imitates "real" pizza crust so well that no one will guess it is gluten-free. The recipe makes one large pizza crust or four small individual pizzas.

INGREDIENTS

1 tablespoon GF dry yeast

100 g (3½ oz) brown rice flour or bean flour

50 g (1¾ oz) tapioca flour

2 tablespoons dried milk powder or nondairy milk powder

2 teaspoons xanthan gum

½ teaspoon salt

1 teaspoon unflavoured gelatine powder

1 teaspoon Italian herb seasoning

160 ml (5½ fl oz) warm water (105°F)

½ teaspoon sugar or ¼ teaspoon honey

1 teaspoon olive oil

1 teaspoon cider vinegar

DIRECTIONS

1. Preheat the oven to 220°C/425°F/gas 7.
2. In a medium mixer bowl using regular beaters (not dough hooks), blend the yeast, flours, milk powder, xanthan gum, salt, gelatine powder and Italian herb seasoning on low speed.

3. Add the water, sugar, oil and vinegar.

4. Beat on high speed for 3 minutes. (*Tip:* If the mixer bounces around the bowl, the dough is too stiff. Add water, if necessary, 1 tablespoon at a time, until the dough does not resist the beaters.)

5. The dough will resemble soft bread dough. (You can also mix it in a bread machine on the dough setting.)

6. Put the mixture onto a baking sheet (for thin, crispy crust), or a 27 × 17 cm (11 × 7 in) cake tin or shallow dish (for a deep-dish version) that has been coated with nonstick cooking spray.

7. Liberally sprinkle rice flour onto the dough, then press the dough into the tin, continuing to sprinkle the dough with flour to prevent it from sticking to your hands.

8. Make the edges slightly higher to contain toppings.

9. Bake for 10 minutes.

10. Remove from the oven.

11. Spread the pizza crust with sauce (below) and toppings.

12. Bake for 20 to 25 minutes longer, or until the top is nicely browned.

Pizza Sauce

Prepare this fat-free sauce while the pizza crust bakes. It fills the kitchen with a delicious aroma.

INGREDIENTS

230 g (8 oz) chopped tinned tomatoes or passata

½ teaspoon dried oregano

½ teaspoon dried basil

½ teaspoon dried rosemary

½ teaspoon fennel seeds

¼ teaspoon garlic granules

2 teaspoons sugar or 1 teaspoon honey (optional)

½ teaspoon salt

DIRECTIONS

1. Combine the chopped tomatoes or passata, oregano, basil, rosemary, fennel, garlic granules, sugar and salt in a small saucepan and bring to the boil over medium heat.
2. Reduce the heat to low and simmer for 15 minutes (Letting it simmer for 15 minutes thickens the sauce, so it won't make the pizza crust soggy.)
3. Top a pizza crust with the sauce and your favourite toppings.

CHAPTER 17

A 14-DAY GF DIET

In the previous chapters in this section, you found mouthwatering recipes that could appeal to you, no matter what level of cooking skill (or interest) you currently have. And you found some recipes for delicious breads. (Don't overdo these, though! This is an ideal time to eat healthy to help your body get well as fast as possible – and then stay well.) So, this chapter aims to provide you with information and tips on healthy eating.

GF "FRIENDLY" FOODS

When you are planning your daily menus, select a variety of proteins, vegetables, salads, GF carbohydrates and fruits. Here is a list of a wide variety of foods from which to select and incorporate into your recipes and meals.

Protein Foods

- Chicken and turkey (without the skin)
- Eggs or egg whites
- Fat-free yogurt, natural
- Fresh fish (salmon, tuna, sardines, flounder, mullet, trout, etc.)
- Lean veal
- Milk and milk substitutes
- Red meats, such as beef, pork, lamb or venison (once or twice a week, as you choose)
- Reduced-fat cheese

- Reduced-fat soya cheese
- Seafood (prawns, scallops, mussels, clams, calamari, octopus, etc.)
- Tinned tuna, salmon, mackerel or sardines (packed in water)
- Tofu, firm or soft

Vegetables and Salad Greens

- Alfalfa sprouts
- Artichokes
- Asparagus
- Aubergine
- Bean sprouts
- Beetroot
- Broccoli
- Brussels sprouts
- Cabbage (red or white)
- Carrots
- Cauliflower
- Celery
- Courgette
- Cucumbers
- Endive
- Green beans
- Hot peppers
- Kale
- Leeks
- Lettuce (all types)
- Mangetout
- Mushrooms
- Okra
- Olives (limit to 5)

- Onions
- Pak choi
- Parsley
- Peppers (red, green, or yellow)
- Radishes
- Rocket
- Sauerkraut (no sugar added)
- Spinach
- Squash, yellow
- Tomato juice (no salt)
- Tomato purée
- Vegetable juice
- Water chestnuts
- Watercress

Carbohydrates

- Beans (black, chickpeas, kidney, haricot, broad, soya)
- Buckwheat (pearled, hulled, roasted)
- Corn
- GF breads
- GF pastas
- Green peas
- Lentils
- Potatoes
- Quinoa
- Rice (white or brown)
- Rice noodles
- Wild rice
- Winter squash (acorn, butternut)
- Yams or sweet potatoes

Fruits

- Apples
- Apricots
- Bananas
- Berries (blueberries, strawberries, raspberries, blackberries)
- Cantaloupe melon
- Cherries
- Currants
- Dates
- Figs
- Grapefruit
- Grapes
- Guava
- Honeydew melon
- Kiwi fruit
- Kumquats
- Lemons
- Lychees
- Mandarin oranges
- Mangoes
- Nectarines
- Oranges
- Papayas
- Peaches
- Pears
- Pineapples
- Plums
- Pomegranates
- Raisins
- Watermelon

Seasonings

- GF stock/bouillon (chicken, vegetable, beef)
- GF soy sauce or tamari sauce
- Lemon juice, vinegar
- Natural extracts (vanilla, almond, orange)
- Spices and herbs (allspice, basil, bay leaf, cardamom, cinnamon, cloves, cumin, curry, dill, fennel, garlic, horseradish, mace, marjoram, mint, mustard, nutmeg, oregano, paprika, parsley, pepper, rosemary, saffron, sage, tarragon, thyme, turmeric)

Special-Occasion Foods

I recognize that from time to time, you may want a treat, such as ice cream, a GF biscuit, GF cake, or even french fries. Special treats are okay – as long as you don't overdo them! Please do not substitute GF "junk" in place of processed foods that you were eating regularly. Take this opportunity to eat healthy to get healthy.

14-Day GF Diet

We provided you with recipes to show you that you *can* eat well on a GF diet. Now, I'd like to give you a 14-day diet to get you started. Mix and match to satisfy your taste buds.

Here are some suggestions about how to use the meal-selection chart in this chapter:

1. **Review the food lists above.** You will find many protein, vegetable, carbohydrate and fruit choices. Substitute whatever you like into any menu or recipe.

2. **Eat your favourites frequently.** Who says you have to eat a different menu every day? If you like a particular meal, feel free to have it more frequently. But it is better to rotate your foods and not eat the same thing all the time.

3. **Don't be stuck on conformities!** You can eat breakfast for dinner and lunch for breakfast! The kind of food we eat at a particular time of day is convention – nothing more.

4. **Don't forget to check out Chapter 14.** This is where you will find many substitutes for cheese and milk, if you also choose to go dairy-free.

5. **Order sauces on the side.** When in doubt while eating out, get your sauces on the side.

6. **Add a salad and/or a vegetable to *any* meal.** And for dessert or a snack, eat fruit.

7. **Experiment with herbs.** Herbs and spices perk up your food. Many have "hidden" health benefits. Don't be afraid to use them liberally.

8. **Think tomato.** Use tomato sauces, salsa and other sauces that are gluten-free to perk up your food.

9. **Drink plenty of water throughout the day.** Avoid tap water. You can also have coffee (if it agrees with you), tea, herbal tea and juice. I would recommend smaller amounts of juice, diluted with sparkling mineral water or still water – usually half juice, half water. Keep away from fizzy drinks (both diet and regular) or any other intensely sweetened beverage.

10. **Plan ahead.** This is extremely important, especially when eating gluten-free for the first time, to make sure you have everything you need. It's also important to plan ahead when eating out. Familiarize yourself with local menus and substitutions. If you frequent a particular restaurant, ask if the cook would prepare a GF pasta that you provide or warm your GF bread.

TRAVELLING? HERE'S WHAT TO DO

One of the biggest fears that individuals with gluten sensitivity harbour is eating out. Their first thought is that there will be nothing that they can order, unless the restaurant has a special GF menu. Their second fear is that someone will "slip" them some gluten.

I am gluten-sensitive, and I can assure you that you *can* eat out! And if you communicate with your waiter and the chef, the problems you encounter will be minimal. Restaurants are very accommodating. Tell your waiter you have a "wheat allergy". You will be amazed. You will find that the waiter (or at least the manager) will steer you away from items containing (or possibly containing) gluten. And they will advise the chef to prepare foods without gluten.

That said, here are some other tips on eating out, especially when you are travelling on holiday or business.

1. **Add a salad or vegetables.** Substitute these for the french fries or crisps that are often served as an accompaniment.

2. **Eat lunch for breakfast.** You can usually find eggs and potatoes on breakfast menus, and they make good choices (especially if you don't have any GF bread with you). But think outside of the breakfast box! Nothing says that you cannot have chicken, turkey or any other protein for breakfast, along with a salad and/or vegetables.

3. **Take GF bread.** If you have bread, you can find a deli counter and buy enough turkey to make a sandwich. All supermarkets have bagged salad, carrots and other vegetables that you can eat as snacks or add to a "takeaway" meal.

4. **Eat fruit.** You can find fresh fruit in any corner shop or supermarket. Eat it as a snack or add it to your meal as an easy dessert.

5. **Carry unsalted nuts.** They make a good snack and can be purchased almost anywhere.

6. **Ask about sauces.** When dining out, ask about the ingredients in the sauce. It's unlikely that tomato sauce will have gluten in it. *Tip:* Most Chinese restaurants will steam your food without any sauce.

7. **Take your own GF soy sauce.** Carry a small container of GF soy sauce with you when you intend to go to an Oriental restaurant.

8. **Enjoy "real" ethnic food!** Sure, the breads and pasta are tempting. But Italian restaurants offer many other fine items that you can eat, such as grilled fish, prawns and meat. If you can tolerate milk products, order risotto; if not, ask for rice. Mexican restaurants usually offer corn tortillas. You can order all types of dishes prepared with beans, rice, salad and vegetables. Avoid soured cream and cheese if you are eating dairy-free, but ask if the restaurant offers nondairy alternatives; many do. Middle Eastern menus offer a lot of protein, salads and vegetables, including items such as hummus (avoid the pitta bread) and stuffed vine leaves.

Breakfast: Week 1

DAY 1	DAY 2	DAY 3	
• Egg omelette with onions, tomatoes, mushrooms • Add potatoes, sweet potatoes or yams to the omelette or have GF toast • Fresh fruit of your choice	• Quinoa Flakes Hot Cereal (Page 170) • Fresh strawberries • Milk of your choice	• Buckwheat pancakes • Fresh blueberries • Natural maple syrup or all-fruit jam	

Breakfast: Week 2 (See Chapter 15 for recipes)

• Hot Buckwheat Breakfast Cereal (Page 169)	• Almond Butter and Banana Toast (Page 165)	• Orange Pink-Grapefruit Smoothie (Page 164)	

Lunch: Week 1

• Tuna or chicken salad made with low-fat mayonnaise, chopped celery and carrots • Romaine lettuce, radish, tomato • GF bread	• Grilled venison burger with onion and tomato • Steamed broccoli • GF burger bun	• Grilled prawns • Mixed green salad with vegetable • Grilled courgettes	

Lunch: Week 2 (See Chapter 15 for recipes)

• Turkey and Bacon Lettuce Wrap (Page 178)	• Chef's Salad to Go (Page 178)	• Open-Faced Toasted Tuna Salad with Cheese (Page 179)	

Dinner: Week 1

• Baked red mullet with onion, cherry tomatoes, red potatoes, extra-virgin olive oil • Mixed salad • Baked yam or sweet potato	• GF penne pasta • Tomato sauce • Grilled prawns • Grilled vegetables: courgette, onion, red and green peppers	• Grilled chicken breast • Steamed broccoli, mangetout, carrots • Butternut squash	

Dinner: Week 2 (See Chapter 15 for recipes. Add salad and/or vegetables to all meals.)

• Vegetable and Beef Salad (Page 206)	• White Bean Soup with Ham and Greens (Page 207)	• Grilled Salmon with Mustard Sauce (Page 200)	

DAY 4	DAY 5	DAY 6	DAY 7
• Egg omelette with courgette, broccoli, onion • Add potatoes or sweet potatoes to the omelette or enjoy GF toast	• Low-fat cheese melted on GF bread with a slice of tomato • Fresh fruit on the side	• GF cereal (hot or cold) • Raspberries and/or raisins • Milk of your choice	• Low-fat or fat-free unsweetened yogurt • Cucumber, radish, green and red peppers, onion • GF bread
• Turkey on Toast (Page 163)	• Goat's Cheese Omelette (Page 168)	• Cooked rice cereal	• Baked Herb Cheese Omelette (Page 169)
• Roast chicken (or meat of your choice) • Steamed mangetout, cabbage and carrots • Baked or boiled sweet potato	• Grilled salmon • Mixed salad • Lentils and brown rice	• Chicken breast breaded in GF flour or breadcrumbs and baked in the oven (you can also melt cheese of your choice over it) • Mixed salad • GF pasta with tomato sauce	• Grilled scallops • Steamed asparagus • Acorn squash
• Chicken Salad Sandwich (Page 184)	• Egg Salad Sandwich (Page 181)	• Asian Salad and Dressing (Page 184)	• Turkey sandwich
• Grilled salmon with lemon and herbs • Mixed salad • Wild rice	• (Chinese takeaway) Steamed prawn with Chinese vegetables • Rice (brown or white) • GF soy sauce	• (Italian restaurant) Veal or chicken pizaiola • Tricoloured salad with rocket, radicchio, endive • Roasted potatoes • Spinach with garlic and olive oil	• (Mexican restaurant) Chicken fajitas with corn tortillas • Beans • Guacamole, pico de gallo • Rice
• Pad Thai with Vegetables (Page 196)	• Sautéed pork or veal over gluten-free pasta	• Turkey Skewers with Mango Salsa (Page 204)	• Spicy Chicken Sesame Fajitas (Page 205)

HELPFUL RESOURCES FOR GLUTEN-FREE LIVING

Many of the sites listed below include links to other gluten-free suppliers

INFORMATION, SUPPORT AND ADVOCACY

Coeliac UK
www.coeliac.co.uk
This charity for people with coeliac disease and dermatitis herpetiformis offers information on gluten-free living, including food lists and contact details for stockists of gluten-free food. They campaign to raise awareness of coeliac disease and offer advice and support to people with the disease, including a listing of support groups throughout the UK.

CORE – The Digestive Disorders Foundation
www.digestivedisorders.org.uk
CORE offers information on a range of digestive disorders, including gluten intolerance. Their website provides useful, downloadable fact-sheets.

The Coeliac Society of Australia
www.coeliac.org.au
The Coeliac Society provides information on coeliac disease and advice on following a gluten-free diet. Each state has its own sub-chapter of the society, which can provide further information and support, including information on eating out.

The Coeliac Society of New Zealand
www.coeliac.co.nz
This society promotes the welfare of children and adults with coeliac disease as well as other people who are following a gluten-free diet. Their website includes information on eating out, a list of food manufacturers and advice on following a gluten-free diet.

Gluten Sensitivity/Coeliac Support Group (South Africa)
www.labspec.co.za/coelic/index.htm
A support group, started by a sufferer, which provides information on the condition, a diet related to South African products, and information on relevant medical articles.

FOOD

Gluten-Free Foods
www.glutenfree-foods.co.uk
This online shop offers a range of gluten-free products, including biscuits, breads and flour.

Gluten-Free Foods Direct
www.glutenfreefoodsdirect.co.uk
This online shop offers a full range of gluten-free foods, including international foods.

G-Free
www.gfree.co.uk
The G-Free site sells a range of gluten-free breads, cakes and ready-roll pastry, and also features a selection of gluten-free recipes.

Leeoras Gluten-Free Ready Meals
www.leeoras.co.uk
Leeoras produces vegetarian gluten-free meals and gourmet foods.

Nutrition Point
www.nutritionpoint.co.uk
Nutrition Point manufactures and sells a range of gluten-free foods.

TruFree
www.trufree.co.uk
TruFree produces a range of gluten-free products, including pasta, breads and desserts. Their products are stocked by major supermarkets and health food stores in the UK.

Doves Farm Gluten Free
www.dovesfarm-glutenfree.co.uk
This useful site includes information on the Doves Farm gluten-free products as well as recipes and general information on the gluten protein and gluten intolerance.

Glutafin
www.glutafin.co.uk
Glutafin produces a range of gluten-free products including breads and baked products.

Village Bakery
www.villagebakery.com
The Village Bakery bakes gluten-free bread made to Codex standards, as well as conventional bread, for purchase online.

Goodness Direct
www.goodnessdirect.co.uk
This online shop offers a range of natural and organic products and has a special section for gluten-free food and drink.

Gluten-Free Shop, Australia
www.glutenfreeshop.com.au
This online shop delivers throughout Australia and offers a range of products, including breads, pastries, beer and more.

Gluten-Free Favourites, Australia
www.glutenfreefavourites.com.au
Everything from baby food to cosmetics, all gluten-free and delivered throughout Australia.

Gluten-Free Foods, Australia

www.glutenfreefoods.com.au

This shop, based in Mornington, Victoria, has a mail-order service. They stock breads, pies, small goods and more.

Gluten-Free Goodies, New Zealand

www.glutenfreegoodies.co.nz

This New Zealand-based company offers a range of gluten-free baked products and bread mixes.

The Gluten-Free Shop, New Zealand

www.glutenfree.co.nz

This New Zealand-based online shop offers a wide range of gluten-free products. They also offer bespoke gluten-free gift boxes.

Glutenex, South Africa

www.glutenex.co.za

Provides a range of everyday gluten-free foods including breads, biscuits and snacks.

GLUTEN-FREE BEER

Green's Gluten-Free Beers

www.glutenfreebeers.co.uk

Green's produces a range of gluten-free beers, which are available to buy online.

O'Brien Brewing, Australia

www.obrienbrewing.com.au

This Australian producer sells gluten-free beer through their website and at stockists throughout Australia.

The Twisted Hop, New Zealand

www.thetwistedhop.co.nz

This retailer can deliver O'Brien's gluten-free beer to addresses throughout New Zealand.

GLUTEN-FREE TRAVEL AND DINING

Gluten-Free-Onthego

www.gluten-free-onthego.com

This searchable directory, run by Coeliac UK, provides details of restaurants, cafes and hotels that can cater to a gluten-free diet.

Gluten-Free Travel, Australia

www.glutenfreetravel.com.au

Information on hotels that cater for gluten-intolerant travellers.

ONLINE FORUMS

www.coeliac.info/suppboard/index.php

General information on gluten sensitivity, plus recipes and advice.

http://members2.boardhost.com/glutenfree/

This discussion board includes questions and advice regarding gluten sensitivity and coeliac disease.

SUPPLEMENTS

Worldwidehealthcenter.net

www.worldwidehealthcenter.net

This website sells a wide range of natural health products and supplements and, as its name suggests, it delivers to the UK and worldwide. It supplies Culturelle, the product that promotes health gut flora.

The Nutri Centre

www.nutricentre.com

Based in London, the nutri centre stocks a very wide range of products, including S. boulardii and phosphatidylcholine.

Complete Health

www.completehealth.com.au

This online shop, based in Australia, stocks a wide range of supplements including S. boulardii (under the BioCenticals SB FlorActiv brand name).

Introduction

1 C. Matteoni, et al., "Celiac Disease Is Highly Prevalent in Lymphocytic Colitis", *Journal of Clinical Gastroenterology,* March 2001, 32(3):25-227.

Chapter 1

1 Marion Zarkadas, et al., "Celiac Disease and the Gluten-Free Diet: An Overview", *Topics in Clinical Nutrition,* April/June 2005, 20(2):127-38.

2 A. Fasano, and C. Catassi, "Current Approaches to Diagnosis and Treatment of Celiac Disease: An Evolving Spectrum", *Gastroenterology* 120 (2001): 636-51.

3 A. Rostom, "Incidence and Prevalence of Celiac Disease", NIH Consensus Development Conference on Celiac Disease, June 28-30, 2004, http://consensus.nih.gov/2004/ 2004CeliacDisease118html.htm (accessed January 2,8, 2006).

4 A. Fasano, and C. Catassi, "Current Approaches to Diagnosis and Treatment of Celiac Disease: An Evolving Spectrum", *Gastroenterology* 120 (2001): 636-51.

5 Alessio Fasano, et al., "Prevalence of Celiac Disease in At-Risk and Not-at-Risk Groups in the United States", *Archives of Internal Medicine* 163 (February 10, 2003): 286.

6 Kenneth Fine, "Early Diagnosis of Gluten Sensitivity: Before the Villi Are Gone", www. enterolab.com/essay/.

7 Kenneth Fine, "Early Diagnosis of Gluten Sensitivity: Before the Villi Are Gone", www. enterolab.com/essay/.

8 J. O'Keefe, and L. Cordain, "Cardiovascular Disease Resulting from a Diet and Lifestyle at Odds with Our Paleolithic Genome: How to Become a 21st-Century Hunter-Gatherer", *Mayo Clinic Proceedings* (2004): 79:101-8.

9 "History of Grains", *The Whole Grain,* University of Minnesota, www.wholegrain.umn. edu/history/index.cfm.

10 *Nutrient Content of the U.S. Food Supply, 1909-2000,* Economic Research Service, U.S. Department of Agriculture, p. 20.

11 S. Eaton, and L. Cordain, "Evolutionary Aspects of Diet: Old Genes, New Fuels", *World Review of Nutrition and Dietetics* (Basel, Karger, 1997): 81:27.

12 "About Dr. Weston A. Price", Weston A. Price Foundation for Wise Traditions, www. westonaprice.org.

13 Samantha Flower, "Nutritional Therapy, Learning from Native Cultures", The Kevala Centre, www.kevala.co.uk (accessed December 17, 2005).

14 Jimaima Lako, "Dietary Trends and Diabetes: Its Association among Indigenous Fijians 1952 to 1994", *Asia Pacific Journal of Clinical Nutrition* 10 (September 2001): 183.

15 J. O'Keefe, and L. Cordain, "Cardiovascular Disease Resulting from a Diet and Lifestyle at Odds with Our Paleolithic Genome: How to Become a 21st-Century Hunter-Gatherer", *Mayo Clinic Proceedings* (2004): 79:101-8.

16 Karen Michel, "Native Americans Discuss a Return to Traditional Natural Foods to Combat Health Problems", *The Washington Post*, September 22, 2004, republished by Organic Consumers Association, www.organicconsumers.org (accessed December 28, 2005).

17 Brenda Norrel, "Leading Degenerative Diseases in Indian Country Can Be Fought with Healthy Diets", *Indian Country Today*, March 1, 2005.

18 "Diabetes Statistics for Native Americans", American Diabetes Association, www.diabetes. org/diabetes-statistics/native-americans.jsp (accessed December 28, 2005).

19 "Diabetes Statistics for Native Americans", American Diabetes Association, www.diabetes. org/diabetes-statistics/native-americans.jsp (accessed December 28, 2005).

Chapter 3

1 The Dermatitis Herpetiformis Online Community, www.dermatitisherpetiformis.org.uk/ whatisdh.html (accessed July 17, 2005).

2 American Osteopathic College of Dermatology (AOCD), Dermatologic Disease Database, Dermatitis Herpetiformis, www.aocd.org/skin/dermatologic_diseases/dermatitis_herpeti. html (accessed August 20, 2005).

3 American Osteopathic College of Dermatology (AOCD), Dermatologic Disease Database, Dermatitis Herpetiformis, www.aocd.org/skin/dermatologic_diseases/dermatitis_herpeti. html (accessed August 20, 2005).

4 The Dermatitis Herpetiformis Online Community, www.dermatitisherpetiformis.org.uk/ whatisdh.html.

5 Medline Plus, U.S. National Library of Medicine and National Institutes of Health, www. nlm.nih.gov/medlineplus/druginfo/medmaster/a601102.html (accessed August 22, 2005).

6 National Institute of Neurological Disorders and Stroke (NINDS), NINDS Shingles Information Page, www.ninds.nih.gov/disorders/shingles/shingles_pr.htm (accessed July 24, 2005).

7 The Net Doctor, www.netdoctor.co.uk/medicines/100001109.html (accessed August 20, 2005).

8 Lionel Fry, MD, "What Is DH?" *Crossed Grain*, summer 2001, reprinted with permission on the Dermatitis Herpetiformis Online Community, www.dermatitisherpetiformis.org. uk/whatisdh.html (accessed August 25, 2005).

9 G. Michaëlson, et al., "Psoriasis Patients with Antibodies to Gliadin Can Be Improved by a Gluten-Free Diet", *British Journal of Dermatology* 142 (2000): 44-51.

10 W. K. Woo, et al., "Celiac Disease-Associated Antibodies Correlate with Psoriasis Activity", *British Journal of Dermatology* 151 (October 2004): (4):891-4, www.blackwell-synergy.com/links/doi/10.1111/j.1365-2133.2004.06137.x (accessed August 27, 2005).

11 G. Michaëlsson, et al., "Gluten-Free Diet in Psoriasis Patients with Antibodies to Gliadin Results in Decreased Expression of Tissue Transglutaminase and Fewer Ki67+ Cells in the Dermis", *Acta Dermato-Venereologica* 83 (2003): 425-9.

12 G. Michaëlson, et al., "Psoriasis Patients with Antibodies to Gliadin Can Be Improved by a Gluten-Free Diet", *British Journal of Dermatology* 142 (2000): 44-51.

13 F. Drago, et al., "Pemphigus Improving with Gluten-free Diet", *Acta Dermato-Venereologica* 85(1) (2005): 84-5.

14 E. Scala, et al., "Urticaria and Adult Celiac Disease", *Allergy* 54 (1999).

15 G. R. Powell, and W. L. Weston, "Dermatitis Herpetiformis Presenting as Chronic Urticaria", *Pediatric Dermatology* 21(5) (September 2004): 564.

16 L. Caminiti, et al., "Chronic Urticaria and Associated Celiac Disease in Children: A Case-Control Study", *Pediatric Allergy and Immunology* 16(5) (August 2005): 428.

Chapter 4

1 National Ataxia Foundation, www.ataxia.org.

2 M. Hadjivassiliou, et al., "Gluten Ataxia in Perspective: Epidemiology Genetic Susceptibility and Clinical Characteristics", *Brain* 126 (2003): 685-91.

3 M. Hadjivassiliou, et al., "Gluten Sensitivity as a Neurological Illness", *Journal of Neurology, Neurosurgery, and Psychiatry* 72 (2002): 560-3.

4 National Institute of Neurological Disorders and Stroke (NINDS), NINDS Peripheral neuropathy fact sheet, www.ninds.nih.gov/disorders/peripheralneuropathy/peripheralneuropathy.htm.

5 M. Hadjivassiliou, et al., "Gluten Sensitivity as a Neurological Illness", *Journal of Neurology, Neurosurgery, and Psychiatry* 72 (2002): 560-3.

6 M. Hadjivassiliou, et al., "Gluten Sensitivity as a Neurological Illness", *Journal of Neurology, Neurosurgery, and Psychiatry* 72 (2002): 560-3.

7 M. Hadjivassiliou, et al., "Dietary Treatment of Gluten Ataxia", *Journal of Neurology, Neurosurgery, and Psychiatry* 74 (2003): 1221-4.

8 N. Zelnick, et al., "Range of Neurologic Disorders in Patients with Celiac Disease", *Pediatrics* 113(6): June 2004.

9 M. Hadjivassiliou, et al., "Headache and CNS White Matter Abnormalities Associated with Gluten Sensitivity", *Neurology* 56 (2001): 386-8.

10 Courier Press, "Gluten-Free Diet May Fight Migraines", www.courierpress.com (accesse October 17, 2005).

11 The National Autistic Society, www.autism.org.uk.

12 Centers for Disease Control, Fact Sheet, CDC Autism Research, May 4, 2006.

13 Centers for Disease Control, Fact Sheet, CDC Autism Research, May 4, 2006.

14 Autism Research Institute, "Parent Ratings of Behavioral Effects of Biomedical Interventions", *Autism Research Institute Publication* 34 (March 2005).

15 "The GF/CF Diet, Success Stories: Dietary Intervention for Autistic Spectrum Disorders", the GF/CF diet support group information website, www.gfcfdiet.com/successstories.htm (accessed January 8, 2006).

16 A. M. Knivsberg, et al., "A Randomized, Controlled Study of Dietary Intervention in Autistic Syndromes", *Nutritional Neuroscience* 5(4) (2002): 251-61.

17 K. L. Reichelt, et al., "Can the Pathophysiology of Autism Be Explained by the Nature of the Discovered Urine Peptides?" *Neuroscience* 6(1) (February 2003): 19-28.

18 A. Vojdani, et al., "Immune Response to Dietary Proteins, Gliadin, and Cerebellar Peptides in Children with Autism", *Nutritional Neuroscience* 7(3) (June 2004): 151-61.

19 A. Vojdani, et al., "Immune Response to Dietary Proteins, Gliadin, and Cerebellar Peptides in Children with Autism", *Nutritional Neuroscience* 7(3) (June 2004): 151-61.

20 Attention Deficit Disorder Association, Fact Sheet on Attention Deficit Hyperactivity Disorder (ADHD/ADD), www.add.org/articles/factsheet.html (accessed November 24, 2005).

21 National Institute of Mental Health, "Attention Deficit Hyperactivity Disorder", www.nimn.nih.gov/pulicat/adhd.cfm (accessed November 24, 2005).

22 Attention Deficit Disorder Association, Fact Sheet on Attention Deficit Hyperactivity Disorder (ADHD/ADD), www.add.org/articles/factsheet.html (accessed November 24, 2005).

23 National Institute for Health and Clinical Excellence (NICE), www.nice.org.uk.

24 N. Zelnik, et al., "Range of Neurologic Disorders in Patients with Celiac Disease", *Pediatrics* 113 (2004): 1672-6.

25 OCD-UK, www.ocduk.org.

26 Päivi Pynnönen, et al., "Untreated Celiac Disease and Development of Mental Disorders in Children and Adolescents", *Psychosomatics* 43(4) (July-August 2002): 331-4.

27 Gluten-Free Celiac Disease Forum at Celiac.com, www.glutenfreeforum.com/.

Chapter 5

1 "Health Topics: Handout on Health: Systemic Lupus Erythematosus", National Institute of Arthritis and Musculoskeletal and Skin Diseases, National Institutes of Health, Department of Health & Human Services, www.niams.nih.gov/hi/topics/lupus/slehandout/ (accessed August 28, 2005).

2 M. J. Rensch, et al., "The Prevalence of Celiac Disease Autoantibodies in Patients with Systemic Lupus Erythematosus", *American Journal of Gastroenterology* 96 (2001): 1113-5.

3 M. Hadjivassiliou, et al., "Gluten Sensitivity Masquerading As Systemic Lupus Erythematosus", *Annals of Rheumatic Diseases* 63 (2004): 1501-3 http://ard.bmjjournals.com (accessed August 4, 2005)

4 National Multiple Sclerosis Society, www.nationalmssociety.org.

5 National Multiple Sclerosis Society, www.nationalmssociety.org.

6 M. Hadjivassiliou, "Multiple Sclerosis and Occult Gluten Sensitivity", author reply, *Neurology* 64(5) (March 8, 2005): 933-4.

7 National Osteoporosis Society, www.nos.org.uk.

8 W. Stenson, et al., "Increased Prevalence of Celiac Disease and Need for Routine Screening among Patients with Osteoporosis", *Archives of Internal Medicine* 165(4) (February 28, 2005).

9 W. Wright, "Personal Story", Osteoporosis Society of Canada, www.osteoporosis.ca (accessed September 22, 2005).

10 T. Valdimarsson, et al., "Reversal of Osteopenia with Diet in Adult Celiac Disease", *Gut* 38:322-7.

11 T. Kemppainen, et al., "Bone Recovery after a Gluten-Free Diet: A 5-Year Follow-Up Study", *Bone* 25(3) (September 1999): 355-60.

12 *The Merck Manual of Health & Aging,* "What Is Osteomalacia?" www.merck.com.

13 R.A. Basu, et al., "Celiac Disease Can Still Present with Osteomalacia!" *Rheumatology* 39 (2000): 335-6.

14 W. DeBoer, et al., "A Patient with Osteomalacia as Single Presenting Symptom of Gluten-Sensitive Enteropathy", Journal of Internal Medicine 232(1) (July 1992): 81-5.

15 A. J. Dorst, and J. D., Ringe, "Severe Osteomalacia in Endemic Sprue. An Important Differential Diagnosis in Osteoporosis", *MMW Fortschr Med* 116(8) (March 20, 1998): 42-5.

16 R. A. Basu, et al., "Celiac Disease Can Still Present with Osteomalacia!" *Rheumatology* 39 (2000): 335-6.

17 Arthritis Research Campaign, www.arc.org.uk

18 "Juvenile Rheumatoid Arthritis", *Kids Health for Parents,* http://kidshealth.org/parent/medical/arthritis/jra.html.

19 Arthritis Foundation, Disease Center, www.arthritis.org.

20 I. Alghafeer, et al., "Rheumatic Manifestations of Gastrointestinal Diseases", *Rheumatic Diseases* 51(2), Arthritis Foundation, www.arthritis.org (accessed September 26, 2005).

21 E. Lubrano et al., "The Arthritis of Celiac Disease: Prevalence and Pattern in 200 Adult Patients", *British Journal of Rheumatology* 35 (1996): 1314-8.

22 I. Hafström, et al., "A Vegan Diet Free of Gluten Improves the Signs and Symptoms of Rheumatoid Arthritis: The Effects on Arthritis Correlate with a Reduction in Antibodies to Food Antigens", *Rheumatology* 40 (2001): 1175-9, http://rheumatology.oxfordjournals. org (accessed September 25, 2005).

23 RemedyFind, www.remedyfind.com.

24 Home Schooler's Curriculum Swap, http://theswap.com/BBS/ForumHome/12798.html.

25 Scleroderma Foundation, "What Is Scleroderma?" www.scleroderma.org/medical/overview.shtm (accessed September 26, 2005).

26 Arthritis Foundation, "Sjögren's Syndrome", www.arthritis.org.

27 D. Slot, and H. Locht, "Arthritis as Presenting Symptom in Silent Adult Celiac Disease", *Scandinavian Journal of Rheumatology* 29 (2000): 260-3.

28 Diabetes UK, www.diabetes.org.uk

29 Vijay Kumar, et al., "Celiac Disease-Associated Autoimmune Endocrinopathies", *Clinical and Diagnostic Laboratory Immunology* (July 2001): 679.

30 M. Addison, "Type 1 Diabetes: New Perspectives on Disease Pathogenesis and Treatment", seminar, *The Lancet* 358 (July 21, 2001): 225.

31 M. Addison, "Type 1 Diabetes: New Perspectives on Disease Pathogenesis and Treatment", seminar, *The Lancet* 358 (July 21, 2001): 225.

32 O. I. Saadah, et. al., "Effect of Gluten-Free Diet and Adherence on Growth and Diabetic Control in Diabetics with Celiac Disease", *Archives of Disease in Childhood* 89 (2004): 871-876, www.abd.bmjournals.com (accessed July 8, 2005).

33 C. E. Counsell, et al., "Celiac Disease and Autoimmune Thyroid Disease", *Gut* 35:844-846 http://gut.bmjjournals.com/cgi/content/abstract/35/6/844 (accessed August 20, 2005).

34 U. Volta, et al., "Celiac Disease in Patients with Autoimmune Thyroiditis", *Digestion* 64 (2001): 61-5.

35 A. Ventura, et al., "Duration of Exposure to Gluten and Risk for Autoimmune Disorders in Patients with Celiac Disease", *Gastroenterology* 117 (1999): 297-303.

36 C. Sategna-Guidetti, et al., "Prevalence of Thyroid Disorders in Untreated Adult Celiac Disease Patients and Effect of Gluten Withdrawal: An Italian Multicenter Study", *American Journal of Gastroenterology* 96(3):75.

Chapter 6

1 P. Green, et al., "Characteristics of Adult Celiac Disease in the USA: Results of a National Survey", *American Journal of Gastroenterology* 96(1) (2001).

2 Coeliac UK, www.coeliac.co.uk.

3 A. Fasano, et al., "Prevalence of Celiac Disease in At-Risk and Not-at-Risk Groups in the United States", *Archives of Internal Medicine* 163(3) (February 10, 2003).

4 G. Corrao, et al., "Mortality in Patients with Celiac Disease and Their Relatives: A Cohort Study", *The Lancet* 358(9279) (August 4, 2001).

5 The IBS Network, www.ibsnetwork.org.uk

6 IBS Tales, "The Tale of Charlene", www.ibstales.com/happy_tales_five.htm (accessed October 6, 2005).

7 D. S. Sanders, et al., "Association of Adult Celiac Disease with Irritable Bowel Syndrome: A Case-Control Study in Patients Fulfilling ROME II Criteria Referred to Secondary Care", *The Lancet* 358 (9292) (November 3, 2001): 1504-8.

8 C. O'Leary, et al., "Celiac Disease and Irritable Bowel-Type Symptoms", *American Journal of Gastroenterology* 97(6) (June 2002): 1463-7.

9 B. Shahbazkhani, et al., "Celiac Disease Presenting with Symptoms of Irritable Bowel Syndrome", *Alimentary Pharmacology & Therapeutics* 18(2) (July 2003): 231.

10 Jen-Paul Achkar, MD, "Inflammatory Bowel Disease", American College of Gastroenterology, www.acag.gi.org/patients/gihealth/ibd.asp (accessed October 2, 2005).

11 A. R. Eurler, and M. E. Ament, "Celiac Sprue and Crohn's Disease: An Association Causing Severe Growth Retardation", *Gastroenterology* 72(4 Pt 1) (April 1977): 729-31.

12 R. Gillberg, et al., "Chronic Inflammatory Bowel Disease in Patients with Celiac Disease", *Scandinavian Journal of Gastroenterology* 17(4) (June 1982): 491-6.

13 E. G. Breen, et al., "Celiac Proctitis", *Scandinavian Journal of Gastroenterology* 22(4) (May 1987): 471-7.

14 A. Sha, et al., "Epidemiological Survey of Celiac Disease and Inflammatory Bowel Disease in First-Degree Relatives of Celiac Patients", *Quarterly Journal of Medicine* 74(275) (March 1990): 283-8.

15 A. Tursi, et al., "High Prevalence of Celiac Disease among Patients Affected by Crohn's Disease", *Inflammatory Bowel Diseases* 11(7) (July 2005): 662-6.

16 A. Kang, et al., "Celiac Sprue and Ulcerative Colitis in Three South Asian Women", Indian Journal of Gastroenterology 23 (2004): 24-5, www.indianjgastro.com (accessed October 8, 2005).

17 P. Iovino, et al., "Esophageal Impairment in Adult Celiac Disease with Steatorrhea", *American Journal of Gastroenterology* 93(8) (August 1998): 1243.

18 A. Cuomo, et al., "Reflux Oesophagitis in Adult Celiac Disease: Beneficial Effect of a Gluten-Free Diet", *Gut* 52 (2003): 514-7.

19 G. R. Corassa, et al., "Celiac Disease in Adults", *Baillieres Clinical Gastroenterology* 9(2) (June 1995): 329-50.

20 P. Collin, et al., "Endocrinological Disorders and Celiac Disease", *Endocrine Reviews* 23(4) (2002): 464-83.

21 I. de Freitas, et al., "Celiac Disease in Brazilian Adults", *Journal of Clinical Gastroenterology* 34 (April 2002): 4.

22 David Wray, "Gluten-Sensitive Recurrent Aphthous Stomatitis", *Digestive Diseases and Sciences (Historical Archive),* Springer Science+Business Media B.V. 26(8) (August 1981): 737-40.

23 Mayo Clinic, "Celiac Disease: Signs and Symptoms", www.mayoclinic.com.

24 Joseph Murray, MD, PhD, "The Widening Spectrum of Celiac Disease", summarized by Jim Lyles (Sprue-nik Press, November 1996).

25 Centers for Disease Control, "Giardiasis Fact Sheet", www.cdc.gov/ncidod/dpd/parasites/giardiasis/factsht_giardia.htm.

26 E. Mastropasqua, and A. Farruggio, "Giardia Duodenalis: A Confounding Factor for the Diagnosis of Celiac Disease", *Journal of Clinical Gastroenterology* 36(2) (2003): 185.

27 B. Landzberg, and B. Connor, "Persistent Diarrhea in the Returning Traveler: Think beyond Persistent Infection", *Scandinavian Journal of Gastroenterology* 40(1) (January 2005): 112-4.

Chapter 7

1 Centers for Disease Control and Prevention, "Chronic Fatigue Syndrome", www.cdc.gov/ncidod/diseases/cfs/.

2 Department of Pain Medicine and Palliative Care, Beth Israel Medical Center, "Fibromyalgia", http://stoppain.org/pain_medicine/.

3 National Institute of Arthritis and Musculoskeletal and Skin Diseases (NIAMS), National Institutes of Health, "Questions and answers about fibromyalgia", www.niams.nih.gov/hi/topics/fibromyalgia/fibrofs.htm.

4 A. Skowera, M. Peakman, et al., "High Prevalence of Serum Markers of Celiac Disease in Patients with Chronic Fatigue Syndrome", *Journal of Clinical Pathology* 54 (2001): 335-6.

5 R. Zipser, et al., "Presentations of Adult Celiac Disease in a Nationwide Patient Support Group", Digestive Diseases and Sciences 48(4) (April 2003): 761-4.

6 National Library of Medicine, "Iron deficiency anemia", www.nlm.nih.gov/.

7 U. Schmitz, et al., "Iron-Deficiency Anemia as the Sole Manifestation of Celiac Disease", *The Journal of Clinical Investigation* 72(7) (July 1994): 519-21.

8 B. Annibale, et al., "Efficacy of Gluten-Free Diet Alone on Recovery from Iron Deficiency Anemia in Adult Celiac Patients", *American Journal of Gastroenterology* 96(1) (January 2001): 132.

9 U. Karnam, et al., "Prevalence of Occult Celiac Disease in Patients with Iron Deficiency Anemia: A Prospective Study", *Southern Medical Journal* 97(1) (January 2004).

10 Medical Journal of Australia 2003 178(10): 483–485.

11 Asthma UK, www.asthma.org.uk.

12 J. Kero, et al., "Could TH1 and TH2 Diseases Coexist? Evaluation of Asthma Incidence in Children with Celiac Disease, Type 1 Diabetes, or Rheumatoid Arthritis: A Register Study", Journal of Allergy and Clinical Immunology 108(5) (November 2001): 781-3.

13 K. Palosuo, et al., "Rye Gamma-70 and Gamma-35 Secalins and Barley Gamma-3 Hordein Cross-React with Omega-5 Gliadin, A Major Allergen in Wheat-Dependent, Exercise-Induced Anaphylaxis", Clinical & Experimental Allergy 31(3) (March 2001): 466-73.

14 G. Kanny, et al., "Chronic Urticaria to Wheat", Allergy 56(4) (April 2001): 356.

15 BrainTalk Communities, http://brain.hstypastry.net/forums (accessed October 19, 2005).

16 U.S. National Library of Medicine and National Institutes of Health, Medline Plus, "Unintentional Weight Loss", www.nlm.nih.gov/medlineplus/ency/article/003107.htm.

17 S. Bode, and E. Gudmand-Hoyer, "Symptoms and Haematologic Features in Consecutive Adult Celiac Patients", Scandinavian Journal of Gastroenterology 31(1) (January 1996): 54-60.

18 J. L. Shaker, et al., "Hypocalcemia and Skeletal Disease As Presenting Features of Celiac Disease", Archives of Internal Medicine 157(9) (May 12, 1997): 1013-6.

19 American Heart Association, "Cardiomyopathy", www.americanheart.org.

20 National Library of Medicine and the National Institutes of Health, "Myocarditis", www. nlm.nih.gov/medlineplus/ency/article/000149.htm.

21 Alessio Fasano, and Carlo Catassi, "Current Approaches to Diagnosis and Treatment of Celiac Disease: An Evolving Spectrum", Gastroenterology 2001 120:636-51.

22 Andrea Frustaci, L. Cuoco, et al., "Celiac Disease Associated with Autoimmune Myocarditis", Circulation 2002 105:2611-8, originally published online May 13, 2002.

23 M. Curione, M. Barbato, et al., "Idiopathic Dilated Cardiomyopathy Associated with Celiac Disease: The Effect of a Gluten-Free Diet on Cardiac Performance", Digestive and Liver Disease 34(12) (December 2002): 866-9.

24 Nisheeth K. Goel, et al., "Cardiomyopathy Associated with Celiac Disease", Mayo Clinic Proceedings 80 (2005): 674-6.

25 Andrea Frustaci, L. Cuoco, et al., "Celiac Disease Associated with Autoimmune Myocarditis", Circulation 2002 105:2611-8, originally published online May 13, 2002.

26 A. Meini, et al., "Prevalence and Diagnosis of Celiac Disease in IgA-Deficient Children", Annals of Allergy, Asthma, & Immunology 77 (October 1996): 333-6.

27 F. Cataldo, et al., "Celiac Disease and Selective Immunoglobulin A Deficiency", Journal of Pediatrics 131(2) (August 1997): 306-8.

28 Peter Arkwright, et al., "Autoimmunity in Human Primary Immunodeficiency Diseases", Blood 99(8) (April 15, 2002): 2694-702.

29 M. Heneghan, et al., "Celiac Sprue and Immunodeficiency States: A 25-Year-Review", Journal of Clinical Gastroenterology 25(2) (September 1997): 421-5.

30 "Rice Study Shows Immune System Evolution Prevents Disease", Rice University, www. media.rice.edu/.

Chapter 8

1 Bari Spielman, "Flatulence in Dogs", PetPlace.com, www.petplace.com/dogs/flatulence-in-dogs/page1.aspx (accessed February 18, 2006).

2 Tim Watson, "Diet and Skin Disease in Dogs and Cats", *American Society for Nutritional Sciences, Journal of Nutrition* 128 (1998): 2783S-9S.

3 Michael Day, "The Canine Model of Dietary Hypersensitivity", *Proceedings of the Nutrition Society* 64(4) (November 2005): 458-64.

4 W. Grant Guilford, et al., "Prevalence and Causes of Food Sensitivity in Cats with Chronic Pruritus, Vomiting, or Diarrhea", *Journal of Nutrition* 128 (1998): 2790S-1S, originally presented as part of the Waltham International Symposium on Pet Nutrition and Health in the 21st Century, Orlando, Florida, May 1997.

5 V.R.M. Batt, and E. J. Hall, "Gluten-Sensitive Enteropathy in the Dog", *Wiener Medizinische Wochenschrift* 79(8) (1992): 242-7.

6 Stanley Marks, "Advances in Dietary Management of Gastrointestinal Disease", presentation at the World Small Animal Veterinary Association, 2003, www.vin.com/proceedings/Proceedings.plx?CID=WSAVA2003&PID=6690&O=Generic (accessed February 18, 2006).

7 Stanley Marks, "Advances in Dietary Management of Gastrointestinal Disease", presentation at the World Small Animal Veterinary Association, 2003.

8 Purina Beneful, http://beneful.com/products/original.aspx.

9 PetSmart, Great Choice, food for dogs, with chunky chicken.

10 Iams, Food for Thought Technical Bulletin No. 38R, "Wheat: Ingredients and Their Use in Our Pet Foods", www.iams.com.

Chapter 9

1 Autism Research Institute, www.autismwebsite.com/.

Chapter 10

1 Kenneth D. Fine, MD, "Frequently Asked Questions about Results Interpretation", Enterolab, www.enterolab.com/What_Happens (accessed January 10, 2006).

2 Kenneth D. Fine, MD, "Frequently Asked Questions about Results Interpretation", Enterolab, www.enterolab.com/What_Happens (accessed January 10, 2006).

3 Dr. Fine is the medical director and director of operations of EnteroLab Reference Laboratory in Texas. He has held staff positions at both Baylor University Medical Center and the University of Texas-Southwestern Medical School. His research has been published in prestigious medical journals, including *Gastroenterology, The New England Journal of Medicine, The Journal of Clinical Investigation*, and *The American Journal of Gastroenterology*.

4 K. D. Fine, and F. Ogunji, "A New Method of Quantitative Fecal Fat Microscopy and Its Correlation with Chemically Measured Fecal Fat Output", *American Journal of Clinical Pathology* 113(4):528-34.

5 Aristo Vojdani, PhD, MSc, MT, is the founder and chief executive officer of Immunosciences Lab, Inc. He is a graduate of Bar Ilan University in Israel, where he studied microbiology, biochemistry, and immunology. In addition to directing Immunosciences Lab, Dr. Vojdani is also assistant research neurobiologist in the Department of Neurobiology, David Geffen School of Medicine, at the University of California in Los Angeles.

Chapter 11

1 Codex Alimentarius, "Understanding the Codex Alimentarius", www.codexalimentarius. net (accessed December 30, 2005).

2 Codex Alimentarius, "Codex Standard for Gluten-Free Foods: Codex Stan 118-1981 (amended 1983)".

3 Celiac.com, "Forbidden list", www.celiac.com.

4 Lone Star Celiac Support Group, www.dfwceliac.org.

5 Lone Star Celiac Support Group, www.dfwceliac.org.

6 Lieberman, S., *Dare to Lose: 4 Simple Steps to a Better Body,* Avery (2003).

7 Information about these flours came from various sources, including The Gluten-Free Pantry, www.glutenfree.com; Celiac.com, www.celiac.com; The Cook's Thesaurus, www. foodsubs.com/; Bob's Red Mill, www.bobsredmill.com.

Chapter 12

1 S. Lieberman, and N. Bruning, *The Real Vitamin & Mineral Book, 2003,* 3rd ed., (Avery/ Penguin Putnam, New York).

2 J. A. Catanzaro, and L. Green, "Microbial Ecology & Probiotics in Human Medicine (Part II)", *Alternative Medicine Review 2001* 2(4):296-305.

3 J. A. Catanzaro, and L. Green, "Microbial Ecology & Probiotics in Human Medicine (Part II)", *Alternative Medicine Review 2001* 2(4):296-305.

4 James E. Williams, "Portal to the Interior: Viral Pathogens and Natural Compounds That Restore Mucosal Integrity and Modulate Inflammation", *Alternative Medicine Review 2003* 8(4):395-409.

5 Alan Miller, The Pathogens, Clinical Implications and Treatment of Intestinal Hyperpermeability. *Alternative Medicine Review 2001* 2(5):330-45.

6 Kathleen A. Head, and Julie S. Jurenka, "Inflammatory Bowel Disease Part I: Ulcerative Colitis—Pathophysiology and Conventional and Alternative Treatment Options", *Alternative Medicine Review 2003* 8(3):247-83.

7 H. J. Cornell, and F. A. Macrae, J. Melney, et al., "Enzyme Therapy for the Management of Celiac Disease", *Scandinavian Journal of Gastroenterology* 40 (2005): 1304-12.

Chapter 13

1 M. Boniotto, et al., "Variant Mannose-Binding Lectin Alleles Are Associated with Celiac Diseases", *Immunogenetics* 54(8) (November 2002): 596-8.

2 N. F. Childers, and M. S. Margoes, "An Apparent Relation of Nightshades (Solanaceae) to Arthritis", *Journal of Neurological and Orthopedic Medical Surgery* 12 (1993): 227-31, http:// noarthritis.com/research.htm.

3 Eric Orr, "Monsanto Re-engineers Nature", *Chattooga Quarterly News,* Chattooga Conservancy, www.chattoogariver.org/index.php?req=monsanto&quart=Su2005 (accessed February 5, 2006).

4 P. Montague, "2005 Was a Very Good Year for the Biotech Food Industry", Rachel's Democracy & Health News #837 (January 5, 2006), Environmental Research Foundation, www.rachel.org.

Chapter 14

Recipes adapted from the following sources:

1 Bette Hagman, *The Gluten-Free Gourmet Bakes Bread* (Owl Books, 1999), 40.

2 This recipe, as well as others for dairy substitutes (unless otherwise noted), were adapted from Go Dairy Free, www.godairyfree.org.

3 Go Dairy Free, www.godairyfree.org/guide/eat/substitutes/sourcream.htm.

Chapter 15

Recipes adapted from the following sources:

1 Wholehealth MD, www.wholehealthmd.com.

2 McCann's Irish Oatmeal, www.mccanns.ie/pages/faq.html.

3 Wegmans, www.wegmans.com/greatMeals/recipes/.

4 RecipeZaar, www.recipezaar.com/150978.

5 RecipeZaar, www.recipezaar.com/106530.

6 Epicurious, Classic Omelette, www.epicurious.com/recipes/recipe_views/views/15068.

7 Zoe Quinta, Bed & Breakfast Inns Online, www.bbonline.com/recipe/quintazoe_qt_recipe2.html.

8 Thurston House, Bed and Breakfast, Bed & Breakfast Inns Online, www.bbonline.com/recipe/thurston_fl_recipe1.html.

9 5 A Day, Recipe America.com, www.recipeamerica.com.

10 Cooks.com, www.cooks.com.

11 Recipe America, www.recipeamerica.com.

12 Amaranth pancakes, All Recipes, http://brunch.allrecipes.com/az/mrnthPncks.asp.

13 Mr. Breakfast, Spinach Soufflé, www.mrbreakfast.com.

14 Cooks.com, www.cooks.com.

15 All Recipes, http://salad.allrecipes.com/az/EggSalad.asp.

16 Fun Lunch Recipes for Vegetarian Kids and their Parents, Better Health USA, www.betterhealthusa.com/public/269.cfm.

17 Fabulous Foods, www.fabulousfoods.com/recipes/main/sandwiches/veggiefetasand.html.

18 Sara Moulton, *Good Morning America,* ABC News, http://i.abcnews.com/GMA/Springtime/story?id=412924&page=1.

19 *Rachael Ray's 30 Minute Meals,* Food TV, www.foodnetwork.com.

20 Bob Blumer, *The Surreal Gourmet,* Food TV, www.foodnetwork.com.

21 Bob Blumer, *The Surreal Gourmet,* Food TV, www.foodnetwork.com.

22 *Better Homes and Gardens New Home Cook Book* (Meredith Corp., 1996).

23 Alaska Smokehouse, www.alaskasmokehouse.com.

24 *Betty Crocker's New Cookbook* (McMillan, 1996).

25 *Rachael Ray's 30-Minute Meals,* Food TV, www.foodnetwork.com.

26 Cooks.com, Turkey Skewers with Mango Salsa, www.cooks.com.

27 RecipeZaar, Spicy Sesame Chicken Fajitas, www.recipezaar.com/92972.

28 Michele O'Sullivan, Creamy Cucumber Dressing, All Recipes, http://salad.allrecipes.com/az/CreamyCucumberDressing.asp.

29 Southern U.S. Cuisine, About.com, http://southernfood.about.com/od/beansoups/r/bl00927c.htm.

30 Tanya Paulsen, Cooks.com, www.cooks.com.

31 *Better Homes and Gardens New Home Cook Book* (Meredith Corp., 1996).

32 *Betty Crocker's New Cookbook* (McMillan, 1996).

33 Starlight Yellow Cake, *Betty Crocker's New Cook Book* (McMillan, 1996).

34 Peter J. D'Adamo, *Eat Right 4 Your Type,* RecipeNet, www.recipenet.org/health/recipes/recipkit/quinoa_applesauce_cake.htm.

35 Fitness and Freebies, www.fitnessandfreebies.com/celiac/cerealsnack.html.

36 Crystal Elizabeth Teed, "Gluten Free Macadamia Pie Crust," All Recipes, http://pie.allrecipes.com/az.76516.asp.

37 Azspirit, GF Pie Crust Recipe, SpiritKeep, http://spiritkeep.net/recipebox/azgfpiecrust1.html.

Chapter 16

Recipes adapted from the following sources:

1 Bette Hagman, *The Gluten-Free Gourmet Bakes Bread* (Owl Books, 1999).

2 Rhonda Johnson, Cole's Flour Blend, New Diets.com, www.newdiets.com.

3 Bette Hagman's Basic Featherlight Rice Bread, *The Gluten-Free Gourmet Bakes Bread* (Owl Books, 1999).

4 Cory Bates, GF Banana Bread, Celiac.com, www.celiac.com.

5 Grit.com,www.grit.com/articles/RecipeBox0506/.

6 Amber Lee, Dinner Rolls, gfutah.org.

7 Carole Fenster, Pizza Crust, Living Without, www.livingwithout.com/special_pizza.htm.

GENERAL INDEX

A

acidophilus 87, 97, 133-4
acne and acne rosea 31-2
Actonel 50
ADD (attention-deficit disorder) 41-3, 88
ADHD (attention-deficit hyperactivity
    disorder) 41-3, 88
adrenalin 18-19
AGA *see under* antibodies
allergies *see* food allergies
almonds 120
amaranth flour 120
anaemia 75-6
anaphylaxis 18-19, 20, 76
ankylosing spondylitis 55
antibiotics/antimicrobials 30, 87
antibodies (immunoglobulins) 15-16, 53-4,
    141
    AGA anti-gliadin antibody 20, 30,
        93, 94, 101-2, 103-4, 105-6, 107
    EMA anti-endomysial antibody 20,
        93, 94, 101-2, 103
    tTGA/ATTA anti-tissue
    transglutaminase antibody 20, 93, 96,
        101-2, 103, 104, 107
    IgA 27-8, 30, 31, 64, 81, 96
    IgE 18, 20
    IgG 30, 31, 64, 96
antigens 15, 18
antihistamine 18, 19, 32
anti-inflammatories 136
antioxidants 132
aphthous stomatitis 70
Arataeos 24
arthritis 52-5
aspartame 117
Asperger's syndrome 88
asthma 18, 76-8
ataxia 21, 35-8, 46, 48
    progressive idiopathic ataxia 94
attention-deficit disorder (ADD) 41-3, 88
attention-deficit hyperactivity disorder
    (ADHD) 41-3, 88
autism 39-41, 88, 90-1

autistic enterocolitis 91
autoimmune diseases
    ankylosing spondylitis 55
    arthritis 52-5
    diabetes 12, 13, 56-7, 104
    lupus 45-7
    multiple sclerosis 47-8
    osteomalacia 51-2
    osteopenia 48-50
    osteoporosis 48-50
    rickets 51
    scleroderma 55
    Sjögren's syndrome 53, 55
    stool tests 106
    thyroid disease 57-9

B

barley 2, 21, 62, 113, 136
behavioural problems
    ADD/ADHD 41-2
    autistic tantrums 40
    OCD 42-3
besan flour 120
beta-carotene 128
beverages 116-17, 126, 161
breakfast
    cereals 119, 160
    importance of 161-2
Bock, Dr. Kenneth 88-91
boron 128
bread 119-21
    see also Recipes Index
broad bean flour 120
buckwheat 120

C

calcium 79, 128, 129
carbohydrates, list of GF friendly 231-2
cardiomyopathy xi, 79-80
carrageenan 85, 143-4
casein/dairy free diet 40, 89, 96-7, 99, 106,
    142, 150

257

RECIPE INDEX

ABOUT THE AUTHOR

Shari Lieberman, PhD, CNS, FACN, has been in private practice as a clinical nutritionist for more than 20 years. She earned a master of science degree in nutrition, food science and dietetics from New York University and a doctoral degree in clinical nutrition and exercise physiology from The Union Institute in Cincinnati. She is a certified nutrition specialist (CNS), a fellow of the American College of Nutrition (FACN), a member of the New York Academy of Science, a member of the American Academy of Anti-Aging Medicine, a former officer and present board member of the Certification Board for Nutrition Specialists, and president of the American Association for Health Freedom. In 2003, she received the Clinician of the Year Award from the National Nutritional Foods Association.

Dr. Lieberman is the founding dean of the master of science programme in clinical nutrition at New York Chiropractic College, a contributing editor to the American Medical Association's *5th Edition of Drug Evaluations*, a peer reviewer for scientific publications, a published scientific researcher and a presenter at numerous scientific conferences. She is a member of the nutrition team for the New York City Marathon.

Dr. Lieberman's bestseller *The Real Vitamin and Mineral Book* is now in its third edition. She also is the author of *Mineral Miracle, User's Guide to Brain-Boosting Supplements, Dare to Lose: 4 Simple Steps to a Better Body, Get Off the Menopause Roller Coaster, Maitake Mushroom and D-Fraction, Maitake: King of Mushrooms,* and *All About Vitamin C.* Dr. Lieberman is a frequent guest on television and radio in the US, and she often is cited in magazine articles as an authority on nutrition.

To learn more about Dr. Lieberman and her work, visit her website at www.drshari.net.